Implementing the Information Literacy Framework

PRACTICAL GUIDES FOR LIBRARIANS

⑥ About the Series

This innovative series written and edited for librarians by librarians provides authoritative, practical information and guidance on a wide spectrum of library processes and operations.

Books in the series are focused, describing practical and innovative solutions to a problem facing today's librarian and delivering step-by-step guidance for planning, creating, implementing, managing, and evaluating a wide range of services and programs.

The books are aimed at beginning and intermediate librarians needing basic instruction/guidance in a specific subject and at experienced librarians who need to gain knowledge in a new area or guidance in implementing a new program/service.

⑥ About the Series Editor

The **Practical Guides for Librarians** series was conceived by and is edited by M. Sandra Wood, MLS, MBA, AHIP, FMLA, Librarian Emerita, Penn State University Libraries.

M. Sandra Wood was a librarian at the George T. Harrell Library, the Milton S. Hershey Medical Center, College of Medicine, Pennsylvania State University, Hershey, PA, for over 35 years, specializing in reference, educational, and database services. Ms. Wood worked for several years as a Development Editor for Neal-Schuman Publishers.

Ms. Wood received a MLS from Indiana University and a MBA from the University of Maryland. She is a Fellow of the Medical Library Association and served as a member of MLA's Board of Directors from 1991 to 1995. Ms. Wood is founding and current editor of *Medical Reference Services Quarterly*, now in its 35th volume. She also was founding editor of the *Journal of Consumer Health on the Internet* and the *Journal of Electronic Resources in Medical Libraries* and served as editor/co-editor of both journals through 2011.

Titles in the Series

1. *How to Teach: A Practical Guide for Librarians* by Beverley E. Crane

2. *Implementing an Inclusive Staffing Model for Today's Reference Services* by Julia K. Nims, Paula Storm, and Robert Stevens

3. *Managing Digital Audiovisual Resources: A Practical Guide for Librarians* by Matthew C. Mariner

4. *Outsourcing Technology: A Practical Guide for Librarians* by Robin Hastings

Implementing the Information Literacy Framework

A Practical Guide for Librarians

Dave Harmeyer
Janice J. Baskin

PRACTICAL GUIDES FOR LIBRARIANS, NO. 40

ROWMAN & LITTLEFIELD
Lanham • Boulder • New York • London

Published by Rowman & Littlefield

An imprint of The Rowman & Littlefield Publishing Group, Inc.

4501 Forbes Boulevard, Suite 200, Lanham, Maryland 20706

www.rowman.com

Unit A, Whitacre Mews, 26-34 Stannary Street, London SE11 4AB

British Library Cataloguing in Publication Information Available

Library of Congress Cataloging-in-Publication Data Available

ISBN 978-1-5381-0757-7 (pbk. : alk. paper) | ISBN 978-1-5381-0758-4 (ebook)

♾™ The paper used in this publication meets the minimum requirements of American National Standard for Information Sciences—Permanence of Paper for Printed Library Materials, ANSI/NISO Z39.48-1992.

Printed in the United States of America

To educators—to the librarians and classroom faculty who understand the importance of information literacy skills in the education of their students and who take the thoughtful time to read, engage, and implement the many tips, steps, tools, and strategies mentioned within these pages.

To the students themselves, who deserve an education that will give them the habits of mind needed to be savvy in managing information in order to be wise consumers, fulfilled individuals, and good citizens.

Contents

Appendixes

Figures, Tables, and Handouts

⑥ Figures

⊚ Tables

⑥ Handouts

Chapter 6

Chapter 8

Chapter 9

Appendix A

Foreword

Dave Harmeyer and Janice Baskin have written an incredibly rich guide for those who would like to incorporate the Association of College & Research Libraries' *Framework for Information Literacy for Higher Education* not only into their own classes but on their campuses more broadly. It is a great strength of the book that it is written by a librarian in conjunction with a classroom faculty member and therefore addresses two core sets of readers who are critical to what needs to be a united effort to advance students' information literacy.

In their preface, the authors note that the conceptual approach of the *Framework* "takes educators deep into the intellectual territory of a liberal education and, as such, requires new ways of doing things among librarians, classroom educators, and administrators." This approach was intentional and was seen as a critical shift during the development of the *Framework*. The information environment today is so vast, so multifaceted, and so full of pitfalls and quicksand that understanding core concepts is critical to maneuvering adeptly and thoughtfully through this landscape. As has become apparent recently, extraordinary discernment is called for—a discernment that must constantly adjust to new threats to our understanding of information sources, veracity, transparency, and purposes. Valuing and using a "set of integrated abilities encompassing the reflective discovery of information, the understanding of how information is produced and valued, and the use of information in creating new knowledge and participating ethically in communities of learning" (information literacy definition in the *Framework* introduction) requires a strong commitment in time, energy, and intellect. Students must be exposed to these ideas in multiple courses and challenged to make them their own. It is clear that learning, and respecting such habits of mind, falls squarely within "the intellectual territory of a liberal education." And while information literacy instruction is important for students' academic endeavors, it is also crucial for their development as informed and responsible citizens. It is, indeed, a significant endeavor.

Ideally, all educators on campus would be aware of the scope and import of information literacy and make robust connections between their disciplines and information literacy when teaching. We do not want information literacy to be categorized as the sole responsibility of librarians, and indeed it is impossible for librarians, given their small numbers and limited prolonged contact with students, to be solely responsible for information literacy instruction. The authors have, by their very collaboration and through the content of this book, addressed the issue of information literacy as the joint responsibility of librarians and classroom educators. They also recognize that this may lead to anxiety, as they note in the preface: "For those used to the one-shot library instruction approach, this can feel daunting—for both classroom instructor and librarian. This book serves to help guide the way."

While the *Framework* has been strongly embraced by many academic librarians, there are questions about how to use it, and it is new to many classroom faculty. What a boon this volume will be in meeting both needs. It does information literacy librarians and classroom faculty the great service of approaching the implementation of the *Framework* in a supportive and structured manner. It provides enough background information to help those less informed about the history and current state of information literacy learn the lay of the land, but not so many details that readers will get bogged down. It addresses issues on both a micro, classroom, level and a macro, campus, level. For those who previously used the *Standards*, this book recognizes the potential need for a transition period before fully implementing the *Framework* and notes how earlier best practices still have relevance today. The wide range of handouts will serve to jump-start brainstorming for one's own situation or discipline, and the distillation of content in the tables, including sample student learning objectives, will be of enormous assistance for all readers. The website that complements the book is yet another supportive resource.

Academic librarians have known for some time that the model of course-related, one-time instruction is broken. It may meet immediate needs for research assignments, but it absolutely cannot accomplish what is needed to help learners become information literate. This book will help to set the course that the *Framework* will take on higher education campuses.

Let me end on a more personal note. It was a pleasure to be asked to write this foreword. One obvious reason is being able to recommend it to readers—it is an incredible resource for navigating the potential of the *Framework*. But there is also a second reason: I had the pleasure of co-chairing with Craig Gibson the task force that developed the *Framework* over the course of 2013 and 2014. Seeing the impact that the *Framework* is having on the profession, and listening to thoughtful and engaged conversations about its potential (and even its hurdles), engenders a feeling of amazement. It was an intense process to get to the point where there was a document to offer academic librarians, classroom faculty, and administrators. The task force brought together a highly motivated and knowledgeable group of people to create a document that reflects both educational theory and practice and the complex challenges of our current information environment. Yet it is not solely the work of the task force. We received more than one thousand pages of feedback on the various drafts. Reviewing and addressing the feedback provided by so many in the profession was exhilarating, confusing, overwhelming, exciting, and daunting. As might be expected, the comments ran the gamut of opinion, and changes that would satisfy one person would be antithetical to another. We read every comment and benefited from many as we shaped the final document. As an example, I was part of a small group within the task force that was initially called Format as Process. The astute feedback we received motivated our renaming it to Information Creation as a Process. The careful review and constructive responses by so many were most appreciated while we were honing the thoughts and language of the *Framework*.

Having a chance to delve into this volume and explore the authors' guidance and resources reignites the sense of discovery and excitement that occurred during the creation of the *Framework*. I expect that you, as readers, will recognize the same potential.

Trudi Jacobson
Distinguished Librarian
Head, Information Literacy Department
University at Albany
State University of New York

Preface

Implementing the Information Literacy Framework: A Practical Guide for Librarians is written with three types of people in mind: librarians, classroom educators, and their students. As accreditation bodies increasingly are focused on assessing education requirements that purposefully create information-literate graduates prepared for today's oversaturated information ecosystem, the Association of College & Research Libraries (ACRL) has created a conceptual framework to help educators meet this instructional challenge. The *Framework for Information Literacy for Higher Education* has rethought information literacy not as a set of practices but rather as a group of interrelated concepts that work whatever the subject matter and whatever the information source—whether a library database, a campaign white paper, or a website on a new product or medical procedure.

The *Framework* takes educators deep into the intellectual territory of a liberal education and, as such, requires new ways of doing things among librarians, classroom educators, and administrators. This is information literacy instruction that very much needs the co-equal collaboration of librarians and classroom educators to embed this instruction into the substance of an academic course, to integrate information literacy experiences within assignments, and to create accessible data from those course assignments. For those used to the one-shot library instruction approach, this can feel daunting—for both classroom instructor and librarian. This book serves to help guide the way.

To illustrate, perhaps your current scenario is something like this: Frustration sets in at the end of a school year. Library faculty had a well-written strategic plan and vision ready to deliver a successful information literacy program at the beginning of the year. But somehow the year ends with the same old scenario—in practice and in everyone's mind, information literacy means someone showing students how to navigate the online databases to get peer-reviewed, scholarly articles in one-shot instruction sessions, on the ground, online, or at the library's reference desk. In this model there is precious little student in-depth, information literacy skill development or critical thinking and scant data available for assessment needs. Leaving the classroom, what do graduates know about managing, evaluating, utilizing, or creating information? How prepared are they to find the right and accurate information they need? In our conversations and in our research, we have seen that librarians and classroom educators alike need and want more guidance and resources for teaching conceptually about information literacy within the classroom.

But at the time of this book, it appears no one seems to care except an occasional campus accreditation liaison, who wants to add to the accreditation report a nicely written paragraph explaining what's been done regarding information literacy on campus.

This book and its website (https://implementingtheinformationliteracyframework .wordpress.com/ or https://tinyurl.com/ya6h4vyq) intend to change that unacceptable scenario forever. One of the few books written jointly by an academic librarian and a classroom faculty member, *Implementing the Information Literacy Framework* packs dozens of how-to ideas and strategies into ten chapters intentionally written for librarians and classroom instructors. This book promises to honor the rescinded 2000 *Information Literacy Competency Standards for Higher Education* and faithfully bring to realization the concepts developed in the 2015 *Framework for Information Literacy for Higher Education*.

If you have been waiting for a no-nonsense, carefully explained, yet practical source for implementing the *Framework*, this book is for you, your faculty colleagues, and students, all in the context of a discipline-specific, co-equal collaboration between library liaison and classroom educator. Relax and let the book and website assist you in deepening your passion and action for implementing the information literacy *Framework*. The goal of the book is to engage every student in a process so that on graduation day, each has: a) the tools to successfully practice information literacy skills, and b) the intellectual capacities to think conceptually as an information-literate person.

The following is a breakdown of what to expect in each chapter.

- Chapter 1 reminds us why information literacy matters within the context of where it came from, where it is today, and how it is moving into every discipline-specific classroom.
- Chapter 2 provides guidance for librarians and educators on how to begin to integrate the new *Framework* into current information literacy instruction programs.
- Chapter 3 discusses how five pre-2015 published best practices for doing information literacy are still relevant today, with step-by-step instructions.
- Chapter 4 covers information literacy from the perspective of the classroom instructor—how they have perceived librarians and how the *Framework* changes that.
- Chapter 5 looks at the librarian's perspective in regard to offering guidance in using the new *Framework*.
- Chapter 6 offers tips for building successful collaborations in implementing a cross-disciplinary program for information literacy instruction toward a *Framework* campus culture.
- Chapter 7 proposes five step-by-step strategies already implemented on campuses since the *Framework*'s adoption in February 2015, followed by a summary of six suggested best practices for implementing the *Framework* by the original co-chairs of the *Framework* committee.
- Chapter 8 unpacks the first three of six *Framework* frames, with a number of suggested learning outcomes and ready-to-use, in-class assignments and corresponding rubrics. The assignments and rubrics are posted on the book's website to copy and change to meet your information literacy needs.
- Chapter 9 continues the same types of tools found in chapter 8, but with the last three of the six *Framework* frames.

- Chapter 10 takes a look back and a look forward at the intellectual culture of information literacy, with recommendations for all stakeholders in the educational process of developing information-literate graduates and citizens.
- The appendixes provide bonus helpful tools (also on the book's website) including six faculty-friendly essays introducing the six frames, with ready-to-use rubrics for assessing each frame in a student assignment; a set of six flashcards designed to fit on business cards to be used to recall the six *Framework* frames and share their concepts with students and faculty; and publicity bookmarks ready to be copied and cut.

It is hoped this book and its many tools and strategies will help you implement a host of *Framework*-based information literacy experiences for students and faculty, creating a campus culture that understands, and thus integrates, information literacy in its educational mission. Share the experience with a faculty or library colleague, read the book together, and discuss your next steps in information literacy. Enjoy the journey.

Acknowledgments

The authors would like to acknowledge the support and influence of a number of individuals in the creation of this book. First is the director of Azusa Pacific University's three main campus libraries and presence at seven regional campuses, Dr. Paul Gray, along with his full-time and part-time library faculty and staff. Without his years-long encouragement and workload provisions to compose the book, it simply would not have been accomplished.

Second is our amazing and endearing series editor, Sandy Wood, and publisher, Charles Harmon, who provided decades of expertise in librarianship and publishing to correct our textual errors and challenge the ebb and flow of our output.

Third, we acknowledge our patient families and friends. For Dave: his wife Sheli and two daughters, Breanna and Sophia, as they tolerated Dad's attention to his laptop in the evenings and weekends. For Janice: her daughter Emily and sons Roger and Eric, for their love and support; her siblings Nancy, Mary Beth, Michael, and Trish, for their validation and high level of tolerance in listening to endless soliloquies on information literacy; and for dear friends Debbie Edens, Karen Drange, and Barbara Kitching for their unwavering friendship and bottomless encouragement throughout the book-writing process.

And finally, we acknowledge an unknown number of Azusa Pacific University faculty colleagues who allowed us the privilege of listening to their advice as we spoke to them time and time again about our passion for information literacy—over lunches, after faculty meetings, and during moments of passing along campus byways and hallways over the years. It is because of all these individuals that we have come to the finish line of a long and enjoyable journey.

CHAPTER 1

At the Crossroads
Reframing Information Literacy Instruction

IN THIS CHAPTER

▷ Why information literacy matters

▷ The origins of information literacy

▷ The evolution of information literacy

▷ Information literacy today

▷ Moving information literacy into the discipline-specific classroom

---

EDUCATORS SHARE A profound responsibility. They don't want to just transfer knowledge; they want to transform the knowledgeable—their graduates—so that they will aspire to and participate in transforming the world. What does information literacy have to do with that? Why has something that had been largely the domain of librarians become so significant today in higher education? Why have accrediting agencies identified information literacy as a "core competency" for student achievement (WASC, 2013; NEASC, 2011; MSCHE, 2014)? And why have many schools and universities pinpointed it as a student learning outcome among their general education requirements? These developments are changing what educators do in the classroom. Information literacy has become cross-disciplinary, increasingly embedded into course curricula, specified, and measured. It is a new requirement, a new obligation for classroom educators at all levels—primary, secondary, and post-secondary.

So, what exactly is information literacy? How is it related to students' learning, to their critical thinking, and to educating and creating lifelong learners? Let's start with what it's not—at least not anymore, if it ever was. Surprising to some, information literacy is not simply knowing how to use the resources in the library or knowing how to cite a source correctly. Nevertheless, by 2015, nearly all universities and schools formally recognized the five information literacy standards developed and approved by the Association of College & Research Libraries (ACRL) in 2000; many institutions had taken these standards virtually verbatim, but others had created their own individual expressions. However, these now are changing from five rather clear-cut, yet somewhat fixed, concepts to a much broader sort of gestalt concept—sometimes referred to as "metaliteracy." Like salt in water, information literacy impacts how people approach new knowledge, how they find it, process it, use it.

In addition, far more important now is the fact that the nation's graduates, the future citizens of the world, need to be measurably competent not only in finding and using information but in how information is "manufactured," if you will, and in how they will be creating new information. These graduates are the future: They will be shaping the future realities of the world, the language, the mental processes, the culture's ethos, pathos, and logos.

So, information literacy is a much larger concept than critically reading a text or appropriately using a source in a paper. Information literacy first of all involves all the information people receive—what they see and what they hear, whether it's an aesthetic message like a painting, an advertisement, or a song; a piece of written argumentation like a legal brief, an insurance policy, or a medical diagnosis; or a set of numbers or variables. It involves perceiving and interpreting non-verbal messages as well as verbal, non-textual as well as textual. It involves the ambiance of the moment, the context, the emotional intelligence, and the environmental scanning. All these things shape knowledge: what people choose to notice; how they categorize an element of information, value it, recall it; how they foreground it or rank its significance; whether they posit it; and ultimately how or what they create from it. It helps determine whom people will vote for, which car they will buy, what food they will eat or not eat, as well as how they will raise their children, how they understand and obey the laws, how they will perform and grow in their jobs or in their calling or mission, how they will practice and grow in their faith traditions.

Secondly, information literacy involves the ability to deconstruct a piece of information, to perceive what's missing, the questions not asked, the evidence not presented, the voice not heard. It can infer intent, understand audience, and detect the influence of subtleties like tone or mood. All these are necessary to understand a piece of information, not in a superficial or literal way (and even beyond the analytical or evaluative level), but rather at the synthetic and creative level.

Thirdly, information literacy understands how information is formed and preserved—or not. It asks who are the gatekeepers, who controls the language; it understands distortion, whether intentional or a parameter of the medium; it accounts for ambiguity, ambivalence, obscurity, deception, and manipulation. It recognizes truth.

Perhaps surprisingly, all this has evolved and can be extrapolated from the ACRL's former five standards of information literacy: (a) knowing you need information, (b) knowing where and how to find the information you need, (c) knowing how to evaluate and analyze information, (d) knowing how to use that information to accomplish your purpose, and (e) knowing how to use information appropriately and ethically. These aspects are embedded and more comprehensively developed and articulated in the new information literacy "framework" now being implemented by ACRL. Central to this new framework are "threshold concepts": authority is constructed and contextual, information creation as a process, information has value, research is inquiry, scholarship is a conversation, and searching is strategic.

So that's the present reality: Information literacy is a core competency that faculty now are expected to embed in their course curriculum and to assess. As the time approaches for preparation of the next local, regional, and national accrediting reports, schools and universities will need information literacy data to report and will turn—in part, if not wholly—to their classroom faculty to help provide it.

But here's a second reality: More than they realize, faculty are already teaching some of the most important aspects of information literacy. That's because information literacy happens when students are educated. When educators think about the successful graduates in their disciplines, they automatically assume these students have acquired the kinds of intellectual skills that define information literacy. Christine Susan Bruce, in her book *Informed Learning*, clearly reflects the perspective of the educator:

> As educators we need to think about information use and its relationship with learning when we design learning. We need to emphasize both discipline and information-use outcomes in our learning design and implementation; discipline mastery is achieved through the processes of creative and reflective information use. Once we recognize what information is and how we are using it, we can be more in charge of the information environment and how we encounter, source, control, engage with, and use information. We cannot assume that learners are aware of these processes or that they are able to implement them. (2008: 3–4)

So, classroom faculty think about and embed in their instruction the concepts of information literacy, but their frame of reference is different. Classroom faculty think more in terms of informed learning, while the term information literacy—until recently—had been more closely associated with a library perspective. Librarians and regular classroom faculty don't use the same language. For many, there has been a gap between the classroom faculty's understanding of how to incorporate and measure information literacy in the classroom and librarians' understanding of student learning in the discipline-specific class period or course. Many classroom instructors just don't know how to move forward to incorporate assessable information literacy instruction within their various courses, and many librarians have been unprepared to more deeply collaborate with classroom faculty.

So, faculty have a new responsibility—information literacy—and yet at the same time they've been doing it at least implicitly within their courses; after all, don't all educators strive to see informed learning in their classrooms? But many faculty don't have a good plan for doing it explicitly—that is, with measurable outcomes. To whom should they turn for assistance but librarians? Librarians are the resident experts in information literacy, can collaborate with classroom faculty to incorporate information literacy goals into course and program student learning outcomes, can help map those student learning outcomes to assignments and other course resources, and can come alongside faculty to help assess information literacy in their classrooms.

See appendix A, "What Is Information Literacy? A Short Guide for Faculty and Librarians," for a series of short discussions of the six ACRL information literacy concepts, or "frames," each accompanied by an example of what a co-equal collaboration between a librarian and a classroom faculty looks like. The book's website also has a color copy of the guide in both a PDF and a changeable Word format for easy tailoring to one's needs. The book's website is located at https://implementingtheinformationliteracyframework .wordpress.com/ or https://tinyurl.com/ya6h4vyq.

⊚ The Origins of Information Literacy

Information literacy as a separate concept first appeared in the 1970s. The term itself is credited to Paul Zurkowski, who used it in his 1974 paper, "The Information Service Environment Relationships and Priorities," written for the National Commission on Libraries and Information Science under the then U.S. Department of Health, Education, and Welfare's National Institute of Education. Zurkowski himself was president of the Information Industry Association, representing at the time some 70 for-profit information service providers. He wrote:

> People trained in the application of information resources to their work can be called information literates. They have learned techniques and skills for utilizing the wide range of information tools as well as primary sources in molding information solutions to their problems. . . . The individuals in the remaining portion of the population, while literate, in the sense that they can read and write, do not have a measure for the value of information, do not have an ability to mold information to their needs, and realistically must be considered to be information illiterates. (1974: 6)

This is the seminal definition of information literacy, its genesis as a concept. It is important to understanding the development of information literacy over the decades, showing how it started, where it went, and to what it returns. This understanding is key to understanding the new *Framework*. While other disciplines have encompassed many of the aspects of information literacy—rhetoric, critical thinking, and communication studies, for example—the unique characteristics of contemporary information literacy spring from the same 1974 reality that people live in an information age—or as some would say, too-much-information age. Their capacity to address, evaluate, process, and use the amount of information—coming at them in a great number of forms and from a great number of sources—is simply inadequate to meet the sheer volume demanding their attention. At the same time, digital technology has created new venues for generating, delivering, and storing information, requiring new skills simply to manipulate the data as well as new knowledge to understand how the medium affects the message. Reminiscent of the shift from the handwritten to printed books, or from horse and buggy to automobile, these new forms have transformed and continue to transform the way people perceive, interpret, and change the knowledge, if not the realities, of the world surrounding them, whether permanent or ephemeral, physical or mental; at some levels, the new forms require people to reformulate the very ways they think.

Information literacy has never been an idea that settled on any one definition as its precepts have been explored and discussed in its various forms over the years, if not centuries. Its meaning has been interpreted and consigned by librarians, by educators in the professional fields and in the liberal arts, and by practitioners in the media arts, in rhetoric, in communication, and in labor, business, politics, and religion. Information literacy is integral to research and scholarship but also to the preservation and persistence of democracy and to the health of a global economy. The raison d'être of information literacy is to create the possibility for citizens to make informed (and presumably right) choices.

During the early part of the twenty-first century, the domain of information literacy was enlarged with the advent of such phenomena as social networks, online "communities of practice," and easy-to-use communication devices, and at the same time spawned such terms as metaliteracy, transliteracy, multiple literacies, and information fluency. Various schemas jostle in the marketplace of ideas with their different renderings of the hierarchies and relationships for these terms, seeking a common cornerstone for scaffolding their new understandings. While the vast majority of the discourse focuses on education and library instruction, it was not originally centered there. Zurkowski was a pragmatist who foresaw the rise of vast information management systems and wanted the government to invest in teaching the population how to use these. He was neither a librarian nor an educator but a lawyer, and as a lawyer he argued that information literacy was essential to the constitutional right of freedom of expression, which in turn is essential for a free and democratic citizenry to remain so. "The infrastructure supporting our information service environment transcends traditional libraries, publishers and schools. It embraces the totality of explicit physical means, formal and informal, for communicating concepts and ideas," he wrote (1974: 1). In a footnote, he then lists as many of those physical means as possible—including such diverse information sources as town criers, audiotapes, and graffiti. If he were writing this paper today, he would surely list the newest information-distributing venues, those created through digital and wireless technologies.

◎ The Evolution of Information Literacy

Closely following Zurkowski's paper, Lee Burchinal's "The Communications Revolution: America's Third Century Challenge" further contextualized the concept of information literacy in terms of the United States transitioning from an industrial economy to an "information-based economy," which clearly mandated that

we should set about systematically to create "information literacy" for all adults in the nation, so each can function effectively in our emerging society. . . . To be information literate requires a new set of skills. These include how to efficiently and effectively locate and use information needed for problem-solving and decision-making. Such skills have wide applicability for occupational as well as personal activities. (1976: 11)

Though his definition of information literacy does expand its uses beyond academic tasks to those of life management outside of it, Burchinal's focus was on the new communication technologies of automated and electronic communications:

[If] our forecasts are correct, computer terminal devices will be common in the home within a decade. From such devices we'll do our banking, shopping, plan vacations, and communicate with friends. We will have our choice of voice, digital, graphic or pictorial forms of presentation. All family members will use such devices, just as preschool children today master the telephone, record and tape players and television sets. (1976: 12)

Burchinal's paper did not consider the more profound implications of evaluating and creating new information. This ability to "mold information" as part of being information literate is key to a third seminal paper from that decade, mass communication research consultant Cees Hamelink's "An Alternative to News," which reasoned from an ideological or political stance that "a new information literacy is necessary for liberation from the oppressive effects of the institutionalized public media" (1976: 120). His frame of reference was the news media or, more broadly, the "processes of public communication," but really, it is *all* information since, as he argued, "what is actually communicated is the outcome of a decision between possible alternatives which is made on the basis of the most powerful interests (economical, hierarchical, intellectual)" (120). That is to say, there are always gatekeepers, whether technological or living, who process and deliver information. Being information literate, then, is being able to read and interpret the forms, content, and source-givers of any information in order to utilize, organize, or create from it. But herein lies the rub, Hamelink writes:

> The outcome of the decision-making process is, in fact, then a gigantic pollution of information—with meaningless messages. Wherever one watches TV or reads a daily newspaper, "information" about the world is presented in incoherent fragments (especially in "newscasts") or in pre-digested explanations which can only be passively filed away. In this way "information" functions as an oppressive tool since, by its manner of presentation, it keeps people from shaping their own world. (1976: 120)

This perspective—aligned with Zurkowski's definition of information literacy and again current in the new ACRL *Framework* (particularly in the frame "Information Creation as a Process") draws on a liberal arts concept of information literacy, one that involves the processes of knowledge, learning, communication, and composition, to name a few, and one that means information literacy is embedded in the general education process, certainly at the college level but practically at the secondary and even primary school level. It unfolds now as an interdisciplinary idea, reinvented as a core value in creating a society whose members are critical thinkers: "If . . . people are to be given the chance to intervene in their reality"—that is, be free and able to determine their future—"then information channels have to be created that do permit the coherent organization of information" (Hamelink, 1976: 120).

This idea of information literacy as a liberal art, and thus part of the general education process, was articulated by Patricia Senn Breivik as early as 1989 and represented by her as an umbrella of related literacies (figure 1.1). Calling herself "an inappropriate speaker" for the seventeenth annual LOEX [Library Information Exchange] Conference on Library Instruction due to her "inability to be a supporter, any longer, of library instruction," she heralded in the larger concept of information literacy along with the call for librarians to "venture out into the larger sea of higher education of which librarianship is only a small part" (1989: 5). Speaking to her fellow librarians in 1989, Breivik wrote:

> There are strong elements of the current information literacy thrust in the old library-college movement. The emphasis in the latter, however, was on the library taking control of the educational process. This approach has no sex appeal for anybody who was not a librarian and, therefore, was doomed to failure. But if we are talking about the restructuring of the learning process, we are talking about turning over to classroom faculty much of our control of what and how information management skills are mastered. . . . You are being asked to convince [your faculty and administration] that information literacy is the very basis by which the learning process can become more active and by which students can be prepared for lifelong learning and active citizenship. (1989: 3, 5)

Figure 1.1. Information literacy umbrella (Breivik, 2005). © 2005 Taylor & Francis Group. *Used with permission.*

Librarians weren't the only group whose understanding needed enlarging. Arguing from the liberal arts side, Breivik and colleague Dan Jones wrote:

In 1989 . . . a report issued by a group of national leaders in education and librarianship [ALA, 1989: 7] called for a learning process that would "actively involve students in the process of knowing when they have a need for information, identifying information needed to address a given problem or issue, finding needed information, evaluating the information, organizing the information, [and] using the needed information effectively to address the problem or issue at hand." Higher education is being called upon to define and develop a new learning style that fosters within students the abilities needed to be information-literate. (1993: 25)

The most popular and frequently cited articulation of information literacy as a liberal art was by Jeremy Shapiro and Shelley Hughes:

What sort of "information literacy"—an often used but dangerously ambiguous concept—should we be promoting, and what should it accomplish? . . . Should it be, something broader, something that enables individuals not only to use information and information technology effectively and adapt to their constant changes, but also to think critically about the entire information enterprise and information society? Something more akin to a "liberal art"—knowledge that is part of what it means to be a free person in the present historical content of the dawn of the information age? (1996: 31)

In the past two and a half decades, headway in making information literacy a liberal art or general education goal has been modest at best. The story of information literacy has been one largely told by librarians and, as faulted by its critics, the most commonly accepted (and recently rescinded) *Standards*, those created by ACRL, had been framed as a skill set within academics, rather than situated for the information-saturated world at large where citizens live and work for many, many years after they leave school.

Given the history, that is to be expected. The early instructional efforts in information use were called "bibliographic instruction sessions" and were developed by librarians in the 1970s; this then evolved into the more comprehensive "library instruction" and "reference services" by the 1980s, and finally the term "information literacy" became common by the 1990s, precipitated in part by the publication in 1987 of Kuhlthau's *Information Skills for an Information Society* and the formation that same year of the American Library Association (ALA) Presidential Committee on Information Literacy. Soon after, in 1990, the ALA formed the National Forum on Information Literacy "to mainstream information literacy philosophy and practices throughout every sector of American society" (NFIL, 2014b). The group now consists of "a robust collaborative of 100+ national and international organizations working together, on various levels, to mainstream this critical, 21st century educational and workforce development concept throughout every segment of society" (NFIL, 2014c).

But now, after decades of a largely library-driven, skills-set approach to information literacy, with the advent of the *Framework* a new age is breaking that, for some, reinvents old concepts in perceiving, interpreting, and synthesizing the information of the world and refocuses the term back to its conceptual roots:

- In an age of too much information, we need more nuanced and comprehensive information management skills than in previous ages.
- The processes for gathering, "publishing," distributing, and accessing information are changing and expanding.
- The critical thinking skills necessary to evaluate and determine how to use information in the older systems of information providers need to be adapted to the new systems of information.
- Information-literate citizens are essential for a free society and a healthy global economy.
- Information literacy is a life skill necessary for lifelong learning and decision making.
- Those who are information literate will define information literacy, not the providers of information.

As Drew Whitworth has stated, "Information is not something that should be given to people, or 'retrieved' by them, but formed by them, as a response to their own needs and through their own efforts" (2013). Given these conditions, information, in the hands of the information-literate population, becomes empowering.

Information Literacy Today

While it is important to remember that this book focuses on the language and organization of the new ACRL *Framework*, the *Framework* itself was created by drawing from the broader traditions of information literacy. Around the globe there are many formal statements defining information literacy, and until the recent *Framework*, one of the most commonly cited definitions in education has been the one codified in 2000 by the ACRL. From its website:

> Information literacy forms the basis for lifelong learning. It is common to all disciplines, to all learning environments, and to all levels of education. It enables learners to master content and extend their investigations, become more self-directed, and assume greater control over their own learning. An information-literate individual is able to:
>
> 1. Determine the extent of information needed
> 2. Access the needed information effectively and efficiently
> 3. Evaluate information and its sources critically
> 4. Incorporate selected information into one's knowledge base
> 5. Use information effectively to accomplish a specific purpose
> 6. Understand the economic, legal, and social issues surrounding the use of information, and access and use information ethically and legally. (ACRL, 2000: 2)

The New ACRL *Framework*

As of 2015, ACRL has extensively revised the definition of information literacy:

> Because this *Framework* envisions information literacy as extending the arc of learning throughout students' academic careers and as converging with other academic and social learning goals, an expanded definition of information literacy is offered here to emphasize dynamism, flexibility, individual growth, and community learning: "Information literacy is the set of integrated abilities encompassing the reflective discovery of information, the understanding of how information is produced and valued, and the use of information in creating new knowledge and participating ethically in communities of learning." (ACRL, 2015: 3)

The task force has moved away from the term "Standards" and instead identified six "Frames" of information literacy, outlined below.

Authority Is Constructed and Contextual: "Information resources reflect their creators' expertise and credibility, and are evaluated based on the information need and the context in which the information will be used. Authority is constructed in that various communities may recognize different types of authority. It is contextual in that the information need may help to determine the level of authority required" (ACRL, 2015: 4).

Information Creation as a Process: "Information in any format is produced intentionally to convey a message and is shared via a selected delivery method. The iterative processes of researching, creating, revising, and disseminating information vary, and the resulting product reflects these differences" (ACRL, 2015: 6).

Information Has Value: "Information possesses several dimensions of value, including as a commodity, as a means of education, as a means to influence, and as a means of negotiating and understanding the world. Legal and socioeconomic interests influence information production and dissemination" (ACRL, 2015: 8).

Research as Inquiry: "Research is iterative and depends upon asking increasingly complex or new questions whose answers in turn develop additional questions or lines of inquiry in any field" (ACRL, 2015: 9).

Scholarship as Conversation: "Communities of scholars, researchers, or professionals engage in sustained discourse with new insights and discoveries occurring over time as a result of varied perspectives and interpretations" (ACRL, 2015: 10).

Searching as Strategic Exploration: "Searching for information is often nonlinear and iterative, requiring the evaluation of a range of information sources and the mental flexibility to pursue alternate avenues as new understanding develops" (ACRL, 2015: 12).

Clearly, the *Framework* is an approach that leans toward the theoretical and is meant to be applicable and relevant to any discipline or situation of inquiry. And just as clearly, it travels into the territory of a liberal art and touches on areas of discourse in such disciplines as communication studies, composition, logic, philosophy, and rhetoric, among others. Implicit is an invitation for collaboration among librarians and classroom educators in these different fields of study; implicit is the understanding that information literacy cannot be contained or owned by any one group or discipline. Given that the ACRL *Framework* is contextualized within higher education, it is useful in the next few pages to scan the work of some of the other key organizations in this field in order to get a broader, more societally based understanding.

United Nations Educational, Scientific and Cultural Organization (UNESCO)

The roots of information literacy in the United Nations Educational, Scientific and Cultural Organization date back to the 1948 UN Universal Declaration of Human Rights, which declared its members' "common desire and commitment to build a people-centered, inclusive, and development-oriented information society, where everyone can create, access, utilize and share information and knowledge" in order to "achieve their full potential in promoting their sustainable development and improving their quality of life" (Moeller, et al., 2011: 9). Adhering to the more recent 2005 Alexandria Proclamation that information literacy is a "basic human right," in 2008, following an international contest, UNESCO created a logo to help identify the organization's efforts to promote information literacy across the globe (figure 1.2). UNESCO, in its "Understanding In-

Figure 1.2. UNESCO international information literacy logo. © *2008 UNESCO. Used with permission.*

formation Literacy: A Primer," identifies 11 "stages" of the information literacy life cycle and describes information literacy as

> the set of skills, attitudes and knowledge necessary to know when information is needed to help solve a problem or make a decision, how to articulate that information need in searchable terms and language, then search efficiently for the information, retrieve it, interpret and understand it, organize it, evaluate its credibility and authenticity, assess its relevance, communicate it to others if necessary, then utilize it to accomplish bottom-line purposes . . . sometimes the terms "Information Competency," or "Information Fluency" or even other terms, are used in different countries, cultures or languages, in preference to the term Information Literacy. (Horton and UNESCO, 2007: 53)

National Forum on Information Literacy (NFIL)

In 1989 the ALA formed the Presidential Committee on Information Literacy, which in turn issued a report of six recommendations for teaching information literacy to students and educators, along with "design[ing] one or more models for information literacy development appropriate to formal and informal learning environments throughout people's lifetimes," and established the National Forum on Information Literacy. NFIL defines information literacy as

> the ability to know when there is a need for information, to identify, locate, evaluate, and use effectively that information for the issue or problem at hand. Simply put, information literacy is the key competency needed to enhance K–16 academic performance, engage patient personal responsibility, improve workplace performance and productivity, and compete effectively in a dynamically evolving world marketplace. (NFIL, 2014a)

NFIL has developed a visual representation of information literacy as an umbrella or roof over four elements or aspects of information literacy: media literacy, research and library skills, critical literacy, and information ethics (figure 1.3).

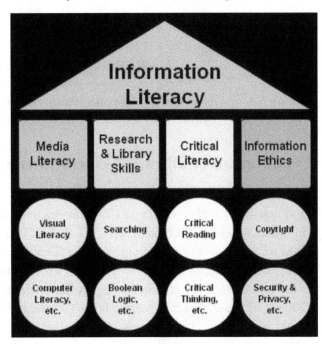

Figure 1.3. NFIL information literacy "umbrella" graphic. © 2011 National Forum on Information Literacy. Used with permission.

Society of College, National and University Libraries (SCONUL)

This group defines information literacy as "an umbrella term which encompasses concepts such as digital, visual and media literacies, academic literacy, information handling, information skills, data curation and data management" (SCONUL, 2011: 3). It identifies seven "pillars" of the "information literacy landscape" (figure 1.4):

1. Identify: able to identify a personal need for information
2. Scope: can assess current knowledge and identify gaps
3. Plan: can construct strategies for locating information and data
4. Gather: can locate and access the information and data they need
5. Evaluate: can review the research process and compare and evaluate information and data
6. Manage: can organize information professionally and ethically
7. Present: can apply the knowledge gained; presenting the results of their research, synthesizing new and old information and data to create new knowledge, and disseminating it in a variety of ways. (SCONUL, 2011)

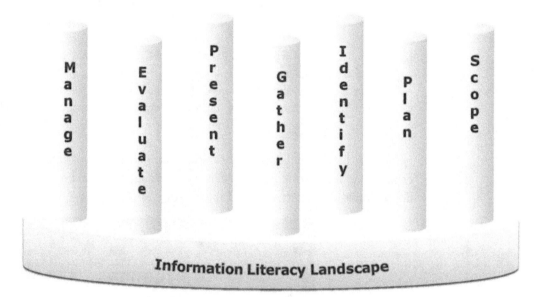

Figure 1.4. Seven pillars of information literacy model. © *2011 Image courtesy of Society of College, National and University Libraries, CC-BY-SA. Used with permission.*

International Federation of Library Associations and Institutions (IFLA)

The International Federation of Library Associations and Institutions was formed in 1927 and now has 1,500 members in 150 countries, representing "the interests of library and information services and their users" (IFLA, 2017). In 2006, Jesús Lau, chair of the IFLA Information Literacy Section, authored the "Guidelines on Information Literacy for Life-long Learning" with the intent to "provid[e] a pragmatic framework for those professionals who need or are interested in starting an information literacy program" (Lau and IFLA, 2006: 1). He pictured information literacy as the hub of eight related skill sets and concepts: information competencies, user training, development of information skills, information fluency, user education, bibliographic instruction, library orientation, and, allowing for the continued evolution of information literacy, "other concepts" (figure 1.5). He wrote:

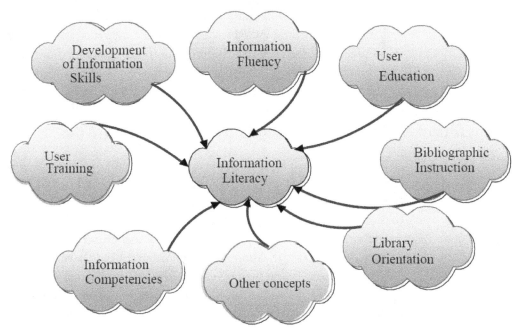

Figure 1.5. The concept of information literacy. © *2006 Lau and IFLA Information Literacy Section. Used with permission.*

In summary, information literacy is assumed to be the knowledge and skills necessary to correctly identify information needed to perform a specific task or solve a problem, cost-efficiently search for information, organize or reorganize it, interpret and analyze it once it is found and retrieved (e.g., downloaded), evaluate the accuracy and reliability of the information, including ethically acknowledging the sources from whence it was obtained, communicate and present the results of analyzing and interpreting it to others if necessary, and then utilize it for achieving actions and results. (Lau and IFLA, 2006: 17)

Project Information Literacy (PIL)

Project Information Literacy is a public benefit, non-profit organization founded in 2008 and funded through the University of Washington Foundation. From December 2013 through 2015, PIL, along with the University of Washington iSchool, conducted a quantitative study on the "information seeking behavior of relatively recent college graduates used for lifelong learning in personal life, the workplace, and the local communities where they lived" (http://projectinfolit.org). Analyzing the results from 1,651 online surveys and 126 telephone interviews from 10 U.S. colleges and universities, PIL's final report concluded:

> As a whole graduates prided themselves on their ability to search, evaluate, and present information, skills they honed during college. Yet far fewer said that their college experience had helped them develop the critical thinking skills of framing and asking questions on their own, which is a skill they inevitably needed in their post-college lives. (Head, 2016)

Thus, its findings support the rationale for the new ACRL *Framework*, particularly as expressed in the frame "Research as Inquiry," and support as well the Association of American Colleges & Universities' (AAC&U) Principles of Excellence 3, "Teach the Arts of Inquiry and Innovation" (https://www.aacu.org/leap/principles-of-excellence).

Though no formal definition for information literacy seems to be present on its website, in a paper for the ACRL 2013 national conference in Indianapolis, PIL Director Alison Head adopted the definition of information literacy from David Bawden (2001): "Information literacy is defined as the competencies an individual summons in order to locate, retrieve, evaluate, select, and use information sources" (Head, 2013: 473).

Association of American Colleges & Universities (AAC&U)

AAC&U has not developed any statements defining information literacy but rather has adapted its definition from NFIL: "The ability to know when there is a need for information, to be able to identify, locate, evaluate, and effectively and responsibly use and share that information for the problem at hand" (AAC&U, 2009). From the work of NFIL as well as ACRL (Lee, 2012: Table 1.1), the association has developed an information literacy rubric that is in common usage. Many colleges have adopted this rubric or used it as a template to create their own. A dozen case studies posted on the AAC&U website have demonstrated some of the ways and the extent to which these rubrics are being used at these institutions (AAC&U, 2011).

National Education Association (NEA)

In 2011, the National Education Association rolled out a publication entitled "Preparing 21st Century Students for a Global Society: An Educator's Guide to the 'Four Cs'" (NEA, 2011). It was the culmination of a more than 10-year process by its Partnership for 21st Century Skills, which began in 2002 with its *Framework for 21st Century Learning* that highlighted 18 different skills and gathered support from 16 states to "build 21st century outcomes into their standards, professional development, and assessments" (NEA, 2011). Eighteen skills proved to be too cumbersome, so with further work and collaboration with dozens of organizations, NEA reduced the number to four "21st century skills that were most important for K–12 education" (NEA, 2011: 3). These were labeled the "Four Cs"—critical thinking, communication, collaboration, and creativity. Information literacy is not mentioned but is implied within the Cs, especially within the critical thinking:

> Today's citizens must be active critical thinkers if they are to compare evidence, evaluate competing claims, and make sensible decisions. Today's 21st century families must sift through a vast array of information regarding financial, health, civic, and even leisure activities to formulate plausible plans of action. (NEA, 2011: 8)

Big6

Big6 is one of the most well-known classroom problem-solving models used by educators, especially at the K–12 level. It is the brainchild of Bob Berkowitz and Mike Eisenberg, nationally recognized information literacy experts. A frequently published writer in the field of information science, Eisenberg is dean emeritus and professor for the University of Washington Information School. With degrees in education, library science, and school administration, Berkowitz is a nationally recognized consultant, educator, speaker, and author in information literacy and information technology. The Big6 website (http://big6.com) gives credit to the ACRL for its definition of information literacy:

There are many different sets of information literacy standards—created by professional organizations, state education departments, school districts, and individual schools and professionals. While the ACRL standards are aimed at college level students, we believe that these standards are relevant to all age and grade levels. (Big6, 2012)

Nonetheless, the Big6 model does deviate from the five ACRL standards, creating six "stages" for "information problem solving":

The Big6 is a process model of how people of all ages solve an information problem. From practice and study, we found that successful information problem-solving encompasses six stages with two sub-stages under each:

1. Task Definition
    1.1 Define the information problem
    1.2 Identify information needed
2. Information Seeking Strategies
    2.1 Determine all possible sources
    2.2 Select the best sources
3. Location and Access
    3.1 Locate sources (intellectually and physically)
    3.2 Find information within sources
4. Use of Information
    4.1 Engage (e.g., read, hear, view, touch)
    4.2 Extract relevant information
5. Synthesis
    5.1 Organize from multiple sources
    5.2 Present the information
6. Evaluation
    6.1 Judge the product (effectiveness)
    6.2 Judge the process (efficiency). (Big6, 2014)

Other Sources of Definitions

Major organizations, mostly library associations, have long histories and vast amounts of writings on information literacy. While many educators and institutions have accepted virtually word-for-word what these library groups have prepared, others have owned the idea for themselves and have created their own materials. One example is the Claremont Colleges in Southern California, a consortium that has created a model for information literacy based on the higher education concept of "habits of mind":

Information literacy is the ability to use critical thinking to create meaningful knowledge from information. The information literate Claremont Colleges student:

- Engages in a process of inquiry in order to frame intellectual challenges and identify research needs;
- Strategically accesses and evaluates information;
- Communicates information effectively;
- Provides clear attribution of source materials used;
- And develops insight into the social, legal, economic, and ethical aspects of information creation, use, access, and durability. (Claremont Colleges Library, 2013)

These organizations discussed are some of the most prominent, significant, and representative in information literacy, but certainly this list is not definitive.

🌀 Moving Information Literacy into the Discipline-Specific Classroom

While librarians may be comfortable and well-versed in the nuances of information literacy, the concept is generally muddier to the classroom instructor. Often the math teacher or the music instructor is far more concerned—and rightly so—about teaching the concepts and principles of their discipline. These instructors are equally comfortable and well-versed in the nuances of their fields and know what they need to do in the classroom to teach their subject. But in the absence of much documented bridge building, they perhaps have limited their understanding of information literacy to only instruction on how to use the library—"librarians just need to show us how to find what we want," it seems to be said, "and we'll take it from there." After all, librarians are rarely mathematicians, chemists, or musicians.

In a recent conversation with a fellow educator in math and physics about the ACRL information literacy standards used at Azusa Pacific University, particularly standards 3, 4, and 5 (evaluate information and its sources critically, incorporate selected information into one's knowledge base, use information effectively to accomplish a specific purpose), the faculty member remarked, "I'm already doing that; that's what I do in the classroom." He had not perceived that aspect of his instruction as being part of teaching information literacy.

That's what makes the new *Framework for Information Literacy for Higher Education* so exciting. While much work remains to be done from discipline to discipline in order to figure out how to practically utilize this new *Framework* within an academic field, there is room now to engage in meaningful discourse about developing coursework strategies to explicitly identify and integrate information literacy instruction into classroom teaching, whatever the discipline, and then assessing student learning outcomes in information literacy competencies for a program, for a grade, or for an institution.

From the perspective of the classroom educator, in the spirit of an invitation for academic discourse, this allows for a non-librarian set of key definitions:

- *Information literacy*: The ability to critically "read" and comprehend, and then effectively act on, all information from any medium (including digital) perceived by any or all of the five senses *either passively or actively*. Key elements include knowing when information is needed, having the intellectual skills to determine the extent and kind of information needed, having the practical skills to find and garner the information wanted *or reject it when not*, having the intellectual abilities to evaluate information received *either passively or actively* in terms of relevance and integrity, knowing how and *when, if at all*, to execute the use of that information effectively and ethically in order to affect one's world, and being able to synthesize and articulate new knowledge from that information.
- *Information literacy competencies*: The specific skills or abilities needed to be information literate.
- *Information literacy frames*: The proposed six "frames" that represent the "core ideas" or "threshold concepts" of information literacy as developed by the ACRL. These six frames are: (a) Authority Is Constructed and Contextual, (b) Informa-

tion Creation as a Process, (c) Information Has Value, (d) Research as Inquiry, (e) Scholarship as Conversation, and (f) Searching as Strategic Exploration.

- *Metaliteracy*: Overarching term referring to different aspects of information literacy—such as computer literacy, visual literacy, digital literacy, media literacy—and expanding the concept of information literacy to include a self-reflective process, that is, *thinking* about the information process itself.
- *Multiple literacies*: A term similar to metaliteracy, but indicating that a separateness and/or equality exists between the various literacies, and that one can have certain literacies but not others, depending on one's context or environment, whether temporary or effectively permanent.
- *Transliteracy*: Generally, the ability to be "literate" across media, to understand how the different literacies interact and impact each other and how this influences meaning, especially in terms of social media. It is a rather new term and thus one that is evolving. It comes from the word "transliterate" itself ("to write words or letters in the characters of another alphabet," Merriam-Webster Online Dictionary, 2014) and originated with a study in online reading begun in 2005 by English professor Alan Liu at the University of California–Santa Barbara. For more information about Dr. Liu's "Transliteracies Project," go to http://transliteracies .english.ucsb.edu/category/about (Liu, 2017). Transliteracy's bearing on the larger discussion of information literacy is yet to be discovered and mapped.

Information literacy to the average person on the street may not seem like a complicated concept. Stated simply, it may mean just being able to find the information you need for whatever purpose is at hand. But to the mind of the educator, that is the tip of the proverbial iceberg. An unquestioning assumption that what you read or see or hear is true or fair, and an uncritical mind that takes whatever floats to the top of the information pile, is not only naïve but a danger to a free society and to the individual who fails to discern.

Key Points

Information literacy began as a concept germinated within the advent of the "Information Age." It epitomized the realization that there was just too much information being produced and too many ways to receive information. People needed a new set of skills to manage, process, and utilize this information, and they needed the intellectual abilities to critically interpret, evaluate, and ethically create information. Libraries by and large soon became the purveyors of information literacy instruction, but by the 1990s it was clear that the intellectual realities of some of its original conceptualization were not being addressed by current methods, as exemplified by the 2000 ACRL *Standards*. Hence, the 2015 *Framework* was created, but the *Framework* requires a significantly different approach to information literacy instruction, and that is what this book is about. Here are the key foundational points to keep in mind when proceeding through this book:

- Information literacy today is understood as a set of both intellectual and practical skills that impact all aspects of life management and human development.
- Information literacy is a core competency in contemporary education that faculty in all disciplines are expected to embed in their curriculum and to assess.

- Faculty already teach some aspects of information literacy, but most do not use the same frame of reference and language as librarians.
- Information literacy has evolved from the dawn of the information age, when it was recognized that the sheer volume of information from an expanding number and types of sources required new and more highly developed information analysis skills and management skills.
- Since it "forms the basis for lifelong learning" (ACRL), information literacy is best conceptualized as a liberal art and as part of the general education process.
- The new ACRL *Framework for Information Literacy for Higher Education* embraces this liberal arts approach, defining information literacy as a "spectrum of abilities, practices, and habits of mind."
- Globally, many groups and organizations, such as UNESCO, actively promote a comprehensive understanding of information literacy as a "basic human right."
- Education in information literacy requires an intentional and systematic cross-disciplinary collaboration among classroom educators, librarians, and education policy makers and administrators.

The chapters that follow will attempt to explicate the most important aspects of teaching information literacy to the future information makers of our society. Chapter 2, "From *Standards* to *Framework*: The Difference and Why It Matters," will describe in more detail the evolution of academic standards for information literacy as formerly represented by the 2000 *Standards*, and now by the new ACRL *Framework*, and will provide guidance for librarians and educators on how to begin to integrate the new *Framework* into current information literacy instruction programs.

References

ALA (American Library Association). 1989. "Presidential Committee on Information Literacy: Final Report." American Library Association. http://www.ala.org/PrinterTemplate.cfm?Section=infolitb&template=/ContentManagement/ContentDisplay.cfm&ContentID=35792.

AAC&U (Association of American Colleges & Universities). 2009. "Information Literacy VALUE Rubric." https://www.aacu.org/value/rubrics/information-literacy.

AAC&U (Association of American Colleges & Universities). 2011. "VALUE Rubrics Case Studies." https://www.aacu.org/value/casestudies.

ACRL (Association of College & Research Libraries). 2000. *Information Literacy Competency Standards for Higher Education*. American Library Association. http://www.ala.org/acrl/standards/informationliteracycompetency.

ACRL (Association of College & Research Libraries). 2015. *Framework for Information Literacy for Higher Education*. American Library Association. http://www.ala.org/acrl/standards/ilframework.

Bawden, David. 2001. "Information and Digital Literacies: A Review of the Concepts." *Journal of Documentation* 57, no. 2: 218–59. doi:10.1108/EUM0000000007083.

Big6. 2012. "Information Literacy & Critical Thinking Connections." http://big6.com/pages/pre-edit-originals/information-literacy.php.

Big6. 2014. "Big6 Skills Overview." http://big6.com/pages/about/big6-skills-overview.php.

Breivik, Patricia Senn. 1989. "Information Literacy: Revolution in Education." *Proceedings of the 17th National LOEX Library Instruction Conference*, Ann Arbor, MI, May 4 and 5.

Breivik, Patricia Senn. 2005. "21st Century Learning and Information Literacy." *Change: The Magazine of Higher Learning* 37, no. 2 (March–April): 21–27.

Breivik, Patricia S., and Dan L. Jones. 1993. "Information Literacy: Liberal Education for the Information Age." *Liberal Education* 79, no. 1 (Winter): 24–29.

Bruce, Christine Susan. 2008. *Informed Learning*. Chicago: Association of College and Research Libraries.

Burchinal, Lee. 1976. "The Communications Revolution: America's Third Century Challenge." Paper presented at the Texas A&M University Library's Centennial Academic Assembly, College Station, TX, September 24.

Claremont Colleges Library. 2013. "Information Literacy at the Claremont Colleges: Critical Habits of Mind and First-Year/Capstone/Graduate Learning Outcomes." http://libraries.claremont .edu/informationliteracy/documents/CCL_Information_Literacy_Habits%20of%20Mind.pdf.

Hamelink, Cees. 1976. "An Alternative to News." *Journal of Communication* 26, no. 4 (Fall): 120–23.

Head, Alison J. 2013. "Project Information Literacy: What Can Be Learned about the Information-Seeking Behavior of Today's College Students?" Paper presented at the annual meeting of the Association of College & Research Libraries, Chicago, July. http://www.ala.org/acrl/ sites/ala.org.acrl/files/content/conferences/confsandpreconfs/2013/papers/Head_Project.pdf.

Head, Alison J. 2016. *Staying Smart: How Today's Graduates Continue to Learn Once They Complete College*. Project Information Literacy. http://www.projectinfolit.org/uploads/2/7/5/4/27541717/ staying_smart_pil_1_5_2016b_fullreport.pdf.

Horton, Forest W., Jr., and UNESCO (United Nations Educational, Scientific and Cultural Organization). 2007. *Understanding Information Literacy: A Primer*. http://www.unesco.org/new/ en/communication-and-information/resources/publications-and-communication-materials/ publications/full-list/understanding-information-literacy-a-primer/.

IFLA (International Federation of Library Associations and Institutions). 2017. "Home Page." https://www.ifla.org/.

Kuhlthau, Carol Collier. 1987. *Information Skills for an Information Society: A Review of Research. An ERIC Information Analysis Product*. Washington, DC: Office of Educational Research and Improvement. ED 297 740.

Lau, Jesús, and IFLA (International Federation of Library Associations and Institutions). 2006. "Guidelines on Information Literacy for Lifelong Learning." http://www.ifla.org/files/assets/ information-literacy/publications/ifla-guidelines-en.pdf.

Lee, Virginia S. 2012. "What Is Inquiry-Guided Learning?" *New Directions for Teaching and Learning* 129 (Spring): 5–14. doi:10.1002/tl.20002.

Liu, Alan. 2017. "Transliteracies Project: Overview." http://transliteracies.english.ucsb.edu/cate gory/about.

Merriam-Webster Online Dictionary. 2014. "Transliterate." https://www.merriam-webster.com/ dictionary/transliterate.

MSCHE (Middle States Commission on Higher Education). 2014. *Standards for Accreditation and Requirements of Affiliation*. 13th ed. Philadelphia, PA: MSCHE. http://www.msche.org/ publications_view.asp?idPublicationType=1&txtPublicationType=Standards+for+Accredita tion+and+Requirements+of+Affiliation.

Moeller, Susan, Ammu Joseph, Jesús Lau, Toni Carbo, and UNESCO (United Nations Educational, Scientific and Cultural Organization). 2011. "Towards Media and Information Literacy Indicators." UNESCO. http://www.unesco.org/new/fileadmin/MULTIMEDIA/HQ/ CI/CI/pdf/unesco_mil_indicators_background_document_2011_final_en.pdf.

NEA (National Education Association). 2011. *Preparing 21st Century Students for a Global Society: An Educator's Guide to the "Four Cs."* National Education Association. http://www.nea.org/ assets/docs/A-Guide-to-Four-Cs.pdf.

NFIL (National Forum on Information Literacy). 2014a. "About the NFIL." http://infolit.org/ about-the-nfil/. (Note: This website ceased to exist May 26, 2016; for more information see https://ojs.lboro.ac.uk/JIL/article/view/PRJ-V9-I2/2246.)

NFIL (National Forum on Information Literacy). 2014b. "Our Mission." http://infolit .org/?s=our+mission.

NFIL (National Forum on Information Literacy). 2014c. "Digital Literacy Resources." https://digitalliteracy.gov/national-forum-information-literacy-nfil.

NEASC (New England Association of Schools and Colleges). 2011. *Standards for Accreditation.* Burlington, MA: NEASC. https://cihe.neasc.org/cihe-publications/standards-accreditation-2011.

Shapiro, Jeremy J., and Shelley K. Hughes. 1996. "Information Literacy as a Liberal Art." *Educom Review* 31, no. 2 (March–April): 31–36.

SCONUL (Society of College, National and University Libraries). 2011. *The SCONUL Seven Pillars of Information Literacy: Core Model for Higher Education.* http://www.sconul.ac.uk/sites/default/files/documents/coremodel.pdf.

WASC (Western Association of Schools and Colleges) Senior College and University Commission. 2013. *2013 Handbook of Accreditation.* Alameda, CA: WASC. http://www.wascsenior.org/.

Whitworth, Drew. 2013. "Cees Hamelink and the Forgotten Political Origins of Information Literacy." *Anarchic Educator* (blog), February 18. http://anarchiceducator.wordpress.com/2013/02/18/cees-hamelink-and-the-forgotten-political-origins-of-information-literacy/.

Zurkowski, Paul G. 1974. "The Information Service Environment Relationships and Priorities. Related Paper No. 5." Washington, DC: National Commission on Libraries and Information Science, National Program for Library and Information Services. ERIC, ED 100 391.

Further Reading

Horton, Forest W., Jr., and UNESCO. 2013. *Overview of Information Literacy Resources Worldwide.* http://www.unesco.org/new/fileadmin/MULTIMEDIA/HQ/CI/CI/pdf/news/overview_info_lit_resources.pdf.

CHAPTER 2

From *Standards* to *Framework*

The Difference and Why It Matters

THIS CHAPTER IS ABOUT coming to a broad understanding of the intellectual evolution in information literacy as the concept moved from its formal beginnings in the *Standards* (2000) to the paradigm shift represented by the 2015 *Framework*. Simply put, the *Framework* cannot be taught like the *Standards* because it is not a shift in content, but a shift in perceptions and mind-set. Conceptualizing a program for instruction must be predicated on this and, thus, the new understanding must be there first before practical steps can be taken.

A Brief Taste of Information Illiteracy

Imagine completing a school assignment that asks you to argue whether the Holocaust, a well-documented historical event for which there are still living witnesses, actually occurred. You are given some sources to help you decide and to help support the position you take. After investigating the given sources, you decide that the Holocaust is a hoax and support your claim from these given sources. You are awarded a passing grade and praised for your well-reasoned arguments.

Sounds too incredible? It happened in a southern California school in 2014 (Yarbrough, 2014). Eighth graders were given several Internet sources to investigate, sources purportedly representing both positions. The critical thinking assignment stemmed from the class reading of *The Diary of Anne Frank*, a book that at the end of the assignment some students concluded was also a hoax. One of the key sources for the writing assignment was the so-called forensic evidence from Holocaust denier Fred A. Leuchter, Jr. (discredited by the 1999 documentary *Mr. Death: The Rise and Fall of Fred A. Leuchter, Jr.*). However, apparently few of the San Bernardino students questioned Leuchter's authority or challenged evidence offered on his website and instead accepted his information at face value. According to the *San Bernardino County Sun* (figure 2.1), the children were not given general access to the Internet or to a library when completing the assignment but rather directed to only certain websites. The children thus were left to their own abilities to evaluate the information they had been given.

THE SUN
EDUCATION

EXCLUSIVE: Holocaust denied by students in Rialto school assignment

By Beau Yarbrough, The Sun

POSTED: 07/11/14, 5:13 PM PDT UPDATED: ON 07/14/2014

225 COMMENTS

Dozens of Rialto eighth-graders questioned whether the Holocaust occurred in essays written for an in-class assignment this spring.

Rialto Unified School District administrators, besieged by criticism after the assignment became public in May, claimed at the time that none of the students who completed the assignment questioned or denied the Holocaust, but a survey of the students' work by this news organization found numerous examples of students expressing doubt or flatly denying that the Holocaust occurred.

"I believe the event was fake, according to source 2 the event was exhaggerated," one student wrote. (Students' and teachers' original spelling and grammar are retained throughout this story.) "I felt that was strong enogh evidence to persuade me the event was a hoax."

In some cases, students earned high marks and praise for arguing the Holocaust never occurred, with teachers praising their well-reasoned arguments: "you did well using the evidence to support your claim," the above student's teacher wrote on his assignment.

Figure 2.1.   News article in the *San Bernardino County Sun. © 2014 Digital First Media. Used with permission.*

What went wrong? Would access to the Internet or a library have allowed them to debunk the deniers? Was it simply a flawed assignment, or does it reveal larger questions about what students need to know about being information literate? What are the larger ramifications of people lacking the skills or "habits of mind" to be able to ask critical questions about the world around them, a world defined by the information drawn from it? A government or society that upholds freedom of information in its laws and courts needs its citizens to be able to exercise that freedom through being information literate. They need to understand how authority is constructed and how it is related to the formation and distribution of information; they need to understand how information is created and how they can be part of that process; they must be able to consider, compute, and manipulate the various values of information; they must be able to make inquiry; they must understand and participate in discourse; they need to be able to recognize the need for information and know how to search for the information that they have the right and responsibility to have.

Information literacy, as a core life skill in today's information-saturated and media-saturated world, is as much about evaluating and rightly using that information as it is about access and discoverability. Using it for school assignments is certainly expected, but information literacy must also be used to create, decide, fight, or change something. To bend an idiom, schools and librarians can "lead a horse to water," but it's the drinking (or not) that's the issue. Every piece of information is filtered by the mind—is it drivel, junk, propaganda fallacy, superstition, or is it truth? Is it a misinterpretation, a delusion, a distortion (figure 2.2)? Information literacy is about having the eyes to see what the nature of a piece of information truly is.

The Holocaust school assignment was, at the least, a missed opportunity to teach about information literacy, to open a discussion on how students can begin to manage the information that confronts and surrounds them every day, to raise their consciousness on the need to be information literate, and even to spark a sense of urgency before the larger issues of life barge into their lives.

⑥ A Good Start—*Standards* for Information Literacy

While this guide focuses more on the ACRL's 2000 *Standards* and its 2015 *Framework*, there are, in fact, a number of information standards or framework efforts from other organizations, educational institutions, and individual scholars and experts. Of particular relevance is the American Association of School Librarians (AASL) publication *Standards for the 21st-Century Learner* (AASL, 2007), which guides many elementary and secondary schools throughout the United States. These standards—or perhaps others like them—could have guided such educators at the San Bernardino grammar school with its Holocaust assignment. As AASL declared in its 2007 publication:

> The definition of information literacy has become more complex as resources and technologies have changed. Information literacy has progressed from the simple definition of using reference resources to find information. Multiple literacies, including digital, visual, textual, and technological, have now joined information literacy as crucial tools for this century.

AASL has articulated four standards or "essential learning skills" that today's learners need and has stated that learners use skills, resources, and tools to:

drivel junk **bunk** hooey HOKUM **baloney**

twaddle **rot** propaganda INDOCTRINATION dogma

brainwash hypocrisy BIAS prejudice

favoritism **partiality** subjective ARBITRARY

fraud scam **rip-off** ploy

schmooze job hoop-la **puffery** hype

SNOW JOB glib superficial **frivolous** phony

OVERSIMPLIFICATION irrelevant out-of-date

fallacy myth SUPERSTITION trickery

deception **manipulation** cover-up WHITEWASH

gloss over error **miscalculation** oversight

BLUNDER omission mistake **misjudgment**

misreading MISINTERPRETATION delusion

illusion **misunderstanding** inaccuracy

HALF-TRUTH distortion spin **hot air** hard sell

Figure 2.2. Common words used to evaluate the character and value of information.

1. Inquire, think critically, and gain knowledge
2. Draw conclusions, make informed decisions, apply knowledge to new situations, and create new knowledge
3. Share knowledge and participate ethically and productively as members of our democratic society
4. Pursue personal and aesthetic growth. (AASL, 2007)

Each of these four broad statements are further defined under the four headings of: *Skills, Dispositions in Action, Responsibilities,* and *Self-Assessment Strategies.* Historically, this 2007 version is an evolution from its 1998 parent document, *Information Literacy Standards for Student Learning: Standards and Indicators*, which AASL co-produced with the Association for Educational Communications and Technology (AECT). Interestingly, the 2007 and 1998 versions differ in ways that are similar to the differences between the 2015 ACRL *Framework* and the 2000 ACRL *Standards*. Unpacking the 1998 document further, AASL and AECT articulated nine *Information Literacy Standards for Student Learning* under three categories:

I.   Information Literacy Standards: The student who is information literate . . .
     Standard 1: accesses information efficiently and effectively.
     Standard 2: evaluates information critically and competently.
     Standard 3: uses information accurately and creatively.
II. Independent Learning Standards: The student who is an independent learner is information literate and . . .
     Standard 4: pursues information related to personal interests.
     Standard 5: appreciates literature and other creative expressions of information.
     Standard 6: strives for excellence in information seeking and knowledge generation.
III. Social Responsibility Standards: The student who contributes positively to the learning community and to society is information literate and . . .
     Standard 7: recognizes the importance of information to a democratic society.
     Standard 8: practices ethical behavior regarding information and information technology.
     Standard 9: participates effectively in groups to pursue and generate information.
     (AASL and AECT, 1998)

These are not unlike the 2000 ACRL *Information Literacy Competency Standards for Higher Education*, as the information-literate student . . .

Standard 1: determines the nature and extent of the information needed. [with four *Performance Indicators*]

Standard 2: accesses needed information effectively and efficiently. [with five *Performance Indicators*]

Standard 3: evaluates information and its sources critically and incorporates selected information into his or her knowledge base and value system. [with seven *Performance Indicators*]

Standard 4: individually or as a member of a group uses information effectively to accomplish a specific purpose. [with three *Performance Indicators*]

Standard 5: understands many of the economic, legal, and social issues surrounding the use of information and accesses and uses information ethically and legally. [with three *Performance Indicators*]

Before the term "information literacy" was first coined in the mid-1970s, thus beginning the information literacy movement in library science, there was the related bibliographic instruction (BI) movement, which began in 1969. BI consisted mainly of library tours, orientations, and "diluted versions of the reference classes that librarians themselves took in library school" (Gilton, 2004). With the advent of the computer and

Internet age, the meaning of what information is and how to manage it changed, and with it so did the science of librarianship as well as broader society itself. In the mid- to late 1980s, terms such as "information superhighway" and "information overload" became common and helped birth the information literacy movement. As Donna Gilton has explained, "The biggest event of the decade was the gradual growth and development of a distinct information literacy movement, which would absorb bibliographic instruction in the 1990s." Librarians and educators soon became aware of the need for a more comprehensive understanding and articulation of society's need not to just know where to find information, but to become information literate. Thus, before the new millennium, the first attempts by educators, librarians, and policy makers to define what it means theoretically and practically to be information literate were put into writing.

⌖ Where the Standards Brought Us

In 2007, rather than define information literacy as primarily a set of skills, AASL attached to its 1998 *Standards* the twenty-first-century requirement—or threshold concept, perhaps—that education should produce "independent learners":

> To become independent learners, students must gain not only the skills but also the disposition to use those skills, along with an understanding of their own responsibilities and self-assessment strategies. Combined, these four elements build a learner who can thrive in a complex information environment. . . . The amount of information available to our learners necessitates that each individual acquire the skills to select, evaluate, and use information appropriately and effectively. (AASL, 2007)

As Lesley Farmer pointed out in her conference paper, "How AASL Learning Standards Inform ACRL's Information Literacy Framework" (2014), AASL's 2007 *Standards* use the term "information literacy" only once and, instead, according to Farmer, "cleverly sidestepped the problematic term 'information literacy' when it reframed the idea in a context of *independent and lifelong learning*." Perhaps the following summary of AASL's (2007) four units can illustrate a change away from demonstrating skills toward teaching a conceptual framework that is contributing to a new era of multiple information literacies. Accessing skills, resources, and tools, the twenty-first-century learner will:

1. Inquire, think critically, and gain knowledge. [nine *Skills*, seven *Dispositions in Action*, five *Responsibilities*, four *Self-Assessment Strategies*]
2. Draw conclusions, make informed decisions, apply knowledge to new situations, and create new knowledge. [six *Skills*, four *Dispositions in Action*, three *Responsibilities*, four *Self-Assessment Strategies*]
3. Share knowledge and participate ethically and productively as members of our democratic society. [six *Skills*, three *Dispositions in Action*, seven *Responsibilities*, three *Self-Assessment Strategies*]
4. Pursue personal and aesthetic growth. [eight *Skills*, four *Dispositions in Action*, four *Responsibilities*, six *Self-Assessment Strategies*]

Similarly, moving away from the *mechanics* of information management toward the *principles* that control information management, in creating the 2015 *Framework*, ACRL has attempted to define the "core ideas" involved in becoming information literate for a "dynamic and often uncertain information ecosystem in which all of us work and live" by creating the following six threshold concepts (called "frames") along with corresponding, brief descriptions:

1. *Authority Is Constructed and Contextual.* Information resources reflect their creators' expertise and credibility and are evaluated based on the information need and the context in which the information will be used. Authority is constructed in that various communities may recognize different types of authority. It is contextual in that the information need may help to determine the level of authority required. [six *Knowledge Practices*, five *Dispositions*]

2. *Information Creation as a Process.* Information in any format is produced to convey a message and is shared via a selected delivery method. The iterative processes of researching, creating, revising, and disseminating information vary, and the resulting product reflects these differences. [eight *Knowledge Practices*, six *Dispositions*]

3. *Information Has Value.* Information possesses several dimensions of value, including as a commodity, as a means of education, as a means to influence, and as a means of negotiating and understanding the world. Legal and socioeconomic interests influence information production and dissemination. [eight *Knowledge Practices*, four *Dispositions*]

4. *Research as Inquiry.* Research is iterative and depends on asking increasingly complex or new questions whose answers in turn develop additional questions or lines of inquiry in any field. [eight *Knowledge Practices*, nine *Dispositions*]

5. *Scholarship as Conversation.* Communities of scholars, researchers, or professionals engage in sustained discourse with new insights and discoveries occurring over time as a result of varied perspectives and interpretations. [seven *Knowledge Practices*, eight *Dispositions*]

6. *Searching as Strategic Exploration.* Searching for information is often nonlinear and iterative, requiring the evaluation of a range of information sources and the mental flexibility to pursue alternate avenues as new understanding develops. [eight *Knowledge Practices*, six *Dispositions*] (ACRL, 2015)

Because their nature is so different from ACRL's 2000 *Standards*, the six frames and their short definitions are not easy to remember. Appendix B provides a set of flashcards that are meant to be used as memory aids to help librarians, classroom faculty, and students in their discourses and activities with the *Framework* for information literacy. The book's website also has color copies of the flashcard template in both a PDF and Microsoft Word version. This website is located at https://implementingtheinformationliteracyframework.wordpress.com/ or https://tinyurl.com/ya6h4vyq.

⑥ The Idea behind the *Framework*

As Farmer (2014) concluded about the rationale for the new library approaches to information literacy by AASL and ACRL, "the underlying principle is that education focuses on student learning, and that library programs—including professional librarians—can play a significant role in optimizing the conditions for learning." In this post-modern age, information literacy, like critical thinking or quantitative reasoning, is part of the education process. Evidence of change can be seen in emerging specialties in library science degree programs such as "critical librarianship," and other fields, such as rhetoric and communication studies, have been focusing more pedagogical attention on information literacy (Norgaard, 2003; 2004).

Recent critiques of the new *Framework* have voiced concerns that it is too theoretical and, consequently, it will be difficult to define student learning outcomes that are practical enough to teach, to map to assignments, and ultimately to assess. As prescriptive as some complained that the 2000 *Standards* were, at least they were practical and, for the most part, assessable. Discourse has grown, not without some controversy, over how the two approaches—the *Standards* and the *Framework*—could work together or whether the 2000 *Standards* should be sunsetted. For the record, the ACRL Board voted to "rescind" the 2000 *Standards* on June 25, 2016 (ACRL, 2016).

Nevertheless, in order to implement the frames of information literacy, and to be involved in the process of general education for that purpose, librarians must be capable of turning theory into application. This is the idea behind the *Framework*: Information literacy, like other core competencies in education, is one of the hallmarks of the educated mind, and thus teaching to that competency is a common thread in all disciplines that have been organized into degree programs. Our educational institutions—which often mean those involved in general education requirements—are moving forward with their charge to teach information literacy as a twenty-first-century general education requirement. Given the evolution of thinking and scholarship on information literacy, most of it in library science, ACRL has seen this as a richly appropriate opportunity for librarians to be deeply involved in this burgeoning educational issue, and it is investing the intellectual capital to help create relevant and timely resources to support the work of educating and assessing students in information literacy. Librarians at all levels and working in all types of libraries need to decide what role they will play in order to fully embrace the *Framework*, become partners in education, and develop pedagogy and deeply collaborative partnerships with fellow educators in the other academic disciplines. Becoming proficient in understanding the distinctions between the *Standards* and the *Framework*'s frames enables the task of defining this role. To help facilitate this understanding, see table 2.1 for a side-by-side comparison of the *Standards* and the *Framework*.

How to "Compare" the *Standards* and the *Framework*

It has been said that the *Standards* and the *Framework* are not comparable, that they are too different, much like comparing how to build a house to the laws of physics that make the building possible. Perhaps it would be more feasible to discuss how the two approaches are related to each other, and through that discussion, identify and articulate some ways they are connected. Mapping the frames to the *Standards* or the *Standards* to the frames can be useful group exercises to develop your library's understanding of these connections. See tables 2.2 and 2.3 for examples, as well as appendix C, "Thematic Coding the 2000 *Standards* as Found in the 2015 *Framework*." A color copy of appendix C can be found on the book's website at https://implementingtheinformationliteracyframework.wordpress.com/ or https://tinyurl.com/ya6h4vyq.

Table 2.1. Side-by-Side Look at the Five Standards and the Six Frames of Information Literacy (ACRL)

THE STUDENT WHO IS INFORMATION LITERATE CAN		THE INFORMATION LITERATE STUDENT UNDERSTANDS	
FIVE STANDARDS OF INFORMATION LITERACY	PERFORMANCE INDICATORS	SIX FRAMES OF INFORMATION LITERACY	KNOWLEDGE PRACTICES
1. Determines the nature and extent of the information needed	1. Defines and articulates the need for information. 2. Identifies a variety of types and formats of potential sources for information. 3. Considers the costs and benefits of acquiring the needed information. 4. Reevaluates the nature and extent of the information need.	1. Authority Is Constructed and Contextual	The student will: 1. Define different types of authority, such as subject expertise (e.g., scholarship), societal position (e.g., public office or title), or special experience (e.g., participating in a historic event). 2. Use research tools and indicators of authority to determine the credibility of sources, understanding the elements that might temper this credibility. 3. Understand that many disciplines have acknowledged authorities in the sense of well-known scholars and publications that are widely considered "standard." Even in those situations, some scholars would challenge the authority of those sources. 4. Recognize that authoritative content may be packaged formally or informally and may include sources of all media types. 5. Acknowledge they are developing their own authoritative voices in a particular area and recognize the responsibilities this entails, including seeking accuracy and reliability, respecting intellectual property, and participating in communities of practice. 6. Understand the increasingly social nature of the information ecosystem where authorities actively connect with one another and sources develop over time.
2. Accesses needed information effectively and efficiently	1. Selects the most appropriate investigative methods or information retrieval systems for accessing the needed information. 2. Constructs and implements effectively-designed search strategies. 3. Retrieves information online or in person using a variety of methods. 4. Refines the search strategy if necessary. 5. Extracts, records, and manages the information and its sources.	2. Information Creation as a Process	The student will: 1. Articulate the capabilities and constraints of information developed through various creation processes. 2. Assess the fit between an information product's creation process and a particular information need. 3. Articulate the traditional and emerging processes of information creation and dissemination in a particular discipline. 4. Recognize that information may be perceived differently based on the format in which it is packaged. 5. Recognize the implications of information formats that contain static or dynamic information. 6. Monitor the value that is placed upon different types of information products in varying contexts. 7. Transfer knowledge of capabilities and constraints to new types of information products. 8. Develop, in their own creation processes, an understanding that their choices impact the purposes for which the information product will be used and the message it conveys.

(continued)

Table 2.1. Continued

FIVE STANDARDS OF INFORMATION LITERACY	PERFORMANCE INDICATORS	SIX FRAMES OF INFORMATION LITERACY	KNOWLEDGE PRACTICES
3. Evaluates information and its sources critically and incorporates selected information into his or her knowledge base and value system	The student will: 1. Summarizes the main ideas to be extracted from the information gathered. 2. Articulates and applies initial criteria for evaluating both the information and its sources. 3. Synthesizes main ideas to construct new concepts. 4. Compares new knowledge with prior knowledge to determine the value added, contradictions, or other unique characteristics of the information. 5. Determines whether the new knowledge has an impact on the individual's value system and takes steps to reconcile differences. 6. Validates understanding and interpretation of the information through discourse with other individuals, subject-area experts, and/or practitioners. 7. Determines whether the initial query should be revised.	3. Information Has Value	The student will: 1. Give credit to the original ideas of others through proper attribution and citation. 2. Understand that intellectual property is a legal and social construct that varies by culture. 3. Articulate the purpose and distinguishing characteristics of copyright, fair use, open access, and the public domain. 4. Understand how and why some individuals or groups of individuals may be underrepresented or systematically marginalized within the systems that produce and disseminate information. 5. Recognize issues of access or lack of access to information sources. 6. Decide where and how their information is published. 7. Understand how the commodification of their personal information and online interactions affects the information they receive and the information they produce or disseminate online. 8. Make informed choices regarding their online actions in full awareness of issues related to privacy and the commodification of personal information.
4. Individually or as a member of a group uses information effectively to accomplish a specific purpose	The student will: 1. Applies new and prior information to the planning and creation of a particular product or performance. 2. Revises the development process for the product or performance. 3. Communicates the product or performance effectively to others.	4. Research as Inquiry	The student will: 1. Formulate questions for research based on information gaps or on reexamination of existing, possibly conflicting, information. 2. Determine an appropriate scope of investigation. 3. Deal with complex research by breaking complex questions into simple ones, limiting the scope of investigations. 4. Use various research methods, based on need, circumstance, and type of inquiry. 5. Monitor gathered information and assess for gaps or weaknesses. 6. Organize information in meaningful ways. 7. Synthesize ideas gathered from multiple sources. 8. Draw reasonable conclusions based on the analysis and interpretation of information.

5. Understands many of the economic, legal, and social issues surrounding the use of information and accesses and uses information ethically and legally	1. Understands many of the ethical, legal, and socioeconomic issues surrounding information technology. 2. Follows laws, regulations, institutional policies, and etiquette related to the access and use of information resources. 3. Acknowledges the use of information sources in communicating the product or performance.
5. Scholarship as Conversation	The student will: 1. Cite the contributing work of others in their own information production. 2. Contribute to scholarly conversation at an appropriate level, such as local online community, guided discussion, undergraduate research journal, conference presentation/poster session. 3. Identify barriers to entering scholarly conversation via various venues. 4. Critically evaluate contributions made by others in participatory information environments. 5. Identify the contribution that particular articles, books, and other scholarly pieces make to disciplinary knowledge. 6. Summarize the changes in scholarly perspective over time on a particular topic within a specific discipline. 7. Recognize that a given scholarly work may not represent the only or even the majority perspective on the issue.
6. Searching as Strategic Exploration	The student will: 1. Determine the initial scope of the task required to meet their information needs. 2. Identify interested parties, such as scholars, organizations, governments, and industries, which might produce information about a topic and determine how to access that information. 3. Utilize divergent (e.g., brainstorming) and convergent (e.g., selecting the best source) thinking when searching. 4. Match information needs and search strategies to search tools. 5. Design and refine needs and search strategies, based on search results. 6. Understand how information systems (i.e., collections of recorded information) are organized to access relevant information. 7. Use different searching language types (e.g., controlled vocabulary, keywords, natural language). 8. Manage searching processes and results.

Table 2.2. Mapping the Frames to the Standards

KEYWORDS	STANDARDS	FRAMES
Information Needed	1	A, B, D, F
Access	2	A, C, F
Evaluate, Analyze	3	A, B, C, D, E
(Use for a) Purpose	4	B, C, D
Ethics	5	A, C, D, E

Key: A = Authority Is Constructed and Contextual; B = Information Creation as a Process; C = Information Has Value; D = Research as Inquiry; E = Scholarship as Conversation; F = Searching as Strategic Exploration.

Hopefully, this book can guide today's librarians and educators in understanding this evolution in information literacy pedagogy to help open pathways for creating the practical means for applying the *Framework* in their instruction and collaborations. This is an uncommon way to use a guide, perhaps, but it is relevant to—and even practical for—the situation. Some librarians and classroom faculty will have little difficulty transitioning into this new age of information literacy instruction, but others may be unable to so easily move from the seeming concreteness of the *Standards* to the more abstract *Framework* in order to extract and implement application from theory. Applying practice from theory is critical for a successful integration of the ACRL *Framework* into information literacy instruction.

Since the ACRL *Framework* is still relatively recent, those who have not been significantly involved in its development—which is nearly all educators, as well as librarians—are still familiarizing themselves with it and, truth be told, waiting for others more expert to plumb the depths of its meanings through future scholarship and general literature. Many librarians and educators are waiting for the pioneers to provide the examples, case studies, and other efforts to work with the *Framework*. This book is one of those efforts and, as such, is expected to be a conversation starter and catalyst, a friendly goad to get you started. To help in a tangible way with this conversation-starting process, appendix D provides a template to create information literacy bookmarks with all six frames of the *Framework* on each bookmark. The book's website also makes available the bookmark template in a color PDF and changeable Microsoft Word version for easy tailoring to specific needs (https://implementingtheinformation literacyframework.wordpress.com/ or https://tinyurl.com/ya6h4vyq). Or, make your own bookmarks and get the conversation started!

As stated earlier, the ACRL Board rescinded the 2000 *Standards*, which it defined as the *Standards* being "no longer in force." While the ACRL chooses to no longer support the *Standards*, removing them from its website in July 2017, it cannot remove them from people's working knowledge. Therefore it is useful to refer to the *Standards* as needed to build transitions, since these are not viewed as being in conflict with the *Framework*'s ideas.

The ACRL assures that the "*Framework* is not intended to be prescriptive but to be used as a guidance document in shaping an institutional program" (ACRL, 2015). So while there is no need to delay getting into the new *Framework*, there are no "*Framework* police" checking up on the progress of librarians and educators to demonstrate compli-

Table 2.3. Mapping the Standards to the Frames

FRAME	KNOWLEDGE PRACTICES	RELATED TO
A. Authority Is Constructed and Contextual	The student will:	
	1. Define different types of authority, such as subject expertise (e.g., scholarship), societal position (e.g., public office or title), or special experience (e.g., participating in a historic event).	1. Standard 1 (2), 3 (2)
	2. Use research tools and indicators of authority to determine the credibility of sources, understanding the elements that might temper this credibility.	2. Standard 3 (2), 5 (1)
	3. Understand that many disciplines have acknowledged authorities in the sense of well-known scholars and publications that are widely considered "standard." Even in those situations, some scholars would challenge the authority of those sources.	3. Standard 3 (4, 6)
	4. Recognize that authoritative content may be packaged formally or informally and may include sources of all media types.	4. Standard 1 (2)
	5. Acknowledge they are developing their own authoritative voices in a particular area and recognize the responsibilities this entails, including seeking accuracy and reliability, respecting intellectual property, and participating in communities of practice.	5. Standard 3 (3), 4 (1, 3), 5 (3)
	6. Understand the increasingly social nature of the information ecosystem where authorities actively connect with one another and sources develop over time.	6. Standard 3 (4, 6)
B. Information Creation as a Process	The student will:	
	1. Articulate the capabilities and constraints of information developed through various creation processes.	1. Standard 1 (2), 5 (1)
	2. Assess the fit between an information product's creation process and a particular information need.	2. Standard 1 (2), 2 (1)
	3. Articulate the traditional and emerging processes of information creation and dissemination in a particular discipline.	3. Standard 3 (6), 4 (1, 2)
	4. Recognize that information may be perceived differently based on the format in which it is packaged.	4. Standard 1 (2), 3 (2)
	5. Recognize the implications of information formats that contain static or dynamic information.	5. Standard 3 (2), 5 (1)
	6. Monitor the value that is placed upon different types of information products in varying contexts.	6. Standard 2 (5), 3 (2, 4, 6), 5 (1)
	7. Transfer knowledge of capabilities and constraints to new types of information products.	7. Standard 3 (3, 4), 4 (1)
	8. Develop, in their own creation processes, an understanding that their choices impact the purposes for which the information product will be used and the message it conveys.	8. Standard 3 (7), 4 (2)
C. Information Has Value	The student will:	
	1. Give credit to the original ideas of others through proper attribution and citation.	1. Standard 5 (2, 3)
	2. Understand that intellectual property is a legal and social construct that varies by culture.	2. Standard 5
	3. Articulate the purpose and distinguishing characteristics of copyright, fair use, open access, and the public domain.	3. Standard 5
	4. Understand how and why some individuals or groups of individuals may be underrepresented or systematically marginalized within the systems that produce and disseminate information.	4. Standard 3 (4, 5), 5
	5. Recognize issues of access or lack of access to information sources.	5. Standard 5
	6. Decide where and how their information is published.	6. Standard 4

(continued)

Table 2.3. *Continued*

FRAME	*KNOWLEDGE PRACTICES*	RELATED TO
	7. Understand how the commodification of their personal information and online interactions affects the information they receive and the information they produce or disseminate online.	7. Standard 5
	8. Make informed choices regarding their online actions in full awareness of issues related to privacy and the commodification of personal information.	8. Standard 5
D. Research as Inquiry	The student will:	
	1. Formulate questions for research based on information gaps or on reexamination of existing, possibly conflicting, information.	1. Standard 1 (1), 3 (4)
	2. Determine an appropriate scope of investigation.	2. Standard 1
	3. Deal with complex research by breaking complex questions into simple ones, limiting the scope of investigations.	3. Standard 1, 3 (7)
	4. Use various research methods, based on need, circumstance, and type of inquiry.	4. Standard 1, 2
	5. Monitor gathered information and assess for gaps or weaknesses.	5. Standard 3
	6. Organize information in meaningful ways.	6. Standard 2
	7. Synthesize ideas gathered from multiple sources.	7. Standard 3 (3)
	8. Draw reasonable conclusions based on the analysis and interpretation of information.	8. Standard 3 (3, 4, 5, 6, 7)
E. Scholarship as Conversation	The student will:	
	1. Cite the contributing work of others in their own information production.	1. Standard 5
	2. Contribute to scholarly conversation at an appropriate level, such as local online community, guided discussion, undergraduate research journal, conference presentation/poster session.	2. Standard 3 (6), 4 (3)
	3. Identify barriers to entering scholarly conversation via various venues.	3. Standard 3 (4), 5
	4. Critically evaluate contributions made by others in participatory information environments.	4. Standard 3
	5. Identify the contribution particular articles, books, and other scholarly pieces make to disciplinary knowledge.	5. Standard 1 (2), 3 (2, 4, 6)
	6. Summarize the changes in scholarly perspective over time on a particular topic within a specific discipline.	6. Standard 3 (1, 3, 4)
	7. Recognize that a given scholarly work may not represent the only or even the majority perspective on the issue.	7. Standard 3 (4, 6)
F. Searching as Strategic Exploration	The student will:	
	1. Determine the initial scope of the task required to meet their information needs.	1. Standard 1 (1)
	2. Identify interested parties, such as scholars, organizations, governments, and industries, which might produce information about a topic and determine how to access that information.	2. Standard 1 (2), 2 (1, 2)
	3. Utilize divergent (e.g., brainstorming) and convergent (e.g., selecting the best source) thinking when searching.	3. Standard 2 (2)
	4. Match information needs and search strategies to search tools.	4. Standard 2 (1, 2, 3)
	5. Design and refine needs and search strategies, based on search results.	5. Standard 2 (5), 3 (7)
	6. Understand how information systems (i.e., collections of recorded information) are organized to access relevant information.	6. Standard 2 (1, 2)
	7. Use different searching language types (e.g., controlled vocabulary, keywords, natural language).	7. Standard 2 (2, 3, 4)
	8. Manage searching processes and results.	8. Standard 2 (5)

ance. These are not new standards in the sense that there was something wrong with the content or ideas of the 2000 *Standards*. The two approaches can be viewed as compatible in principle, and neither are considered exhaustive. Indeed, many institutions and organizations have developed and used their own ideas in teaching information literacy before and after the 2000 *Standards* were published, and there is no sign that they would be less independent in their use or non-use of the *Framework*. Rather, to use the language of ACRL, the new *Framework* is really just a new and exciting development in the ongoing scholarly conversation on information literacy.

But this is not said to diminish the *Framework*'s usefulness. The *Standards* have created the necessary cornerstone to legitimize information literacy as a core educational issue, which fostered deeper, more critical conversations and led to the intellectual development that then created the *Framework*. For those scholars and educators who count information literacy as one of their passions, the *Framework* is a beautiful edifice built from that cornerstone, and librarians can hardly wait to open all of its doors and windows to see what's inside.

Working through One Approach to Another

The next decade will be a time of exploring the *Framework*, connecting more dots in other disciplines, and refining the ideas and concepts the *Framework* has articulated. It also will be a time of integrating with the *Framework* the work of years past with the *Standards*. Brown-bag or special meetings among librarians to discuss the ways that the *Framework* can draw on this significant work in information literacy is a common way to begin work on the future of information literacy instruction in individual universities, colleges, and schools. Unless there is already a strong infrastructure for librarian-classroom instructor collaborations, these discussions ideally should be held before any collaborations take place with individual departments or schools across the campus.

Questions to Consider in Changing Your Information Literacy Instruction Program

Time needs to be spent thinking through what the future of information literacy instruction at your institution will be. You can't get to where you want to go unless you know where you are at, so assessing the status of your current program comes first—that is, not what you want to do, but what you are actually doing now and how it is working. What is well established in practice? Where are the gaps? What is feasible for your culture and situation? Inventory your resources, your activities, the people in the library who are involved, and the people outside the library who have been involved. Make some comparisons to other schools or institutions similar to your own. Try to get as clear a picture as possible of the whole effort being made. The clearer your understanding, the easier it will be to create a roadmap for change, no matter how small or large. And it does not need to be large in the beginning. Small successes are better than large failures.

Then it is time for librarians to ask questions—and to gather the information needed to answer them as explicitly and specifically as possible:

1. In what ways is the *Framework* compatible with information literacy instruction now being done?
2. In what ways does the *Framework* impact the overall information literacy program?

3. After identifying changes to be made, how should they be prioritized?
4. Depending on where the library is at in its current strategic plan, what long-term changes should be made, and how should they be prioritized?
5. What support or leadership can you expect from others, such as your general education people, your principal, provost, or other administrators?
6. Depending on the level of development in collaborations with other departments, what are the first steps to take to incorporate the *Framework* material into these collaborations?
7. Start where you are more likely to succeed—which departments or programs are the best candidates to begin or deepen collaborations with their classroom faculty?
8. What resources or personnel are needed to begin adaptations to the new *Framework*?
9. After the first changes to be made are determined, what is a reasonable timeline for implementing them?
10. What additional training or education will librarians need to help them successfully implement change? For example, would training in collaboration and teamwork be beneficial?

Just as good research is careful, methodical, and well documented, so should planning be for a new type of information literacy instruction program. There is no harm in continuing what is currently being done as a new plan is made; there is no harm in continuing with just the *Standards* until you know how you will integrate the *Framework*. The future still arrives one step at a time.

◎ Key Points

To utilize the new *Framework* in instruction, it's important to first comprehend the ways it is different from the *Standards*. This comprehension is more easily attained once there is a clear understanding of how the concept of information literacy itself has evolved and why the *Framework* came into being. Some key steps to bear in mind:

- After years of scholarly discussion and evolving instruction practices, information literacy *Standards* were first organized and nationally recognized at the turn of the millennium by the AASL and the ACRL, among other groups.
- As the understanding evolved and scholarship developed, librarians and educators saw the need to articulate a more comprehensive set of concepts or principles to better master information literacy; thus, the AASL created the 2007 *Standards for the 21st-Century Learner* and ACRL created the 2015 *Framework for Information Literacy for Higher Education*.
- The newer work builds on the previous work; it does not negate it.
- The remainder of the current decade is a time of exploration and experimentation with the *Framework* for both educators and librarians; librarians should be proactive in defining their new role during this time.
- The work of the *Standards* will inform the work of the *Framework* as a major resource in information literacy instruction. ACRL is devoting its future work toward implementing the new *Framework*, just as a software developer might support its newest version, and not create new resources for any older versions. At the

same time, the *Framework* has been developed as a guide; institutions should focus on their culture and their needs and define their terms for success accordingly.

• While some may feel they should wait for others to blaze the new paths, librarians and educators should spend time now thinking through what the future of information literacy instruction at their institutions will be.

In the next chapter, "Pre-*Framework* Ideas to Do This Year," you will read a brief history of information literacy in college and K–12 settings and see how five pre-2015 published best practices for doing information literacy are still relevant today—with step-by-step instructions. Some of these proven techniques include: a) a successful faculty collaboration model, b) the creation of a K–12 information literacy community, and c) a credit-bearing information literacy course.

References

AASL (American Association of School Librarians). 2007. *Standards for the 21st-Century Learner.* American Library Association. http://www.ala.org/aasl/sites/ala.org.aasl/files/content/guide linesandstandards/learningstandards/AASL_LearningStandards.pdf.

AASL (American Association of School Librarians) and AECT (Association for Educational Communications and Technology). 1998. *Information Literacy Standards for Student Learning: Standards and Indicators.* https://www.ala.org/ala/aasl/aaslproftools/informationpower/Infor mationLiteracyStandards_final.pdf.

ACRL (Association of College & Research Libraries). 2000. *Information Literacy Competency Standards for Higher Education.* American Library Association. http://www.ala.org/acrl/stan dards/informationliteracycompetency.

ACRL (Association of College & Research Libraries). 2015. *Framework for Information Literacy for Higher Education.* American Library Association. http://www.ala.org/acrl/standards/ ilframework.

ACRL (Association of College & Research Libraries). 2016. "ACRL Board Takes Action on Information Literacy Standards." *ACRL Insider* (blog), June 25. American Library Association. http://www.acrl.ala.org/acrlinsider/archives/12126.

Farmer, Lesley. 2014. "How AASL Learning Standards Inform ACRL's Information Literacy Framework." Paper presented at the World Library and Information Congress of the International Federation of Library Associations and Institutions (IFLA), Lyon, France. http:// library.ifla.org/id/eprint/831.

Gilton, Donna L. 2004. "Information Literacy Instruction: A History in Context." . http://www .uri.edu/artsci/lsc/Faculty/gilton/InformationLiteracyInstruction-AHistoryinContext.htm (Note: page has been removed; no longer available.)

Norgaard, Rolf. 2003. "Writing Information Literacy: Contributions to a Concept." *Reference & User Services Quarterly* 43, no. 2 (Winter): 124–30.

Norgaard, Rolf. 2004. "Writing Information Literacy in the Classroom: Pedagogical Enactments and Implications." *Reference & User Services Quarterly* 43 no. 3 (Spring): 220–26.

Yarbrough, Beau. 2014. "Exclusive: Holocaust Denied by Students in Rialto School Assignment." *San Bernardino Sun*, July 11. http://www.sbsun.com/social-affairs/20140711/exclusive-holo caust-denied-by-students-in-rialto-school-assignment.

Pre-*Framework* Ideas to Do This Year

N FEBRUARY 2, 2015, the Association of College & Research Libraries Board filed the new *Framework for Information Literacy for Higher Education* "as one of the constellation of information literacy documents from the association" (ACRL, 2015). The board took the parliamentary procedure of *filing* the *Framework* for three reasons: a) to formally show approval of the document, b) to allow future changes to the document without needing to go through another vote and full board approval, and c) to allow the living document to accomplish its full potential. Subsequently, on June 25, 2016, the board "voted to rescind the *Information Literacy Competency Standards for Higher Education*," making the *Framework* the single ACRL model available to academic librarians to guide them in their role as information literacy promoters (ACRL, 2016). Even though there is a compelling need to turn a corner and move forward with the *Framework*, there are also many exemplary ideas and strategies that need to be carefully reviewed, tweaked, and practiced as part of the new campus culture of the *Framework for Information Literacy in Higher Education*.

For this reason, this chapter will first review five foundational milestones of information literacy in librarianship that helped inform the new *Framework*. Following the brief history, attention is given to five pre-*Framework* best practices published in information literacy literature and presented as strategies to be used in your *Framework* campus program. Each approach begins with a backstory for context, followed by step-by-step instructions as solutions for your own information literacy needs.

⊚ Five Milestones of Library Information Literacy

By the year 2000, the higher education library community had more than 10 years to think about and experiment with the initial information literacy standards adopted by the American Library Association in 1989 (ALA, 1989). A number of rich efforts were in circulation before the more prescriptive five *Standards* of information literacy were formalized by the ACRL and adopted in 2000 (ACRL, 2000). These pre-2000 ideas helped inform the information literacy movement that was during this time reaching critical mass within the library profession. An important influence in the mix was Patricia Breivik's 1998 book, *Student Learning in the Information Age*. Breivik questioned the stereotype within libraries that information literacy was largely the librarian's responsibility, to be delivered solely by the librarian's proactive energy and, when possible, collaborative attempts with teachers and faculty (Breivik, 1998). She persuasively demonstrated that "extreme" forces outside higher education (such as technology, the rate of information growth, electronics, speed of communication, portability of record keeping, and the blending of computer and multimedia science) began to shift the perception that information literacy instruction, in the form of in-class bibliographic instruction, was the exclusive responsibility of librarians toward (instead) a shared responsibility among librarians and classroom educators. This obligation also has come to include students as they perform the role of becoming self-learning, competent, information-literate citizens.

Moving forward, in the 15 years since the 2000 rollout of ACRL's *Standards*, more than 1.6 million articles, books, presentations, and other documents have been published on information literacy and higher education, or information literacy and academics. From the perspective of the K–12 community, in the years since the 1998 publication of the book *Information Power: Building Partnerships for Learning* from the American Association of School Librarians and the Association for Educational Communications and Technology (a kind of school librarians' equivalent to the 2000 *Standards*), more than 9,600 publications have filled the literature pages and databases on the topic of information literacy and school libraries. This enormous output demonstrates both the importance of information literacy and the prominence it now holds and will hold in the future of primary and secondary education. Sampling such a large volume of scholarship for practical examples is mind-boggling. Nevertheless, we present here four universities and one high school that practiced exemplary information literacy before the 2015 *Framework*. The lessons learned from these kinds of best practices can be continued on our college, university, and K–12 school campuses as librarians and other educators unpack the fifth and newest milestone, ACRL's 2015 *Framework for Information Literacy for Higher Education*. A short review of library information literacy's high points over the past 27 years is described below, followed by the five information literacy models, each with clear step-by-step instructions to implement on your campus.

Milestone 1, 1989: ALA's Five Information Competencies

Although the genesis of the modern information literacy movement began with theorists in the liberal arts and in information technology in the 1970s, much of the work was thoughtfully accomplished by United States, United Kingdom, and Australian library professionals and education leaders since that time. In the United States, the definition of information literacy from the perspective of professional librarianship was formally established by the American Library Association's Presidential Committee on Information Literacy and published in its *Final Report* on January 10, 1989. Much, if not all, of

THE FIVE INFORMATION COMPETENCIES

- Knowing when there is a need for information
- Identifying information needed to address a given problem or issue
- Finding needed information and evaluating the information
- Organizing the information
- Using the information effectively to address the problem or issue at hand

Source: American Library Association. 1989. "Presidential Committee on Information Literacy: *Final Report.*" http://www.ala.org/acrl/publications/whitepapers/presidential. Used with permission from the American Library Association.

the five-part statement (see the textbox "The Five Information Competencies") is still embodied in library information literacy definitions today.

One impact of ALA's 1989 statement has been its encouragement to all librarians—school librarians, special, medical, academic, and law—to move philosophically toward becoming change agents and advocates of information literacy as a movement. In practice, in academic libraries this has meant integrating information literacy instruction into many aspects of the general education curriculum. Also, since this 1989 definition, regional accrediting agencies have included information literacy language in their top criteria for assessing universities and colleges as well as K–12 schools (Breivik, 1998; Accrediting Commission for Schools, WASC, 2014).

Milestone 2, 1998: AASL and AECT's *Information Power: Building Partnerships for Learning*

Professionals in school librarianship have an extensive history in developing standards dating back to 1920. Six decades later, a joint venture between the American Association of School Librarians (AASL) and the Association for Educational Communications and Technology (AECT) crafted a forward-thinking book titled *Information Power: Guidelines for School Library Media Programs* (AASL and AECT, 1988).

As ALA's direction began to focus on information competencies, so did the leaders of K–12 library media centers. It took another 10 years before an updated 1998 edition was published, with a different subtitle highlighting the critical concept of collaboration, *Information Power: Building Partnerships for Learning.* The new work represented countless hours of experts studying and evaluating the explosive changes in the fields of library science and educational technology since the first edition. The result was a text that has stood the test of time, as it is still used by school librarians some 19 years later. The book combines a core set of nine information literacy standards, each followed by practical grade-level curricular examples.

Milestone 3, 2000: ACRL's *Information Literacy Competency Standards for Higher Education*

The information literacy movement, as no surprise, also captured the attention of the academic library community. One source traces the teaching of information skills by higher

INFORMATION LITERACY COMPETENCY STANDARDS FOR HIGHER EDUCATION

An information-literate student:

- defines and articulates the need for information
- accesses needed information effectively and efficiently
- evaluates information and its sources critically and incorporates selected information into his or her knowledge base
- individually, or as a member of a group, uses information effectively to accomplish a specific purpose
- understands many of the economic, legal, and social issues surrounding the use of information and accesses and uses information ethically and legally.

Source: Association of College & Research Libraries. 2000. *Information Literacy Competency Standards for Higher Education*. http://www.ala.org/acrl/standards/informationliteracy competency. Used with permission from the American Library Association.

education librarians to a symposium titled Libraries and the Search for Academic Excellence, co-sponsored by Columbia University and the University of Colorado in March 1987 (Eisenberg, Lowe, and Spitzer, 2004). During that event, attendees deliberated about the future role of librarians and set forth information literacy as a core competency to be taught in colleges and universities. Two years later in 1989, Breivik and Elwood Gee published the book *Information Literacy: Revolution in the Library*, which moved forward an agenda to act on the symposium's recommendations and to meet the growing information literacy needs of faculty and students. During the next ten years (1990–1999), no less than 2,500 articles and books were published covering information literacy and academic topics. Then in 2000, the ACRL adopted the landmark *Information Literacy Competency Standards for Higher Education*, a document of five relatively easy-to-measure standards (see the textbox "Information Literacy Competency Standards for Higher Education") that has maintained prominence for more than 17 years. The five standards symbolize the ever-developing efforts by academic librarians to embed information literacy into the student learning outcomes at as many colleges and universities as possible.

Milestone 4, 2007: AASL's *Standards for the 21st-Century Learner*

A different approach to packaging information literacy was introduced by school librarian leaders in 2007, nine years after the successful 1998 book *Information Power*. A colorful eight-page summary of learning standards was created as a keepsake pamphlet titled *Standards for the 21st-Century Learner* (AASL, 2007) with two supporting books and a web-based tool. Although the 2007 brochure included all of the 1989 standards found in *Information Power*, it also prophetically broadened the definition of information literacy, made clear by the following statement: "Multiple literacies, including digital, visual, textual, and technological, have now joined information literacy as crucial skills for this century." The two published supporting texts were *Standards for the 21st-Century Learner in Action* (AASL, 2009b), that elaborated on the standards with benchmarking and lesson plans by grade level, and *Empowering Learners: Guidelines for School Library Programs* (AASL, 2009a) that offered a big-picture perspective for laying a program foundation on which the standards could be taught and benchmarks could be reached more successfully. Finally, *A Planning Guide for Empowering Learners* (AASL, 2010) was an online interactive service designed to help the school librarian organize and implement the 2007 standards into a school-wide library program.

Milestone 5, 2015: ACRL's *Framework for Information Literacy for Higher Education*

The next, and most recent, declaration of information literacy guidelines in academic librarianship is what this book is about—the *Framework for Information Literacy for Higher Education*. An ACRL Board-approved task force began work on the project in March 2013 and submitted the final draft, after a very transparent process, to ACRL in early January 2015. On February 2, 2015, the Board decided to invoke a parliamentary procedure to officially file the *Framework* document to allow for "its intended flexibility and potential" and subsequently did not recommend a timeline for sunsetting the 2000 *Standards* (Williams, 2015a). ACRL President Karen Williams clarified the decision by stating that "this means that we have accepted the *Framework* and it will assume its place among the constellation of documents used by information literacy practitioners" (Williams, 2015a). Four months later, on June 16, 2015, the ACRL Board announced the creation of a Framework for Information Literacy Advisory Board "to offer a range of expertise and perspectives that can positively and strategically shape the growth and development of the *Framework*" (Williams, 2015b). Then, on June 25, 2016, less than 17 months after the acceptance of the *Framework* coexisting with the *Standards*, the Board "rescinded" the 2000 *Information Literacy Competency Standards for Higher Education*, making the *Framework* the ACRL default document-guide for integrating information literacy on university and college campus across the United States.

These five historic high points are indicators of careful, successful librarian investments in information literacy over 27 years. The academic library profession is also fortunate to have such continuing momentum of energy, moving beyond these dedicated foundations and leading up to the 2015 *Framework* and beyond. Nevertheless, because past efforts are so rich in exceptional examples of implementing information literacy, it's useful to maintain some of these ideas within a *Framework* campus integration. The following five pre-*Framework* strategies for information literacy are presented in a step-by-step style for easy application, even this year!

◎ Five Great Information Literacy Ideas, Pre-*Framework*

In the more than 25 years prior to the 2015 *Framework*, librarians were engaged in collaborating with higher education faculty and school teachers on information literacy in successful ways. The pre-2015 literature provides a wealth of practical examples showcasing librarians working with university professors and classroom teachers that informed and nurtured the evolving information literacy movement. Presented for consideration are five valuable strategies for helping you fulfill your own information literacy goals. Following brief backgrounds for each example, a number of step-by-step plans for applying each model to your own information literacy choices and needs are suggested.

Strategy #1: Dakota State University

Rise Smith and Karl Mundt (1997) described for its time an innovative if not controversial approach to meeting the information literacy needs of students, which was to focus mostly on training faculty and not librarians to teach students information literacy. The thinking at Dakota State University (DSU) seemed valid: There's so much information literacy instruction to go around, and with a supportive university goal for developing information literacy, faculty should include it in their student learning outcomes and teach it. The method involved five points:

1. Influence faculty to recognize information literacy and to get it into the school's strategic plan as an institutional goal
2. Help faculty develop a clearer understanding of how to use information systems and services for their students
3. Provide faculty with workshops, explaining information literacy strategies that they could easily adapt to their discipline and classroom teaching (see "Further Reading" at the end of this chapter for resources on discipline-specific information literacy ideas in areas of business, psychology, nursing, art history, and others)
4. Be pro-faculty development and pro-collaboration
5. Ensure the library is both physically and virtually ready for the information literacy cultural challenge.

Developing Strategy #1: A Step-by-Step Plan to Empower Faculty to Teach Information Literacy

Step 1: Get Recognized

Using a website, Twitter, Instagram, or Facebook accounts, create links to 30-second faculty testimonials from faculty who are passionate about information literacy. One way to do this is to generate six short, ad-like scripts based on each of the six frames in the *Framework* (2015) and use a smartphone (or other technology) to record one or more faculty members, administrators, or students using the scripts as prompts. Do not use librarians or library staff, but recruit members of your target audiences. Then create a YouTube channel and upload the testimonials. If information literacy is not yet a part of your campus strategic plan, follow protocols to make such a request. Think smarter, not harder, as you plan out librarian involvement on faculty committees that cover student learning outcomes, strategic planning, or faculty development.

Step 2: Connect Dots

Conduct frequent but brief (10- to 15-minute) faculty-friendly workshops within the rhythms of your campus calendar that will help instructors connect their students to no more than one *Framework* concept, or explain one discipline-specific information literacy resource, or share about one resource per workshop. Create a colorful, ready-to-hand-to-students brochure or handout describing the topic covered in the workshop. Another idea is for librarians to visit faculty during their non-student office hours and share one search tip that helps them find resources for their next lecture or current scholarship, and use that opportunity to collaborate on ideas for the frame "Searching as Strategic Exploration." In addition, librarians should get to know the faculty leadership at the department level, usually a chair, with the intention of identifying occasions to regularly engage with faculty at departmental meetings, new faculty orientations, and other appropriate get-togethers. For example, a librarian could give an 18-minute TED talk on a discipline-relevant library database or an upgraded service with the goal of developing information literacy competencies.

Step 3: Consult

Whether initiated by the librarian or the department, consultations with librarians can be scheduled within small faculty groups or individually to brainstorm together through one or more current assignments and design an information literacy exercise that is class- or discipline-specific, one that will provide assessment data that is easy to record for future reports. See "Further Reading" at the end of this chapter for discipline-specific information literacy articles, studies, standards, and more ideas.

Step 4: Initiate Faculty Development

Librarians have untapped expertise that can benefit faculty or classroom teachers in their professional development. To understand this step in the context of information literacy, think outside the box. For example, if librarians put on their technology hat, so to speak, they can probably develop a mini-presentation on time-saving techniques for managing email. Another idea is developing an online library guide on how to use text polling within an online or face-to-face class (examples of free, text polling sites: smpoll.net and easypolls.net). Your IT department may already provide something like this. But, with proper permissions (which you must obtain), these are two genuine needs for a number of faculty—managing email, adding text polling to a class—that your IT team might not take the time to address. Librarians can fulfill such professional development within their skill set and, in a broader sense, be better understood as part of the information literacy scope on campus.

As another example, per faculty interest, the librarian could put on his or her search-a-topic hat. In this case, it shouldn't take much to find a couple of best practices for classroom management and use current preferred communication to deliver it. For example, as need becomes apparent, faculty might appreciate the librarian sending an occasional link to short blog posts on tips for classroom management. As mentioned earlier, this might be a faculty development matter addressed by campus curriculum experts or centers for teaching and learning. However, with proper permissions, librarians can be viewed as additional go-to sources for information on classroom management with up-to-date, evidence-based ideas that really work. It's taking something librarians do well (searching and narrowing with great results) and applying it toward a legitimate faculty need like maintaining successful class environments. All literacies, including information literacy, are taught better in a well-managed class than an unruly one.

As a final example for step 4, the librarian can put on his or her copyright hat. What faculty member wouldn't welcome a brief note on a current fair-use issue, such as a judge's final decision on a lawsuit regarding fair use at one of your rival universities (academically and maybe sports-wise)? Or faculty could view a two-minute Internet video created by a campus librarian in which one or more scenarios are acted out on topics faculty may be uninformed about—say, copyright law (the number of pages a department can legally copy on a faculty member's behalf from an out-of-print book). The librarian could also send to classroom instructors an email link to a library's blog posting explaining how faculty members can more efficiently apply a fair-use checklist, such as the one created at Columbia University (Crews and Buttler, 2008). Of course, such shared knowledge easily falls into the context of information literacy.

Step 5: Become a Change Agent

Smith and Mundt (1997) remind us that the library should be a model example on campuses where information literacy takes place and where the library and its staff play the part of change agents based on the *Framework* concepts. Is your school ready for growth in information literacy? For example, are group spaces in the library adequate and flexible, with whiteboards, computer technology, Wi-Fi, and large monitors for group work? If not, what alternatives to these common information literacy–enhancing technologies can be added? How about creating a makerspace (space where patrons use tools, raw supplies, and equipment to create imaginative processes and products)? Can a student smoothly go from digital technology to print technology in the building or are there physical and technological barriers? When was the last time anyone logged on to a patron library computer and took note of what it's like to be an end user? Are public computers two or three years older than typical faculty and staff computers? Do these devices have updated software or are they running older versions? Another thought: How ready is your library to handle unscheduled information literacy instruction, whether inside or outside the classroom space? Unscheduled instruction would not be something to encourage, but what a perfect, although disruptive, opportunity to expand the culture of information literacy. Try testing the library's web-based resources. Are they easy to teach—by a non-librarian? Observe your student employees as they try to find a resource in a database on a topic without help. If you see roadblocks, talk with the library web developer about changes or computer-embedded help guides on individual databases. If there is any place on campus that should be information literacy–ready, it's the library.

Strategy #2: Florida International University

One of the most cited studies on information literacy and collaboration involves librarians working with faculty at Florida International University (FIU) (Iannuzzi, 1998). FIU librarians came to understand that information literacy was much larger than the professional model of librarians coordinating all information activities. They learned to let go of the idea that librarians were the major gatekeepers over library and information sources, as well as the stereotype that librarian-taught instruction was the sole means for fulfilling information literacy outcomes. Patricia Iannuzzi summed it up by stating, "In order to broaden ownership of the information literacy agenda, librarians needed to move from a model of coordination to a model of collaboration" (1998: 100).

As you will see, FIU's model for information literacy serves as an attractive, time-saving, win-win partnership among classroom faculty, administration, and campus librarians. The focus was a well-planned and intentional effort by library personnel to promote information literacy with three campus-wide, non-library (at least they appear to be at first glance) initiatives: a) regional accreditation, b) student retention, and c) classroom technology.

Most higher education campuses and K–12 schools have ongoing engagement with accreditation criteria to maintain credibility for everyone associated with the institution.

In regard to FIU's accreditation responsibilities, the Southern Association of Colleges and Schools required a competency that was interpreted to mean assessing student computer skills. One FIU librarian's timely research project convinced classroom faculty that "the type of computer literacy skills incorporated in information literacy skills . . . could help anticipate changes in the accreditation criteria" (Iannuzzi, 1998: 101). As a result, the librarian's recommendation was approved and information literacy instruction sessions were conducted along with assessment criteria in four lower-division classes and three upper-division classes. Not only did an important accreditation criterion get addressed, but librarians received a positive invitation to conduct information literacy instruction.

The second of three library-advanced initiatives involved student retention. This took place as FIU librarians became active in committees addressing low student retention. Along the way, librarians suggested strengthening information literacy language in a particular section of freshmen classes. Engagement in library involvement with campus-wide initiatives like retention, with information literacy recommended as a piece of the solution, helps faculty recognize librarians as proactive team players in an academic community rather than dogmatically tied to a perceived library agenda. The purpose of Iannuzzi's second example was not to show a relationship between retention and information literacy (apparently there is none), but to show that librarians who are involved in mission-critical, campus-wide initiatives like retention have opened the door for embedding information literacy in a part of the curriculum that otherwise may not have been possible.

This theme of librarians helping others succeed in typically non-librarian roles introduces the last of the three partnership ideas. Librarians at FIU made it a top objective to help faculty thrive. This is most evident in a series of thoughtfully designed workshops as a result of a joint brainstorming session between the library and the campus's Academy for the Art of Teaching (Iannuzzi, 1998). The topics designed and implemented by librarians addressed the challenges faculty face in the classroom, such as motivating students to use technology, refining critical thinking techniques, improving student learning with technology and fact-based assignments, learning for long-term retention, and explaining how information literacy relates to intellectual development (Iannuzzi, 1998). FIU educators, both librarians and classroom instructors, used partnerships to improve personal and professional plans while benefiting students and faculty within the context of information literacy.

Developing Strategy #2: A Step-by-Step Plan to Make Information Literacy a Campus-Wide Initiative

Step 1: Be Proactive

Through appropriate channels, librarians should be invited to potentially influential meetings on campus. In fact, librarians should forget about not being invited and instead become proactive, looking for and expecting opportunities to be legitimately engaged in policy- and decision-making events at school.

Step 2: Change Your Mind-set

As difficult as it may feel, the library needs to move away from expecting to be the sole gatekeeper of library and information resources. This means moving toward providing places for non-library professionals to teach information literacy (as elaborated in Strategy #1). The task of creating an information-literate population takes more than librarians to accomplish. Change your mind-set; it cannot be done by librarians alone.

Step 3: Determine Campus-Wide Initiatives

Every campus has a strategic plan. Find it and study it through the eyes of information literacy. Don't give up, but let the plan percolate in the back of your mind. The FIU librarians found at least three institutional strategies that information literacy could address—some directly, some indirectly: accreditation, retention, and technology. Admittedly, these are not easy connections to see at first. Your campus may have similar ones or very different strategic goals that information literacy could address. But the idea is to take on the challenge and reinvent current campus strategic goals into information literacy–friendly initiatives.

Step 4: Know Your Accreditation Criteria

In FIU's situation, the campus leadership interpreted a required accreditation competency to mean assessing student computer skills. If you do not know your school's accreditation bodies, learn these, and find out when the next report or visit is due. There will be a regional one and possibly a number of program-specific national organizations. Access current accreditation guidelines and note criteria that information literacy might address. As you may know, some higher education regional accreditation bodies include information literacy as a required condition or use related language such as critical thinking, research effectiveness, technology literacy, or information problem solving. If so, librarians and classroom faculty need to be actively engaged in fulfilling that particular initiative. This typically means providing data on information literacy such as an accurate count of relevant information literacy resources, personnel and instruction details, and resource usage statistics. Be prepared.

Step 5: Think Longitudinally

The FIU library recommendation to meet computer literacy skills (an accreditation requirement) included assessing lower-division and upper-division information literacy. Taking this a bit further, if privacy issues can be resolved, assessing the same students as freshmen and then again as, say, juniors, on the same information literacy skills, can provide rich longitudinal data on the success or failure of information literacy being integrated in the lives of these students and on improving assessment tools and, of course, information literacy instruction. This represents the kind of data your accreditation bodies and your school administrators might expect. So, do not plan only a series of one-time information literacy efforts, but include longitudinal ones as well.

Step 6: Help Classroom Faculty and Teachers Thrive

One technique FIU librarians used was to meet the unique needs of faculty by helping them thrive. Campus faculty and teachers have needs. Librarians can collaborate with faculty to create faculty-specific training that meets their needs, rather than focusing on training only related to traditional library resources and services. Because librarians are not fully aware of every faculty need, they should, with an attitude of professional humility, work within existing faculty structures, such as faculty development departments or centers for teaching and learning, to gain appropriate permissions (as also described in Strategy #1). Topics could include how to motivate students through time-saving searching ideas, how to improve student learning with fact-based assignments, or how information literacy can affect intellectual development.

Strategy #3: Redwood High School

Action research is a cyclic approach to solving a problem commonly found in the fields of business and public relations. The three-part method begins with finding gaps in expectations, then designing solutions to meet those gaps, and finally repeating the cycle by observing the success or failure of those changes and continuing to improve them—in other words, continual improvement. In this third of five pre-*Framework* models to consider, Lesley Farmer (2001) reported on applying action research to improve information literacy competencies at Redwood High School in California. Farmer began by calling together a study group of teachers, students, and the school librarian with the goal of improving student information competency based on answering two questions: a) What information skills do students need to demonstrate? and b) What interventions will improve those student skills?

Following the action research model, the next step involved the group agreeing on a list of expected skills. The teachers were next asked to match items on the skill list with specific class assignments. The study group was also asked to identify possible interventions that would help students meet a level of competency for each item on the list. The school librarian was tasked with developing a new or updating a current set of research guides to help lead students in each intervention. The group of teachers and the librarian pilot-tested these tools, and based on results, made some changes. The study group also designed rubrics for research that aligned with the list of expected skills and created a detailed teacher's guide.

Finally, the group took the parts of the process and created a number of in-service teacher workshops covering the overall plan and each topic on the list. Some of the more interesting findings in the study included the following: a) research guides were heavily used; b) during implementation, students were found asking higher levels of questions; c) more students successfully completed a larger number of assignments; plagiarism was less prevalent; and the school librarian became more active in the research process.

Developing Strategy #3: A Step-by-Step Plan for Creating a Collaborative K–12 Information Literacy Community

Step 1: Form a Study Group

Call together a study group made up of teachers, students, and the school librarian with the goal of improving information literacy on campus. The group begins by answering two questions: a) What information skills do our students need to demonstrate? and b) What interventions do our students need to improve these skills? The group also has access to reviews relevant to K–12 library standards resources such as the *Standards for the 21st-Century Learner* (AASL, 2007), *Standards for the 21st-Century Learner in Action* (AASL, 2009b), and *Empowering Learners: Guidelines for School Library Programs* (AASL, 2009a).

Step 2: List Skills

The study group creates and agrees on a list of skills to be taught based on answers to the two questions and the study of relevant standards. Examples of skills could be: evaluate the trustworthiness of a website, determine the credibility of a source, cite sources correctly according to a citation style, or create an annotated bibliography.

Step 3: Match Skills

Teachers in the study group take each of the skills and carefully match them to specific assignments they have in class. For example, an assignment where students create a mythical species of animal by combining two known species would be backed up by citing sources about inheritance from those known species. Another idea might be included in a student-written book report, such as listing three other books that have a similar theme following correct Modern Language Association (MLA) or American Psychological Association (APA) citation style.

Step 4: Develop Interventions

The study group takes each skill and comes up with one or more interventions to help students meet a level of competency for each skill. These interventions could include the development of citation models, the creation of a scope and sequence instruction across the curriculum on information literacy, or applying an information literacy research model such as Big6 (http://big6.com/). As stated earlier, the strategies discussed here are all pre-*Framework* interventions, but ideas coming out of the new *Framework* could certainly be included.

Step 5: Develop Tools

The school librarian takes these interventions and develops information literacy tools that address the gaps between where students likely are and new levels of competency. These tools could be one-page style guides for MLA or APA citations or electronic catalog search techniques for finding books on a topic. In this step, the study group of teachers and librarian would then pilot-test the tools and make improvements, as well as create rubrics for each of the skills agreed on in step 2. A suggested source for more ideas is Kathy Schrock's website, Guide to Everything (http://www.schrockguide.net/).

Step 6: Provide In-Service Events

Finally, the list of skills, accommodations, rubrics, and tools would be written up in a detailed teacher's guide. One or more in-service events for teachers could be provided where other teachers can benefit from the work of the study group, and these teachers can then begin to partner with the school librarian to grow an information literacy community for their campus.

Strategy #4: Washington State University Vancouver

An important part of information literacy is assessment—knowing if what is being done for students is effective and, if not, making changes. Measuring success and interpret-

Table 3.1. Sample of Diller and Phelps's Information Literacy Rubric

Uses information effectively, ethically, and legally to accomplish a purpose.

EMERGING 12	DEVELOPING 34	INTEGRATING 56
Uses information without referencing the source or without abiding by established etiquette, institutional policies, or legal regulations related to the use of that information.	Acknowledges the source of information and uses it in ways that comply with established etiquette, institutional policies, and/or legal regulations related to the use of that information.	Demonstrates a thorough understanding of the established etiquette, institutional policies, and/or legal regulations related to the use of that information.
Uses sources out of context.	Demonstrates some understanding of how context is important when using sources to support arguments.	Respects the context and integrity of sources of information.
Fails to acknowledge or distorts opposing viewpoints.	Acknowledges opposing viewpoints.	Integrates opposing viewpoints into broader contexts.
Relies heavily on quotes.	Uses more paraphrasing than quotes.	Integrates quotes and paraphrases appropriately to formulate an argument.
Makes multiple errors when citing sources.	Makes minimal errors when citing sources.	Makes no errors when citing sources.

Source: Karen R. Diller and Sue F. Phelps. 2008. "Learning Outcomes, Portfolios, and Rubrics, Oh My! Authentic Assessment of an Information Literacy Program." *portal: Libraries and the Academy* 8, no. 1 (January): 87. Used with permission.

ing data for informed improvement is necessary for any ongoing educational endeavor. According to Karen Diller and Sue Phelps (2008), the librarians and classroom faculty at Washington State University Vancouver (WSU Vancouver) have participated in an assessment method worth noting. In their process, a faculty-librarian committee created a statistically tested information literacy rubric.

A sample of Diller and Phelps's rubric can be seen in table 3.1. Their rubric is based on the ACRL's 2000 *Standards*; nevertheless, the principles are useful as an example in a *Framework* context (such as the frame "Research as Inquiry"). WSU Vancouver students take three one-credit learning goal courses, one at the beginning, middle, and end of their education, posting class work and experiences into their personal electronic portfolios. As part of their entries, students include two pieces of evidence for each of six campus-wide learning goals, one being information literacy. A representative sample of these student portfolios is then evaluated by the committee that created the rubric along a six-point Likert scale within three levels of competencies: *emerging*, *developing*, and *integrating*.

Developing Strategy #4: A Step-by-Step Plan for Information Literacy Assessment

Step 1: Think about Scalability

If you are just starting out, or are building on results of past information literacy assessments, consider thinking about scalability. Begin by investing in planning and in people toward a thoughtful pilot project that can later be implemented in limitless ways (examples: random sampling, spot checks, or following a statistically relevant sample of individual freshmen through all four years, with their consent). For another idea, by individual choice or by a committee, determine: a) one student learning community or population to test (e.g., freshmen English classes, adult learning evening courses), b) one information literacy piece to assess (e.g., reliability of web resources, quality and efficiency of finding techniques used), c) two or three class sections, d) one information literacy instruction guideline (e.g., tips for web resource credibility, correct citation style format), and e) a rubric to score one student learning artifact (e.g., a web resource reliability form that students fill out, student-created MLA- or APA-style citations). Do a post-evaluation of your model, improve the process, and grow into including other student communities using scalability.

Step 2: Use Data

Assessment requires data. If you have access to past data on information literacy, consider using that as a guide for current and future measures. Also, think of the end first; that is, what outcome would be most useful for your campus situation? Examples might include raising database search strategy effectiveness or increasing student assignment products and ways those products are delivered. Consider what you can realistically achieve as data results (numeric or maybe a narrative account) that can meet the following two assessment goals:

- In what ways are information literacy efforts for students effective?
- How can results of an assessment be used to improve your information literacy efforts?

Step 3: Assess the Proper Citation Style

Begin with an assignment where students pick from a list of topics (approved by the faculty member) and turn in a preliminary bibliography of 10–20 citations on that topic in the required style (APA, MLA, Chicago, etc.). An assessment of the accuracy of each citation is another measure of information literacy success in education. As noted for other assessment pieces, before students begin the citation assignment, an information literacy session would have been conducted explaining the details of the correct citation style as well as useful resources for students to consult for such an assignment. If the citation style is graded, all student citations would be assessed. If not, then a random sample of student bibliographies could be used. It is suggested that the faculty member or the librarian conduct the assessment for each list of student citations, rather than a faculty-librarian approach. In other words, it is not recommended that the faculty look over the same list of citations for review that the librarian would also look over for a review. Moving on, allow points for each citation (say 10 points) and take points off for missing a style's requirements or completeness. Those requirements could include:

- punctuation (periods and commas in correct places)
- spelling
- italics
- parentheses
- proper display of author and/or editor
- proper use of *and* or the ampersand (&)

- capitalization
- URL (uniform resource locator)
- DOI (digital object identifier) number.

See the "Sample of a Librarian Feedback on a Citation Style Assignment" textbox for an example of graded feedback from a librarian.

Step 4: Assess a Search Plan

Start this step by developing a search plan assignment for students to fill out and a corresponding rubric to assess the work. For an example of this type of rubric or form, see the "Search Plan Assignment with Rubrics for Grading" textbox.

Again, as a pilot project, determine a random sample of filled-out student forms that can be scored by faculty and/or librarians who, in a timely manner, return the plans with constructive comments. If only the librarian (or if only the faculty member) scores this form, the other educator should be sent a copy and have the freedom to comment on each student's response as well. For an example of grader comments, see figure 3.1. A record of the rubric data can be kept for later analysis. Parts of the search plan could include: selecting a discipline-specific topic (from a faculty-created list or chosen by the student with approval by the faculty member), listing keywords and finding synonyms for the keywords, narrowing a broad topic to a more manageable one, writing out a discipline-specific research question, using keywords/synonyms to create a preliminary search string with connectors AND/OR/NOT, using the search string to search the library's book catalog and list the number of results, narrowing a larger number of catalog search results by using database fields (such as date range, peer-reviewed, language, geography, and subjects), repeating this search string in a journal database and listing numerical results, limiting article results by scholarly peer-reviewed sources, determining full-text availability, and clicking on a record result that has no full text and describing how to access the text from other sources. As shared in previous steps, this step would also be preceded by an information literacy session on conducting an effective and efficient search on a topic.

SEARCH PLAN ASSIGNMENT WITH RUBRICS FOR GRADING

After filling out your search plan, turn it in to your professor. Feedback and suggestions on your plan will be returned to you within one week.

Name: **Date:**   **Course:**

1. Mark one of the following for your topic:

Learning Styles   Brain Research & Learning
Critical Thinking Skills   Character Development
Special Education   Multicultural Education

2. What are the main keywords or concepts for the topic you have selected?
Exemplary (3 points): Lists more than 3 keywords or concepts, all are relevant to the topic
Satisfactory (2): Lists 2–3 keywords or concepts, all are relevant to the topic
Needs Improvement (1): Lists 1–2 keywords or concepts, one or both keywords are not relevant to the topic

3. List at least one synonym or related concept for each keyword identified in question 2.
Exemplary (3 points): Lists more than 3 synonyms or concepts, all are relevant to the topic
Satisfactory (2): Lists 2–3 synonyms or concepts, all are relevant to the topic
Needs Improvement (1): Lists 1–2 synonyms or concepts, one or both synonyms are not relevant to the topic

4. Based on 2 and 3 above, write out a specific research question. Your research question illustrates the point you are going to make in your paper.

5. Next, combine your keywords into a search string using the connectors AND, OR, NOT as appropriate. Then write out your search string here:
Exemplary (3 points): Lists keywords with uppercase Boolean operators in between, uses more than one Boolean operator (AND, OR, NOT), uses another limit feature (date, geographic location, language, etc.)
Satisfactory (2): Lists keywords with uppercase or lowercase Boolean operators in between (AND, and, OR, or, NOT, not)
Needs Improvement (1): Lists keywords but without Boolean operators in between, no other limit features are included

6. Using your search string, do a keyword search for your topic in the library's online catalog. How many results did you find? Did you find both books and media? If so, how many of each?

7. List specific ways you can narrow your topic when searching the online catalog or other databases.
Exemplary (3 points): Uses search string in #5, uses the online catalog, lists the correct number of results for books and/or media (you will need to perform the search to verify this)
Satisfactory (2): Uses search string in #5, uses the online catalog, does not list the correct number of results for books and/or media
Needs Improvement (1): Does not use search string in #5, and/or does not use the online catalog, and/or does not list the correct number of results for books and/or media

8. Using your search string, do a keyword search for your topic in one of the databases recommended in the search presentation. Give the database name and list how many results your search returned.

Exemplary (3 points): Uses search string in #5, uses two or more appropriate databases, lists the correct number of results

Satisfactory (2): Uses the search string in #5, uses only one appropriate database, and/or does not list correct number of results

Needs Improvement (1): Does not use search string in #5, and/or uses an inappropriate database, and/or appears to have used no databases (used the web), and/or did not list results or results were incorrect

9. Now, limit your results to scholarly (peer-reviewed) resources only. How many results did you get?

10. Click on the first result in #9. Is the full text of the item available? Note: You may need to click on the Full Text Finder link to determine this.

Exemplary (3 points): Locates full text of more than one article by using or not using (full text available in the record) Full Text Finder link

Satisfactory (2): Locates full text of one article

Needs Improvement (1): Was not able to locate full text of one article, did not use Full Text Finder

Source: Adapted from Stephenson, Kimberley Wilcox. 2013. "Online Search Plan Rubric 7-8-2013 DRAFT." Azusa Pacific University. Used with permission.

Library Orientation: *Search Plan*

After filling out your search plan turn it into your professor. A librarian will offer feedback and suggestions on your plan and return it to you within one week.

NAME: Student   **DATE:** 2/20/2016   **Course: Writing A**

1. Mark one of the following for your topic:

Learning Styles	Brain Research & Learning
Critical Thinking Skills	Character Development
Special Education	XX Multicultural Education

2. What are the main keywords or concepts for the topic you have selected?

Character Development and Young Children, Character Development and Elementary Grades, Character Development and High Performance

> **Commented [s1]:** These appear to be good keywords for narrowing Character Development.

3. List at least one synonym or related concept for each keyword identified in question 2.

Integrity training/growth, Kindergarten through 5th grade, pre-adolescent/elementary age, leader/accomplished/skills, academic performance/moral values

> **Commented [s2]:** In some databases you can narrow by individual grade but K-5 or K-6 will do as well.

> **Commented [s3]:** You could have included an age group like in the previous two. Without the age specification "High Performance" would likely retrieve items outside of elementary/young children. But there's a database that allows narrowing by age in the initial search screen.

4. Based on 2 and 3 above, write out a specific research question. Your research question illustrates the point you are going to make in your paper.

A structured Character Development curriculum in early primary grades will lead to higher performance.

> **Commented [s4]:** Your synonyms broaden the population of your study and can be easily adjusted as you go along in your search.

5. Next, combine your keywords into a search string using the connectors AND, OR, NOT as appropriate. Then write out your search string here:

Character development AND young children. Character curriculum AND elementary grades.

Character development AND leadership. Character development AND higher performance.

> **Commented [s5]:** All synonyms appear to be what could be expected with your original keywords. The concept of "values" may be your best word in getting at character development.

> **Commented [s6]:** Nicely stated. Now I see what you're aiming for (at least for this assignment). So "early primary grades" could be K, 1, 2, 3, probably not 4th grade. Again, you can designate to the grade level in some databases.

> **Commented [s7]:** These appear to be all good search strings to begin with.

6. Using your search string, do a keyword search for your topic in the library's online catalog. How many results did you find? Did you find both books and media? If so, how many of each?

Character development and young children yielded 4 results, all books

Character curriculum AND elementary grades yielded 2 results, both books

Character development AND leadership yielded 10 results, all books

Character development AND higher performance, 1 film

> **Commented [s8]:** The relatively low numbers of hits (4 and 2) makes me think there are other terms that can be used to produce a larger results. There are probably many more resources on this topic, it's just a matter of approaching more relevant keywords.

> **Commented [s9]:** I would assume that many of the 10 are outside your target audience.

Figure 3.1. Sample of librarian feedback on a search plan assignment.

Step 6: Assess the Quality of Access

As conditions permit, working within a faculty-librarian, co-equal collaboration model, take a random sample of turned-in, first-draft papers on topics. Using Diller and Phelps's rubric sample (see table 3.1), or other rubrics in this book, the librarian can help analyze the information literacy component of student drafts, possibly provide some feedback (with faculty approval), and code each paper numerically using the weighted points under each of the three levels of competencies found in Diller and Phelps's rubric: 12 points for papers following the *emerging* qualities, 34 points for papers all in the *developing* category, and 56 points for those qualifying as *integrating*. This information can then be compared with a similar process for a different student population on campus (juniors, seniors, adult learners, master's degree students, doctoral students). Outcomes could demonstrate where on campus there are strengths and weaknesses with regard to information literacy efforts. Again, all of these assessments would be preceded by an information literacy lecture or tutorial on, for example, "Research as Inquiry" (see chapter 9).

Strategy #5: New York City College of Technology, City University of New York

A fifth and final pre-2015 practice used in higher education, and a sustainable choice for years to come, is the stand-alone, for-credit information literacy course. Such a course would usually be a one- to three-unit college course, team-taught by faculty and librarians or, in certain settings, by librarians alone.

One dilemma librarians find when teaching information literacy is the lack of time to reflect on and discuss important social issues. To be more specific, those social elements include: the general ethical use of information, the impact of media and politics on information, the information gap or digital divide between the haves and the have-nots, the intersection of information literacy and social justice, detecting bias, evidence of poor reasoning (fallacies), and evaluating methodologies. In short, *habits of mind*.

Anne Leonard and Maura Smale, both librarians at New York City College of Technology, City University of New York, taught a three-unit, full-semester course titled "Research & Documentation for the Information Age." The course covered the usual things like using databases and finding books, but the main goal of the course was not to introduce students to library searching skills. The authors explained, "In this course we have the time to encourage thoughtful engagement by students with a wide variety of information sources and media, as both content consumers and producers" (Leonard and Smale, 2013: 143), which places the classroom experience in the relatively new subdiscipline of *critical* information literacy in the field of information science. The authors quote James Elmborg to explain the purpose of *critical* information literacy: "Rather than focus on knowledge acquisition, students identify and engage significant problems in the world. By developing critical consciousness, students learn to take control of their lives and their own learning to become active agents, asking and answering questions that matter to them and the world around them" (Elmborg, 2006: 193). Although the course was designed and executed during the tenure of the 2000 *Standards*, it more closely aligns with principles and goals found in the *Framework*, particularly the frames "Information Creation as a Process" and "Authority Is Constructed and Contextual."

In creating their syllabus, Leonard and Smale searched other schools' information literacy curricula for ideas. These other information literacy courses influenced the final

COURSE GOALS FOR RESEARCH & DOCUMENTATION FOR THE INFORMATION AGE

Goals: To introduce you to the theory and practice of research and documentation for all information and media, including:

- Cultural, economic, and political factors that affect information and media
- The organization of information in multiple formats
- Developing methods for finding information that is relevant to you
- Critically evaluating information and its sources
- Copyright, fair use, and ethical use of information and media
- The role of documentation and citation in scholarly, professional, and public work

Source: Leonard, Anne, and Maura A. Smale. 2013. "The Three-Credit Solution: Social Justice in an Information Literacy Course." In *Information Literacy and Social Justice: Radical Professional Praxis,* edited by Lua Gregory and Shana Higgins, 149. Sacramento, CA: Library Juice Press. Used with permission.

structure of their class. They found that these courses were able to merge "both research skills and critical information literacy and social justice components, including topics such as the political aspects of scholarly research and publishing, and the role of alternative presses and knowledge producers as compared to the mainstream media" (Leonard and Smale, 2013: 151). The textbox "Course Goals for Research & Documentation for the Information Age" provides an example of goals from the three-credit course that integrates two concepts: critical information literacy and social justice.

Developing Strategy #5: A Step-by-Step Plan for a Credit-Bearing Information Literacy Course

Step 1: List Learning Goals

Assuming that a process would soon be taken for university approval of a course on information literacy as a one-, two-, or three-unit elective or requirement for general education, begin with a thoughtful list of learning outcomes. These would then need to be approved by a faculty governance process, often including consistency with department and program outcomes. Leonard and Smale's six goals provide a useful outline. They are (paraphrased in the form of measurable goals):

- Determine influences on information from cultural, economic, and political perspectives.
- Know the many shapes information takes.
- Practice a set of search techniques that are learner-centered.
- Be a critical evaluator of information and where it comes from.
- Know the ethical use of information in the context of copyright and fair use.
- Demonstrate how to construct accurate attribution. (Leonard and Smale, 2013)

Faculty in many other academic disciplines have thought deeply about information literacy and such related topics as critical thinking, problem solving, assumptions, and values. Because of this, it is recommended that those seeking to create and teach a course on information literacy have meaningful dialog about the course's content with faculty on their campus in such departments as communications, rhetoric, and others within the general education requirements. The following six steps (2 through 7) are presented as ideas on how to flesh out Leonard and Smale's six goals.

Step 2: Culture Club

Teaching a course on information literacy could begin by understanding the cultural, economic, and political influences on information. One idea for introducing students to the complexity and diversity of today's influences on information could be illustrated by showing one or more brief takes on American culture found on YouTube. After the examples are shown, students could then discuss the types of information showcased by answering the following questions:

- What factors influence our information today (political, economic, and cultural)?
- What is the value of looking at information literacy at this multidisciplinary level?
- Is there a difference between the concept of information and the concept of media that contain information, and if so, what is the difference?

Another idea might be to assign students to three groups, one each on the influences of politics, economics, and culture on information and then have spokespersons share the groups' findings and how they obtained their results.

Step 3: Making Sense of Chaos

A second goal to cover in a course on information literacy might be to explain how current structures of information came to be. A historical perspective can be helpful by reviewing the development of libraries, education, politics, and mass media. Broadly speaking, libraries are just one result of chaos becoming organized in ways that make sense. Consider this library-centric chronological list of information literacy influences: Begin in the third century BCE with the Royal Library of Alexandria, its papyrus scrolls, notoriety, and demise. Travel through the Middle Ages and the invention of the printing press with the capacity for unlimited information to the masses, and yet also large expensive books being chained to shelves and accessible only to the elite few. Continue to the early twentieth century and the creation of the Library of Congress subject headings, the Dewey Decimal System and corresponding call numbers, and the development of the card catalog. Move on to the mid-1990s with the information explosion, including digital information at people's fingertips. Then do the same (construct a simple timeline of high points throughout history) for the other structures of information mentioned above (education, politics, and mass media). Such a discussion would also acknowledge print materials (book, newspapers, magazines, journals), the diversity of non-book items (paintings, sound recordings, cassette tapes, CDs, DVDs), and all things digital that can be disseminated on the global Internet. The mess of chaos is organized to make sense. This explains, in part, "the organization of information in multiple formats" (Leonard and Smale, 2013: 149).

Step 4: Finding Preferences of Users

A third goal for an information literacy course might be to describe the *finding* methods used to discover and retrieve information, as well as to consider today's preferred information-seeking behavior. That's a lot to cover! Begin by reviewing some of the more popular research methods such as Big6 (developed by Eisenberg and Berkowitz, 2015), Bloom's revised Taxonomy (remembering, understanding, applying, analyzing, evaluating, creating), perhaps include the alignment of *Standards for the 21st-Century Learner* found at http://www.ala.org/aasl/standards/learning and the *Common Core State Standards* found at http://www.corestandards.org/read-the-standards/ (for an example, search the Internet for AASL and Common Core crosswalk), as well as examining the finding methods used by young adults in studies like Project Information Literacy (http://www.projectinfolit .org/) at the University of Washington's iSchool. Continue by assigning a few readings and discussions about searching techniques and finding behaviors using Dave Harmeyer's *The Reference Interview Today: Negotiating and Answering Questions Face to Face, on the Phone, and Virtually* (2014). Finish by dividing students into groups of two or three individuals with a computer and have them document the precise steps they would take to find three current documents (their choice) on information literacy. After the exercise, have group spokespersons share their steps and findings with the rest of the class.

Step 5: Cookie Jar Mouse

A fourth goal for a course on information literacy is critical evaluation. Just because a source appears high on an Internet or database search doesn't make it reliable or valid—much like the proverbial mouse in a cookie jar doesn't make it a cookie. It might be easy to detect that a mouse is not a cookie, but in contrast, it's not always apparent if a search result is valid. To help in understanding this, assign students to groups, with one student the recorder, to find examples of bogus research on the Internet. Then have the recorder share with the rest of the class what was discovered. One popular and well-documented research counterfeit is the phony cancer study organized by *Science* magazine and described in a *National Geographic* online feature: "Fake Cancer Study Spotlights Bogus Science Journals" (Vergano, 2013).

Humor aside, attempting to assess truth should be no joke. The frame, "Authority Is Constructed and Contextual," is rich with principles on validity and credibility and would make a good read-reflect exercise. As a follow-up, ask students to create a list of tips that they would use to critically evaluate their next online resources.

Step 6: Copyright Conundrums

The fifth goal used to plan a unit-based course on information literacy might cover copyright, fair use, and the ethical use of information. Copyright is complicated. However, there are three tools that can help move students in the right direction. First, instruct students to go to the University of Texas Copyright Tutorial (University of Texas System Digital Library, 2013). Have them begin by taking the 12-part test or wait until after going through the tutorial (or simply have them do both). Students' saved test scores can inform the instructor on which items on copyright need more review. Second, instruct students about the copyright exception allowed under the limits of fair use. No one can be 100 percent confident that his or her interpretation of fair use will keep them in copyright compliance, except in the context of a judge's decision. However, for practical use, make students aware of a fair-use checklist such as the one created by Crews and Buttler on the Columbia University Libraries website (Crews and Buttler, 2008). Third, help students understand when a work is in the public domain, and therefore not subject to copyright law, by viewing and discussing with particular examples Lolly Gasaway's Public Domain Chart (Gasaway, 2003).

Step 7: Never Go out of Style

The sixth and final goal in conducting a course on information literacy might be an antidote for plagiarism: proper citation style for accurate attribution and knowing when to cite. Whatever style is appropriate for the course—MLA, APA, Chicago, or others—provide students with a review of the important parts of that style, particularly for books and online journal articles. Finally, point students to sources to help them create correct style. Some of these would include the library's copy of the style manual (or make it a textbook in the course) or the library's own website citation resources such as online video tutorials or LibGuides. Other places for citation creation help can be found in the "Cite" feature found in most library databases, the cite functions in proprietary bibliographic software such as BibBase, EndNote, and RefWorks, as well as free web tools such as Purdue University's style pages (search for Purdue + the style abbreviation), and the cite feature found in Google Scholar (scholar.google.com), Zotero, Citation Machine, and EasyBib. However, bear in mind that creating a proper citation remains the student's responsibility. None of these resources are 100 percent correct all the time. Use of these tools is no excuse for students not knowing the correct style details. Students need to conceptually understand the citation process in order to improvise on citing the more challenging types of resources, particularly those found only on the Internet. And most important of all, becoming information literate means knowing when to give credit when credit is justly due.

ⓖ Key Points

Chapter 3 has been about maintaining some of the great ideas for practicing information literacy on campuses that were published before the 2015 *Framework*. The following is a summary of what was learned, including a brief description of the five strategies.

- With the ACRL Board's decision to rescind the 2000 *Standards*, its default document-guide for integrating information literacy on university and college campuses across the United States is the 2015 *Framework*. To appreciate the rich library history of information literacy in the context of moving forward, five milestones of influential standards, books, and frameworks were presented as high-water marks of librarian leadership over a more than 25-year history.
- Of the five strategies presented as pre-2015 best practices to continue using with the *Framework*, Strategy #1 focused on training and assisting faculty in teaching students library information literacy, noting that librarians cannot create a culture of information literacy all by themselves.
- Strategy #2 used information literacy attributes to address non-library, campus-wide needs to build credibility with the academic campus community. Those needs included accreditation, student retention, and classroom technology.

- Strategy #3 established a study group of high school classroom instructors and the librarian to answer two questions: What information skills do students need to demonstrate? And what interventions will improve those student skills? Based on what was learned, the librarian created intervention tools that were tied to classroom assignments.
- Strategy #4 assessed information literacy success and improved the process by applying thoughtful learning rubrics within three levels of student competencies: *emerging*, *developing*, and *integrating*.
- Strategy #5 launched a three-credit course on information literacy based on six curricular goals: understand the culture's influence on information, know the shapes information takes, practice search techniques that are learner-centered, evaluate information critically, use information ethically, and construct attribution accurately.

In Chapter 4 you will learn about information literacy from the perspective of the classroom instructor—how instructors have perceived librarians and how the *Framework* may change that.

References

Accrediting Commission for Schools, WASC (Western Association of Schools and Colleges). 2014. "Accreditation Process Overview." http://www.acswasc.org/pdf_general/WASC_Pro cessOverview.pdf.

AASL (American Association of School Librarians). 2007. *Standards for the 21st-Century Learner*. American Library Association. http://www.ala.org/aasl/standards/learning.

AASL (American Association of School Librarians). 2009a. *Empowering Learners: Guidelines for School Library Programs*. Chicago: American Association of School Librarians.

AASL (American Association of School Librarians). 2009b. *Standards for the 21st-Century Learner in Action*. Chicago: American Association of School Librarians.

AASL (American Association of School Librarians). 2010. *Planning Guide for Empowering Learners*. Chicago: American Association of School Librarians. http://aasl.eb.com/show Login.htm.

AASL and AECT (American Association of School Librarians and Association for Educational Communications and Technology). 1988. *Information Power: Guidelines for School Library Media Programs*. Chicago: American Library Association.

AASL and AECT. 1998. *Information Power: Building Partnerships for Learning*. Chicago: American Library Association.

ALA (American Library Association). 1989. "Presidential Committee on Information Literacy: *Final Report*." American Library Association. http://www.ala.org/acrl/publications/whitepapers/presidential.

ACRL (Association of College & Research Libraries). 2000. *Information Literacy Competency Standards for Higher Education*. American Library Association. http://www.ala.org/acrl/standards/informationliteracycompetency.

ACRL (Association of College & Research Libraries). 2015. *Framework for Information Literacy for Higher Education*. American Library Association. http://www.ala.org/acrl/standards/ilframework.

ACRL (Association of College & Research Libraries). 2016. "ACRL Board Takes Action on Information Literacy Standards." *ACRL Insider* (blog), June 25. http://www.acrl.ala.org/acrlinsider/archives/12126.

Breivik, Patricia Senn. 1998. *Student Learning in the Information Age*. Phoenix, AZ: American Council on Education/Oryx Press.

Breivik, Patricia Senn, and Elwood Gordon Gee. 1989. *Information Literacy: Revolution in the Library*. New York: American Council on Education.

Crews, Kenneth D., and Dwayne K. Buttler. 2008. "Fair Use Checklist." Columbia University Libraries. https://copyright.columbia.edu/basics/fair-use/fair-use-checklist.html.

Diller, Karen R., and Sue F. Phelps. 2008. "Learning Outcomes, Portfolios, and Rubrics, Oh My! Authentic Assessment of an Information Literacy Program." *portal: Libraries and the Academy* 8, no. 1 (January): 75–89.

Eisenberg, Michael, Carrie A. Lowe, and Kathleen L. Spitzer. 2004. *Information Literacy: Essential Skills for the Information Age*. Westport, CT: Libraries Unlimited.

Eisenberg, Mike, and Robert E. Berkowitz. 2015. "Welcome to the Big6." http://big6.com/.

Elmborg, James. 2006. "Critical Information Literacy: Implications for Instruction and Practice." *Journal of Academic Librarianship* 32, no. 2 (March): 192–99.

Farmer, Lesley. 2001. "Information Literacy: A Whole School Reform Approach." In *Libraries and Librarians: Making a Difference in the Knowledge Age*. IFLA Council and General Conference: Conference Programme and Proceedings, Boston (August 16–25), 1–7. http://archive.ifla.org/IV/ifla67/papers/019-106e.pdf.

Gasaway, Lolly. 2003. "When U.S. Works Pass into the Public Domain." University of North Carolina. http://www.unc.edu/~unclng/public-d.htm.

Harmeyer, Dave. 2014. *The Reference Interview Today: Negotiating and Answering Questions Face to Face, on the Phone, and Virtually*. Lanham, MD: Rowman & Littlefield.

Iannuzzi, Patricia. 1998. "Faculty Development and Information Literacy: Establishing Campus Partnerships." *Reference Services Review* 26, no. 3/4: 97–102.

Leonard, Anne, and Maura A. Smale. 2013. "The Three-Credit Solution: Social Justice in an Information Literacy Course." In *Information Literacy and Social Justice: Radical Professional Praxis*, edited by Lua Gregory and Shana Higgins, 143–61. Sacramento, CA: Library Juice Press.

Smith, Rise L., and Karl E. Mundt. 1997. "Philosophical Shift: Teach the Faculty to Teach Information Literacy." Paper presented at the Annual Conference of the Association of College & Research Libraries, Nashville, TN, April 13. http://www.ala.org/acrl/publications/white papers/nashville/smith.

Stephenson, Kimberley Wilcox. 2013. "Online Search Plan Rubric 7-8-2013 DRAFT." Unpublished online rubric for grading "Library Orientation: Search Plan," Azusa Pacific University.

University of Texas System Digital Library, University of Texas at Austin. 2013. "Copyright Tutorial." UT Libraries. http://www.lib.utsystem.edu/copyright/.

Vergano, Dan. 2013. "Fake Cancer Study Spotlights Bogus Science Journals" *National Geographic*, October 4. http://news.nationalgeographic.com/news/2013/10/131003-bohannon-science -spoof-open-access-peer-review-cancer/.

Williams, Karen. 2015a. "More from the ACRL Board on the *Framework for Information Literacy for Higher Education*." *ACRL Insider* (blog), February 4. http://www.acrl.ala.org/acrlinsider/archives/9814.

Williams, Karen. 2015b. "Framework for Information Literacy Advisory Board." *ACRL Insider* (blog), June 16. http://www.acrl.ala.org/acrlinsider/archives/10426.

⑥ Further Reading: Discipline-Specific Information Literacy

ACRL (Association of College & Research Libraries). 2008. "Information Literacy Standards for Anthropology and Sociology Students." American Library Association. http://www.ala.org/acrl/standards/anthro_soc_standards.

ACRL (Association of College & Research Libraries). 2011. "Information Literacy Competency Standards for Journalism Students and Professionals." American Library Association. http://www.ala.org/acrl/sites/ala.org.acrl/files/content/standards/il_journalism.pdf.

ACRL (Association of College & Research Libraries). 2013. "Information Literacy Competency Standards for Nursing." American Library Association. http://www.ala.org/acrl/standards/nursing.

ACRL (Association of College & Research Libraries). 2015. "Information Literacy Standards for Science and Engineering/Technology." American Library Association. http://www.ala.org/acrl/standards/infolitscitech.

Diamond, Kelly, and Lisa Weihman. 2015. "The Best Laid Plans of Librarians and Faculty: Information Literacy Instruction in a General Education Literature Course, Difficulties and Successes." Presentation at the Georgia International Conference on Information Literacy, Savannah, GA, September 25–26.

Ferrer-Vinent, Ignacio J., Margaret Bruehl, Denise Pan, and Galin L. Jones. 2015. "Introducing Scientific Literature to Honors General Chemistry Students: Teaching Information Literacy and the Nature of Research to First-Year Chemistry Students." *Journal of Chemical Education* 92, no. 4 (January): 617–24.

Johns, Liz. 2014. "Preparing English-Language Learners for the American Academy: New and Evolving Practices in Course-Integrated Information Literacy in International Student Programming." Poster session, Western Libraries, Western University, May 21–23. http://ir.lib.uwo.ca/cgi/viewcontent.cgi?article=1109&context=wilu.

Milczarski, Vivian, and Amanda Maynard. 2015. "Improving Information Literacy Skills for Psychology Majors: The Development of a Case Study Technique." *College & Undergraduate Libraries* 22, no. 1 (January–March): 35–44.

O'Neill, Terence William. 2015. "The Business Model Canvas as a Platform for Business Information Literacy Instruction." *Reference Services Review* 43, no. 3: 450–60.

Phelps, Sue F., Loree Hyde, and Julie Planchon Wolf. 2015. "Introducing Information Literacy Competency Standards for Nursing." *Nurse Educator* 40, no. 6 (November–December): 278–80.

Reymond, Rhonda L., and Beth Royall. 2011. "Information Literacy in Art History." *Academic Exchange Quarterly* 15, no. 4 (Winter): 53–62.

Thompson, Leigh, and Lisa Ann Blankinship. 2015. "Teaching Information Literacy Skills to Sophomore-Level Biology Majors." *Journal of Microbiology & Biology Education* 16, no. 1 (May): 29–33.

Watkins, Alexander, and Katherine Morrison. 2015. "Can Only Librarians Do Library Instruction? Collaborating with Graduate Students to Teach Discipline-Specific Information Literacy." *Journal of Creative Library Practice* (February 27). http://creativelibrarypractice.org/2015/02/27/can-only-librarians-do-library-instruction/.

The Culture in the Classroom

The Life of a Classroom Teacher

BOY, I WISH I COULD BE a teacher. You get the summers off plus a couple weeks at Christmas. You get to leave in the middle of the afternoon. Teachers sure have it easy."

Who among educators hasn't heard that? Who, in fact, entered the profession thinking that it had to be one of the less stressful ones around? However, it can be a serious wake-up call to find your "summers off" reviewing textbooks, writing syllabi and lesson plans, researching and writing, catching up on professional reading, planning professional development, and more, while your school-year nights and weekends slip away as you once again try to meet grading deadlines.

Even if the modern teacher or professor only had to teach, that would be more than enough to do. Stuffed into the teaching bag are concepts such as flipped classrooms, active learning, learning communities, learner-centered teaching, teaching with technology, collaborative teaching, strengths-based teaching, blended learning, and teaching to learning styles. And what about giving feedback, creating learning outcomes, mapping them to assignments, and assessing them. As educators think over what they are there to teach—math, biology, economics, music—the distinct vocabulary, the decades—even centuries—old principles, the core concepts, new theories, and basic facts—just how much time is there to reflect on those? It's maddening.

Historian Jacques Barzun said, "Teaching is not a lost art, but the regard for it is a lost tradition" (1945: 12). More than a few of today's educators fear he is still right. The significance of what most instructors feel called to deliver in the classroom is not diminished. But added to their burden as they tend the front lines of education is all the rest—navigating administrators, policies, governments, the parents, and certainly the students themselves, and what all feel is owed to them. Teachers must find time for committee assignments and professional development, perhaps governance responsibilities, time for conferences and maybe occasional scholarly output. Their agenda is full and complicated.

Enter into this overcrowded world of expectations a "new" idea: information literacy, whose flame has been slowly, faithfully tended by a group of individuals largely seen as mild-mannered technicians who take care of library books and magazines. Nevertheless, as stated in previous chapters, much of what information literacy instruction involves—finding a topic, locating resources, evaluating sources, synthesizing information—is already part of regular classroom instruction, and faculty often do not collaborate with others, including librarians (Bury, 2011; Nilsen, 2012; Weiner, 2014). Typical faculty are not generally concerned with teaching information literacy as a separate subject; their frame of reference is built on the cornerstone of student learning outcomes. Thus, information literacy instruction may be implicit in the classroom, but it is uncommon for it to be explicit. So, if the teaching of information literacy is to be included in curricula across disciplines, it needs to be embedded in an individual course or a full program's student learning outcomes. Typically, these outcomes are then mapped to course assignments and, once an assignment is successfully completed, information literacy, like other aspects of an outcome, is assumed to have been learned (McGuinness, 2006; Saunders, 2012).

What Teachers Expect to Do

Not surprisingly, teachers and educators see themselves as experts in terms of pedagogy, in terms of curriculum development, and in terms of their subject matter (Beijaard, Verloop, and Vermunt, 2000). Experienced teachers know that on a day-to-day basis they must establish and maintain authority and control—that is, manage their classroom. They are the gatekeepers of what happens in the classroom. This is part of an instructor's professional identity, and when this identity is perceived as threatened, he or she may respond accordingly (Hardesty, 1991; Beijaard, Verloop, and Vermunt, 2000; McGuinness, 2006; Gardner and White-Farnham, 2013). Any suggestion that they are less than that, that they don't know what they are about, is apt to be met with resistance and will probably trigger responses meant to clarify who is in charge. Thus, teaching-educators expect to be the ones who plan their curricula, who create their lesson plans, and who choose their resources and the presentation and utilization of those resources. It is their authority that determines what happens in the classroom—no one else's.

At times, an instructor's approach to outside resources such as librarians may be collaborative, yet it is often from a perspective of "Here's what I need to accomplish," or "Show me what you have to help me," or "Show me how what you have can help me." In effect, they are the "purchaser," and all others are vendors. At other times, they may want a plug-and-play approach—"Come do a library session." But rare is the attitude one of professional humility—"Please help me, teach me, lead me, tell me if I'm doing this right"—as that contradicts their professional identity (Beijaard, Verloop, and Vermunt, 2000; Steh and Pozarnik, 2005; Okas, van der Schaaf, and Krull, 2014). This is no different from professionalism in any other fields, including librarianship.

We (teachers, instructors, professors, librarians) own the tent of our profession, though where exactly the tent pegs have been staked can be vague and changeable, especially to others. Nevertheless, disrespect or disregard for one's sense of professionalism inhibits the collaborative spirit.

In addition, when much of what information literacy means is part of what it means to create a liberally educated mind, classroom educators then clearly see themselves as owning that subject matter and may be left wondering how more library instruction sessions will help them reach more information literacy threshold moments with their students, whatever the discipline. Such is the perception of many classroom educators, and one not likely to change quickly. For example, librarians may be able to help the teacher locate "good" resources in a discipline, but by *good* the instructor means that, at best, these are *likely* credible articles, books, or whatever. The judgment of whether any particular source is valuable to any given situation—which is one attribute of being information literate—is a call made not by a librarian, but by the individual needing that information. It is a discipline-driven decision. And the ability to make that decision, to learn that lifelong skill, is something the teacher in the classroom expects to make and then integrate into his or her teaching. In this way, in the teacher's mind, this is how information literacy becomes a student learning outcome. However, no matter how strongly classroom instructors feel that they rule their domain, many, quite unlike the librarian, are in a place of unrelenting scrutiny by outsiders.

What Others Expect of Teachers

Results of public opinion surveys on teachers and the quality of work they do has been mixed, even contradictory. In general, results lean toward the negative while at the same time some data indicate that those polled—parents, in particular—do not have a clear idea of what teachers do. (Sound familiar?) And while one poll clearly showed that a majority believe that more *parent* involvement was the key to students achieving more, an even larger majority believed that to improve education, more *teacher* training was needed ("TIME Poll Results," 2010). Other polls show that the majority of the public respects and trusts teachers and would support even higher taxes to raise teacher salaries (Henderson, Peterson, and West, 2014). Overall, polls have revealed the high demands the public places on teachers, and the public's expectation that not only is education overwhelmingly the responsibility of teachers, but what a teacher should teach goes far beyond reading, writing, and arithmetic.

One of the oldest and most respected polls on American Education, the PDK/Gallup Poll in its most recent survey (Bushaw and Calderon, 2014) reveals, by the questions it asks, some of the high expectations that parents have of their schools, if not their teachers: that students should be taught how to manage finances, to maintain a healthy lifestyle, and to be an active community member. Eighty percent believe teachers should pass board certification and be licensed; 60 percent want entrance standards for teacher education programs to be more rigorous. And while 82 percent support using teacher performance to set salaries or bonuses, 61 percent oppose using student performance on standardized tests as a way to gauge teacher effectiveness. Nonetheless, the poll results clearly show that most Americans believe that improving teachers will improve student performance, though absent are the opinions on how this claim should be tested or measured.

While polls tend to show that the public holds a very critical eye on teachers, teachers don't necessarily agree. Another survey from Education*Next* shows that only about half of the public gave teachers a grade of A or B for the quality of their work, while about 69 percent of the teachers polled gave themselves an A or B (Henderson, Peterson, and West, 2014). In measuring career satisfaction among teachers, the MetLife Survey of the American Teacher found that 69 percent of the teachers surveyed disagreed with the statement that "thinking about the current debate on education, teachers' voices in general have been adequately heard" (2010: 49). As education blogger Tracy Dell'Angela points out, "We know that the public spends more time talking *about* teachers than *with* teachers" (2014).

Although the environment for those who teach apparently is not evenly positive or supportive, it is surprising that so many teachers polled (59 percent) in the MetLife survey indicated they were "very satisfied" with their teaching career. However, the characteristics of this satisfied group is important to the task of information literacy instruction: "Highly satisfied teachers have a stronger belief in their students, are more confident in their own ability to help their students succeed, and have more support for and experience with collaboration in schools" (MetLife, 2010: 46).

Teachers may feel pressured from many sides in their jobs, which could lead to their defensiveness and resistance, but if librarians come alongside them as collaborators and as partners in student-centered learning, effective classroom instruction in information literacy can happen.

A Teacher's Perspective and Threshold Concepts

The first development of the idea of "threshold concepts" is credited to Jan Meyer and Ray Land in their Occasional Report 4, wherein they have given this definition:

> A threshold concept can be considered as akin to a portal, opening up a new and previously inaccessible way of thinking about something. It represents a transformed way of understanding or interpreting, or viewing something without which the learner cannot progress. . . . Such a transformed view or landscape may represent how people "think" in a particular discipline, or how they perceive, apprehend, or experience particular phenomena within that discipline (or more generally). (2003: 1)

Threshold concepts are considered "troublesome" because they are "alien, or counter-intuitive or even intellectually absurd at face value" (Meyer and Land, 2003: 2). They are not, as Meyer and Land have explained, simply core concepts, but rather have the distinct attributes of being: a) transformative, leading to a "transformation of personal identity, a reconstruction of subjectivity," and are "likely to involve a . . . shift in values, feeling or attitude"; b) irreversible, "unlikely to be forgotten" or "unlearned"; c) integrative, "expos[ing] the previously hidden interrelatedness of something"; d) bounded, "constitut[ing] the demarcation between disciplinary areas . . . defin[ing] academic territories"; and—to repeat—e) problematic for learners because they struggle to gain the "big picture" and to understand perspectives not their own or ideas that seem foreign or even nonsensical from their pre-threshold understanding (Meyer and Land, 2003: 4–5).

Meyer and Land have given such examples of threshold concepts as *sampling distribution* in statistics, *opportunity cost* in economics, *tuning methodologies* in music, *metabolism* in exercise physiology, *deconstruction* in literary studies, *limit* in pure mathematics, and *heat transfer* in cooking! See table 4.1.

Table 4.1. Some Examples of Threshold Concepts by Discipline

DISCIPLINE	THRESHOLD CONCEPT
Statistics	Sampling Distribution
Economics	Opportunity Cost
Music	Tuning Methodologies
Exercise Physiology	Metabolism
Literary Studies	Deconstruction
Mathematics	Limit
Culinary Arts	Heat Transfer

Source: Jan Meyer and Ray Land. 2003. "Threshold Concepts and Troublesome Knowledge: Linkages to Ways of Thinking and Practicing within the Disciplines." *Enhancing Teaching-Learning Environments in Undergraduate Courses Project.* Occasional Report 4. Edinburgh, Scotland: School of Education, University of Edinburgh.

Meyer and Land admit that threshold concepts are "more readily identifiable within disciplinary contexts where there is a relatively greater degree of consensus on what constitutes a body of knowledge (for example, Mathematics, Physics, Medicine)" (2003: 9). And they point to a concern over a "colonizing" effect on curricula, as a power struggle may develop among academicians over intellectual ownership: "*Whose* threshold concepts then becomes a salient question" (2003: 10). "It appears," they concluded, "that threshold concepts are more readily identifiable in some disciplines (such as Physics) than in others (such as History)" (2003: 11). One might further observe that the "hard" sciences are perhaps more conducive to codifying threshold concepts than the "soft" ones, whose very natures lend themselves to the vagaries of "truth" or "fact."

Since 2003, the literatures of many disciplines have explored, discussed, and attempted to codify and apply to their particular pedagogies an understanding of threshold concepts (Lucas and Mladenovic, 2007; Rodger, Turpin, and O'Brien, 2015). While recognized as a popular topic in higher education, it seems less so in secondary education, and, in any case, there appears to be no solid indication of how comprehensively the concept has been implemented across disciplines, education levels, or geographic areas (Irvine and Carmichael, 2009; Walker, 2013). It may be safe to say that if you have heard of the idea of a threshold concept, then it is a hot topic in your field. It is certainly prominent in the field of library science with the advent of the new *Framework for Information Literacy for Higher Education* from the Association of College & Research Libraries (ACRL, 2015), which has drawn heavily on the threshold concept, and perhaps from this point forward, any collaboration between librarians and faculty in information literacy should begin with a discussion on the threshold concept of threshold concepts!

Student Learning Outcomes

To understand education today is to understand student learning outcomes; it is a threshold concept. This is particularly true at the higher education level, where increasingly

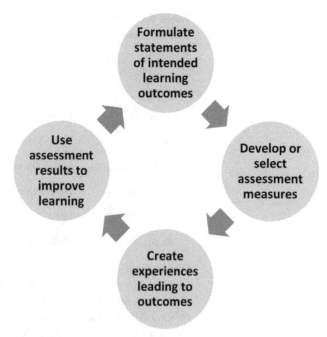

Figure 4.1. The assessment process.

institutions are driven by their accreditation requirements. Accreditation requirements themselves have become more stringent and clearly are anchored to the assessment of successful student learning, which in turn is measured through student learning outcomes. An educator today who is not creating curricula and syllabi with well-defined and measurable student learning outcomes is simply not paying attention. The assessment mantra is: (a) plan—what do you want your students to learn? (b) assess—how are you going to measure it? (c) analyze—what does the assessment tell you? and (d) improve—how are you going to change what you teach? Student learning outcomes are the cornerstone of that process (figure 4.1).

Every teacher, professor, and instructor then steps into the classroom with his or her work defined by the course's student learning outcomes. Nothing happens in the classroom that isn't related to its student learning outcomes. Thus, to include information literacy in a classroom curriculum means: (a) it must be embedded in the coursework, (b) it must be explicit and visible in its student learning outcomes, (c) it must be clearly mapped to assignments, and (d) ultimately, it must be measurable. Some subjects or courses are far more adaptable to embedding information literacy principles, such as those in writing, rhetoric, communications and media courses, and any writing-intensive or research-intensive course or program. Ways to incorporate information literacy in, say, a math or music class, are less apparent—but it has and can be done (Kimball and O'Connor, 2010), especially as a discipline grasps the importance of threshold concepts of information literacy and what it means in terms of pedagogy and course content in order to accomplish an information-literate musician, economist, physicist, physical therapist, and so on.

Nevertheless, creating student learning outcomes are to a greater degree created by the academic or subject department and to a lesser degree by the individual instructor (see figure 4.2 for a list of sample student learning outcomes). Thus, changing a student learning outcome of a course or program is a curricular process, one not owned by librarians but in which their involvement, when including information literacy, would be critical. The librarians' involvement is still mostly undeveloped ground for the classroom educator due largely to the average perception of what a librarian does.

Student Learning Outcomes

Art History

The student will be able to compare and contrast various periods in European art, distinguishing historic influences of the major art epochs.

English

The student will be able to write multiple-page essays that meet college-level academic standards for content, organization, style, grammar, mechanics, and format.

Economics

Use an appropriate analytic frame to predict the impact of policy proposals on social welfare.

Chemistry

Students demonstrate understanding of fundamental concepts of chemistry by definition, explanation, and use of these ideas in examinations and laboratory exercises.

Physics

The physics graduate student will have a specialized knowledge in one of the sub-fields of physics, such as atomic and molecular physics, condensed matter physics, nuclear and particle physics. In addition, the physics graduate will be able to demonstrate a basic knowledge in all the subfields mentioned above.

Music

Upon graduation, most majors will have the ability to design and carry out an ethnographic research project with a focus on musical performance or musical experience (defined broadly).

Basic Computer Skills

Give a sample dataset, the student will use *Excel* to create a spreadsheet that incorporates simple mathematical formulas.

Library and Research

Given specific websites to evaluate, students will be able to assess each website's authority, currency, bias, and accuracy.

Figure 4.2. Sample student learning outcomes. © *2010/2011 Azusa Pacific University, Office of Institutional Research and Assessment. Used with permission.*

Librarians

As librarians transition from a role more commonly perceived as conducting so-called one-shots and on-demand reference interviews toward a collaborative, embedded role that requires far more involvement in curricular development and, for some, a more traditional classroom presence—the old perceptions persist. For many classroom faculty, librarians may be perceived as professionals, but not really teaching faculty (Nilsen, 2012; Gardner and White-Farnham, 2013). Indeed, many librarians do not teach any traditional courses or engage in research, and in some places either do not have faculty status or have lost such status (Coker, vanDuinkerken, and Bales, 2010; Bryan, 2007).

The thought of having academic discourse with someone largely perceived as a technician is at best strange to the classroom teacher. The idea has been fortified by the reality that using today's library has become so technological that it requires strong technical expertise, but not the intellectual engagement of the librarian. So, classroom faculty and teachers come to librarians for service, not academic discourse. And the prescriptive, skills-driven nature of the "older" ACRL *Standards* (2000) for information literacy, while revolutionary at the time, may have helped solidify this characterization.

Information Literacy as a Core Competency

As discussed in chapter 1, information literacy is now recognized as a "core competency" in education, closely tied to critical thinking and essential for lifelong learning. It is what helps make the educated person a good citizen, a wise consumer, and a self-fulfilled individual. While the library profession has embraced information literacy from the time the term was first used (although going through its own evolution from basic library instruction to its current framework), the education profession has only recently become involved in the ramifications of the concept, characterizing it more as a liberal arts and general education requirement. The literature on information literacy in library and information science is robust; by comparison, information literacy literature in education or in individual disciplines is scant. The common observation in what limited literature exists in other disciplines seems to show that faculty know that information literacy is important, but are not very explicit in teaching it, and instead seem to believe that in the process of completing assignments, students will assimilate information literacy (Markless and Streatfield, 1992; McGuinness, 2006).

But this is destined to change as librarians become more familiar and practiced with the new *Framework* for information literacy and classroom faculty are compelled to meet information literacy standards in their courses; deep collaboration ensues, and a new paradigm is realized.

How Classroom Teachers Understand Information Literacy

"School days, school days, dear old Golden Rule days. Reading and 'riting and 'rithmetic, taught to the tune of a hick'ry stick" (Cobb and Edwards, 1907). My, how education has changed. Teachers don't want their students to just read; they—along with national standards movements like the Common Core Initiative—need them to read critically, to deconstruct the text, to be able to analyze it from different perspectives, and to synthesize from it. Writing isn't limited to completing a job application or giving directions to the party; students need to be able to argue and speculate and perform any rhetorical strategy needed to be persuasive and effective in whatever the communication task. As for 'rithmetic, there's one word—well, maybe two: college algebra.

To do any of those complex tasks requires a number of intellectual skills, including competency in information literacy, now recognized as a "core competency" in many education systems. However, like other core competencies—examples include written and oral communication, quantitative reasoning, and critical thinking—they are assumed to be part of the education process; it is what teachers are expected to accomplish as they teach, part of the gestalt of what it means to become educated. But unlike critical thinking or quantitative reasoning, which are easily recognized as the skills of an educated mind, information literacy is less known—partly, I would argue, because of its evolution from bibliographic instruction (how to use a library) and its history with the skill-set approach of ACRL's earlier information literacy *Standards*. The deeper issues of information literacy, which are so adroitly addressed in the new *Framework*, are not as apparent as *information literacy issues* to the classroom educator, as indicated by the relative lack of education and higher education scholarship on the issue.

But an in-depth discussion with an educator on some of the individual facets of information literacy, with the term itself set aside, would reveal a rich understanding of its relevance to the education process and a deep desire to imbue into their students the principles—indeed, the threshold concept—of information literacy.

New Perspectives, New Roles

Making information literacy instruction happen in the classroom requires new perspectives and new roles for both librarians and classroom instructors. Information literacy, especially as understood through the new *Framework*, won't be advanced like the Old World conquering the New World. It will be something morphed out of the perspectives, knowledge, and experiences of all the various stakeholders. Chief among its characteristics will be that it is a) collaborative, b) proactive, c) discipline-specific, d) embedded within curricula, e) classroom- and student-centric, and f) ongoing.

Collaborative

Classroom instructors may not understand or know all that a librarian does, but they understand collaboration and cross-disciplinary partnerships. These are key elements for both parties that can help create a robust and successful alliance. Effective collaboration is not necessarily something that comes naturally. It takes above-average interpersonal communication skills, which is not normally a part of a person's discipline unless, for example, her discipline is communication studies in interpersonal communication. The simplest of missteps can derail meetings and create personality conflicts between the nicest people with the best intentions. Taking time to learn or familiarize oneself with basic collaborative methods can increase the likelihood of a lasting partnership that successfully completes its mission. Indeed, the more complex or developmental a collaboration is, the more critical it is to know the basic skills. And certainly, implementing the new *Framework* for information literacy instruction in the classroom qualifies as both complex and developmental.

Teachers, particularly those engaged in research and scholarly activities, have certain expectations in collaboration. Thus, one of the first keys in beginning to collaborate is to clarify expectations (figure 4.3). These expectations include not just considering who does what in a collaboration and what the goals of the collaboration will be, but also asking what are the perceived values of each member of the collaboration. This determines, among other issues, how communications are handled, how decisions are made, and how conflicts are resolved. A thorough and respectful discussion of expectations should also reveal the values of each person's perspective so that egocentric misunderstandings are minimized. That is, when each person's perspective is known, acknowledged, and valued, it is less likely that motives are misconstrued and more likely that members of a collaboration will trust their fellow collaborators.

A second key is to take the time to build a peer relationship, learning how other individuals in the collaboration work, what specific demands are in their lives both professionally and personally, and what is unique and specific to their situation and to their

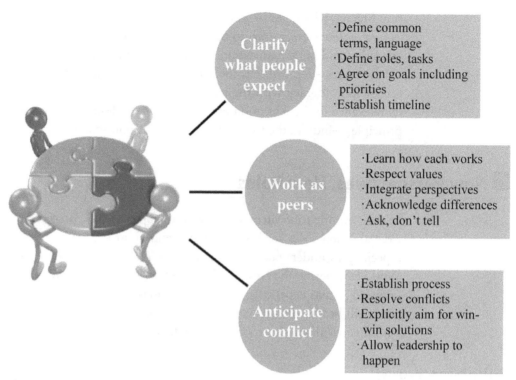

Figure 4.3. Keys to collaboration.

discipline. Contextualizing how they work and understanding what is important in their domain and how they are prioritizing their responsibilities and passions can open the door for meaningful dialog that gets to the heart of what matters to each person. In such an environment, people feel heard and are more willing to share their concerns and ideas.

It is essential to treat the other person as a colleague and a peer, an intellectual equal. Even if he has not put much work as yet into whatever issue is at hand, he anticipates engaging as a professional, as a critical thinker, and as a stakeholder. He anticipates gathering information, evaluating it, constructing his understanding, drawing his own conclusions, and owning his decisions to come from this process. He is not present for a lecture but for discourse, and his discoveries will reveal new things to his collaborators as well. He would rather be asked, not told.

A third key is to anticipate conflict. As differences are revealed and people discourse about the right solutions, conflict is inevitable. But the knowledge and insight gained from conflict properly managed often means that the best solutions—not just the good—are achieved, and that satisfaction among all members of the group is higher. Conflict successfully navigated actually strengthens the collaboration through building trust and confidence among the participants, enabling them to take on even larger challenges. So, before getting too far in the collaborative process, when goodwill and cooperativeness are still fresh, participants should take the time to establish their process for handling conflict. They should aim to resolve problems explicitly: to specifically identify and articulate problems, to identify and explore possible solutions, and clearly—involving all voices—choose one solution and then agree to let it be. Staying inclusive and working for win-win solutions whenever possible are also important.

Conflict often causes the leaders of the group to emerge, those who are the most adept at guiding the group to finding its own way. Allow this to happen, even if it's not you. Like collaboration, leadership is a concept that can be misunderstood. Effective leadership does not mean one person is boss and the others are minions. A leader is less like the head and more like the feet, someone who captures the vision of the team and with courage, conviction, and clarity pushes it forward. As *Forbes* writer J. Maureen Henderson explains, "It's great when everyone's equal, but it's even better when the some who are more equal than others have the strongest time management skills and a meticulous attention to detail" (2011). For further resources on collaboration, see the "Further Reading" list at the end of this chapter.

Proactive

No news may be good news, but patrons without reference questions does *not* mean students are information literate. That is the plight of the uninformed. Just as a person can't make a choice that is not known, no one can ask a question that he or she doesn't know how to ask. Thus, classroom educators are not predisposed to seek out librarians to help them with embedding information literacy in their discipline and in their classroom. As educators, teachers may have thought deeply and critically about informed learning, critical thinking, research, and scholarship; these facets of information literacy are neither new nor foreign to them. In fact, classroom faculty have much to offer librarians to enrich their understanding of information literacy in their own discipline. And librarians who proactively approach classroom faculty as a cross-disciplinary collaboration will find that these faculty will welcome the invitation for discourse on concepts that are just as important to them, though they may not call such concepts by the same name.

Likewise, administrators and faculty developers need to be proactive in providing ways for their faculty to seek out librarians for their information literacy needs and in raising awareness of the broader world of library science and of the kind and depths of knowledge and experience professional librarians possess and are eager to share.

Discipline-Specific

Information literacy, as encompassed by the new *Framework*, is not a one-size-fits-all approach. It must be discipline-specific and, at least in part, the classroom faculty must provide the leadership in this specificity because the ramifications of what it means to be information literate in biology, history, the arts, and other fields are more intimately known by *that* faculty or teacher. At the beginning of a collaboration, as difficult as it may be, librarians need to be asking and listening, and the classroom faculty must be forthcoming with the knowledge and experience she has in the how and where and when of her classroom information literacy instruction. It is a time of finding and mapping common ground, of reconciling language or terminology differences, and clarifying expectations.

Embedded within Curricula

The new *Framework for Information Literacy for Higher Education* (ACRL, 2015) cannot be adequately addressed in one-shot library instruction (Gardner and White-Farnham, 2013). It must be integrated at the course and program levels in the curricula. So, in addition to being by its very nature a collaborative process, information literacy instruction, as guided by the new *Framework*, requires what library science offers in order for an institution to achieve information-literate graduates.

At least until templates, rubrics, assessment tools, and systems are developed and routinely utilized, information literacy instruction within the new *Framework* will be missionary work. Once information literacy instruction is mapped into a course or program, librarians will need to stay in the loop throughout the academic year within their assigned discipline areas, regularly monitoring feedback from their subject discipline liaisons and acting as guides and consultants to the classroom instructors. Their work must be allowed to be a consistent and timely attention to what the instructors see happening in their classrooms throughout a course or year as it relates to information literacy instruction.

Classroom- and Student-Centric

For those librarians whose jobs *do not* entail traditional classroom instruction over the course of a term, the task of creating a syllabus with student learning outcomes, developing assignments mapped to those outcomes, and preparing the requisite lesson plans and various learning activities—including lectures to cover upwards of 32–48 classes—the idea of embedding information literacy instruction throughout the lifetime of a course may seem daunting. Librarians who *do* regularly teach traditional courses are far more comfortable with the idea. But what may be more difficult to grasp and to practice for both the librarian and the classroom teacher is the idea of embedding information literacy instruction in a course whose focus *is not* information literacy, but some other discipline like history or biology. It is to be only one thread in the fabric of the course. At the same time, librarians are challenged to somehow be a part of a classroom that isn't theirs, while teachers must incorporate something of another discipline into their own.

One way to look at this rather peculiar situation is to remember that in today's education, the classroom has moved to where it now is owned by the students; all of its activities are shaped by how students learn and how they are motivated to learn. Faculty are not free to create the learning environment in their own images. So the teacher is something like a ship's captain in charge of bringing the students to their educational destinations, through shifting and sometimes enigmatic currents and forces, and perhaps the librarian is also somewhat like a navigator—though not the teacher's only one—who is familiar with the sea and therefore an invaluable informer to the captain, but who knows better than to tell the captain where to go and how to get there.

Ongoing

Good pedagogy will tell you that a classroom is dynamic; it fluctuates while it develops. The students change over time as they learn new things and cross new thresholds of understanding. In a successful classroom, they are not the same people at the end of a course that they were at the beginning of a course. Instruction in information literacy, like all instruction in the classroom, must be fluid and responsive to this shifting yet malleable environment. Thus, a common statement on a syllabus is something like "Subject to change as the course progresses." Each classroom is unique not just in character but in the way it responds to challenges and in the way it moves through change; in fact, it may respond differently from one situation to the next, and the logic to how it changes can seem imperceptible. That is part of what makes teaching so interesting.

However, this means that the teacher must be nimble and flexible while remaining attentive throughout the life of the course, and so must the companion librarian. Instruction is progressive, and thus to be progressive, it is ongoing. Armed with their learning outcomes, in every class period teachers look for those teachable moments, which literally can be moments—quickly there, like a break in the clouds, then gone. Just as teachers must maintain a certain vigilance to their students' receptiveness, so too should librarians be proactive in staying tuned to teachers' recurring information literacy instruction needs throughout their courses. This is especially important for two reasons. First is the new information literacy *Framework*, which, as it is being implemented, creates a paradigm shift in information literacy instruction. Second, along with that, a proactive approach from librarians will eventually bring an end to the missionary phase of introducing the new *Framework* and establish a new cultural expectation in which classroom faculty more naturally turn to librarians for collaboration on their classroom information literacy instruction.

Key Points

Successfully teaching information literacy as defined and unfolded by the ACRL *Framework* involves librarians collaborating with classroom faculty as an integral part of the classroom culture. This means understanding the following:

- Information literacy instruction in the classroom is *not* taught as a separate subject nor typically taught explicitly, but is implicit throughout the instruction in a course or school year.
- Classroom instructors expect to be the ones to plan the curricula, create lesson plans, and choose their resources and the presentation of those resources.
- The pedagogy of teaching to threshold concepts is not uniformly implemented across disciplines, across levels of education, and across the country; thus, collaboration between librarians and faculty on the threshold concepts of information literacy may need to start with the threshold concept of a threshold concept.
- Today a teacher's work in the classroom is defined by student learning outcomes and the assessment of those outcomes; information literacy instruction must be included in these outcomes.
- Many classroom faculty perceive librarians as professionals but not faculty and come to them for service, not academic discourse or instruction in instruction, regardless of the topic.
- Classroom faculty recognize the importance of information literacy but may assume that, as a result of completing their assignments, students will become information literate.
- Teachers understand bibliographic instruction by the librarian (how to use the library), but the deeper issues of information literacy as newly framed are not as apparent (or recognizable) to them, nonetheless they *include information literacy elements in their instruction.*
- Explicit information literacy instruction in the classroom will morph, or come to be, out of the perspectives, knowledge, and experiences of the various stakeholders.
- Characteristics of the new information literacy instruction are that it will be a) collaborative, b) proactive, c) discipline-specific, d) embedded within curricula, e) classroom- and student-centric, and f) ongoing.

Chapter 5, "Joining the Information Literacy Conversation in Education," will take a look at the librarians' perspective in regard to integrating information literacy instruction into the classroom, particularly the viewpoints of the early adopters and ACRL leadership. From that perspective, the chapter offers guidance in preparing information literacy instruction using the new *Framework*.

⊚ References

ACRL (Association of College & Research Libraries). 2000. *Information Literacy Competency Standards for Higher Education*. American Library Association. January 18. http://www.ala.org/acrl/standards/informationliteracycompetency.

ACRL (Association of College & Research Libraries). 2015. *Framework for Information Literacy for Higher Education*. American Library Association. http://www.ala.org/acrl/standards/ilframework.

Barzun, Jacques. 1945. *Teacher in America*. Boston: Little, Brown and Company.

Beijaard, Douwe, Nico Verloop, and Jan D. Vermunt, 2000. "Teachers' Perceptions of Professional Identity: An Exploratory Study from a Personal Knowledge Perspective." *Teaching and Teacher Education* 16, no. 7: 749–64.

Bryan, Jacalyn E. 2007. "The Question of Faculty Status for Academic Librarians." *Library Review* 56, no. 9: 781–87.

Bury, Sophie. 2011. "Faculty Attitudes, Perceptions and Experiences of Information Literacy: A Study across Multiple Disciplines at York University, Canada." *Journal of Information Literacy* 5, no. 1 (May): 45–64.

Bushaw, William J., and Valerie J. Calderon. 2014. "Americans Put Teacher Quality on Center Stage: The 46th Annual PDK/Gallup Poll of the Public's Attitudes toward the Public Schools, Part II." *Phi Delta Kappan* 96, no. 2: 48–59. http://journals.sagepub.com/doi/10.1177/0031721714553411.

Cobb, Will, and Gus Edwards. 1907. *School Days*. The Lester S. Levy Sheet Music Collection, Sheridan Libraries Special Collections. Baltimore: Johns Hopkins University. http://levysheetmusic.mse.jhu.edu/catalog/levy:149.077.

Coker, Catherine, Wyoma vanDuinkerken, and Stephen Bales. 2010. "Seeking Full Citizenship: A Defense of Tenure Faculty Status for Librarians." *College & Research Libraries* 71, no. 5: 406–20.

Dell'Angela, Tracy. 2014. "What Do Teachers Think about Public Opinion Polls on Teachers?" *Education Post* (blog), September 16. http://educationpost.org/teachers-think-public-opinion-poll-teachers/#.VW-Qss9Viko.

Gardner, Carolyn C., and Jamie White-Farnham. 2013. "'She Has a Vocabulary I Just Don't Have': Faculty Culture and Information Literacy Collaboration." *Collaborative Librarianship* 5, no. 4: 235–42.

Hardesty, Larry. 1991. *Faculty and the Library: The Undergraduate Experience*. Norwood, NJ: Ablex Publishing.

Henderson, J. Maureen. 2011. "How to Collaborate without Killing Someone." *Forbeswoman* (blog). Forbes, September 13. http://www.forbes.com/sites/jmaureenhenderson/2011/09/13/how-to-collaborate-without-killing-someone/.

Henderson, Michael B., Paul E. Peterson, and Martin R. West. 2014. "No Common Opinion on the Common Core." Education*Next*, August 19. http://educationnext.org/2014-education-next-survey-visual-breakdown/.

Irvine, Naomi, and Patrick Carmichael. 2009. "Threshold Concepts: A Point of Focus for Practitioner Research." *Active Learning in Higher Education* 10, no. 2: 103–19.

Kimball, Katherine, and Lisa O'Connor. 2010. "Engaging Auditory Modalities through the Use of Music in Information Literacy Instruction." *Reference & User Services Quarterly* 49, no. 4: 316–19.

Lucas, Ursala, and Rosina Mladenovic. 2007. "The Potential of Threshold Concepts: An Emerging Framework for Education Research and Practice." *London Review of Education* 5, no. 3: 237–48.

Markless, Sharon, and David Streatfield. 1992. *Cultivating Information Skills in Further Education: Eleven Case Studies.* London: British Library Research and Development Department.

McGuinness, Claire. 2006. "What Faculty Think: Exploring the Barriers to Information Literacy Development in Undergraduate Education." *Journal of Academic Librarianship* 32, no. 6 (November): 573–82.

MetLife (Metropolitan Life Insurance Company). 2010. *MetLife Survey of the American Teacher: Collaborating for Student Success.* http://files.eric.ed.gov/fulltext/ED509650.pdf.

Meyer, Jan, and Ray Land. 2003. "Threshold Concepts and Troublesome Knowledge: Linkages to Ways of Thinking and Practicing within the Disciplines." *Enhancing Teaching-Learning Environments in Undergraduate Courses Project.* Occasional Report 4. Edinburgh, Scotland: School of Education, University of Edinburgh.

Nilsen, Christina. 2012. "Faculty Perceptions of Librarian-Led Information Literacy Instruction in Postsecondary Education." Paper presented at the 78th IFLA General Conference and Assembly, Helsinki, Finland, June.

Okas, Anne, Marieke van der Schaaf, and Edgar Krull. 2014. "Novice and Experienced Teachers' Views on Professionalism." *Trames: A Journal of the Humanities and Social Sciences* 18, no. 4: 327–44.

Rodger, Sylvia, Merrill Turpin, and Mia O'Brien. 2015. "Experiences of Academic Staff in Using Threshold Concepts within a Reformed Curriculum." *Studies in Higher Education* 40, no. 4: 545–60.

Saunders, Laura. 2012. "Faculty Perspectives on Information Literacy as a Student Learning Outcome." *Journal of Academic Librarianship* 38, no. 4 (July): 226–36.

Steh, Barbara, and Patricia Marentic Pozarnik. 2005. "Teachers' Perceptions of Their Professional Autonomy in the Environment of Systemic Change." In *Teacher Professional Development in Changing Conditions*, edited by Douwe Beijaard, Paulien C. Meijer, Greta Morine-Dershimer, and Harm Tillema, 343–63. Dordrecht: Springer.

"TIME Poll Results: Americans' View on Teacher Tenure, Merit Pay and Other Education Reforms." 2010. *Time*, September 9. http://content.time.com/time/nation/article/0,8599,2016994,00.html.

Walker, Guy. 2013. "A Cognitive Approach to Threshold Concepts." *Higher Education* 65, no. 2: 247–63.

Weiner, Sharon A. 2014. "Who Teaches Information Literacy Competencies? Report of a Study of Faculty." *College Teaching* 62, no. 1: 5–12.

Further Reading

Brasley, Stephanie S. 2008. "Effective Librarian and Discipline Faculty Collaboration Models for Integrating Information Literacy into the Fabric of an Institution." *New Directions for Teaching and Learning* 114, no. 7: 71–88.

Carr, Jo Ann, and Ilene F. Rickman. 2003. "Information Literacy Collaboration: A Shared Responsibility." *American Libraries* 34, no. 8: 52–54.

Dubicki, Eleanora. 2013. "Faculty Perceptions of Students' Information Literacy Skills Competencies." *Journal of Information Literacy* 7, no. 2: 97–125.

Gullikson, Shelley. 2006. "Faculty Perceptions of ACRL's Information Literacy Competency Standards for Higher Education." *Journal of Academic Librarianship* 32, no. 6: 583–92.

Mackey, Thomas P., and Trudi E. Jacobson. 2005. "Information Literacy: A Collaborative Endeavor." *College Teaching* 53, no. 4: 140–44.

Mazella, David, Laura Heidel, and Irene Ke. 2011. "Integrating Reading, Information Literacy, and Literary Studies Instruction in a Three-Way Collaboration." *Learning Assistance Review* 16, no. 2 (Fall): 41–53.

Montiel-Overall, Patricia. 2005. "Toward a Theory of Collaboration for Teachers and Librarians." *School Library Media Research* 8. http://www.ala.org/aasl/sites/ala.org.aasl/files/content/aasl pubsandjournals/slr/vol8/SLMR_TheoryofCollaboration_V8.pdf.

Oakleaf, Megan. 2014. "A Roadmap for Assessing Student Learning Using the New Framework for Information Literacy for Higher Education. *Journal of Academic Librarianship* 40, no. 5 (September): 510–14.

Peters, Madalienne, and Suzanne Roybal. 2011. *Faculty-Library Collaboration: Embedding Information Literacy in Educational Research Graduate Classes.* July. ERIC, ED 521 660.

Raspa, Dick, and Dane Ward. 2000. *The Collaborative Imperative: Librarians and Faculty Working Together in the Information Universe.* Chicago: American Library Association.

Rockman, Ilene F. 2002. "Strengthening Connections between Information Literacy, General Education, and Assessment Efforts." *Library Trends* 51, no. 2 (Fall): 185–98.

Sanker, Dan. 2013. *Collaboration: The Art of We.* San Francisco: Jossey-Bass.

Sawyer, Keith. 2007. *Group Genius: The Creative Power of Collaboration.* New York: Basic Books.

Schein, Edgar H. 2013. *Humble Inquiry: The Gentle Art of Asking instead of Telling.* San Francisco: Berrett-Koehler Publishers.

Straus, David. 2002. *How to Make Collaboration Work.* San Francisco: Berrett-Koehler Publishers.

Wang, Li. 2011. "An Information Literacy Integration Model and Its Application in Higher Education." *Reference Services Review* 39, no. 4: 703–20.

Joining the Information Literacy Conversation in Education

Faculty Perspectives on Information Literacy

AS NOTED EARLIER in this book, classroom faculty, particularly those in the humanities, already implicitly teach many of the concepts found in the new *Framework* created by the ACRL. With the new *Framework*, the teaching of information literacy has become a matter of co-equal collaboration between librarians and classroom faculty as information literacy instruction shifts to being more explicit within the various disciplines, rather than only one-shot library instruction or bibliographic instruction sessions devised and executed exclusively by librarians.

This chapter attempts to crack open the classroom door enough to highlight, for both librarians and classroom instructors, how some of the concepts of information literacy as captured by the *Framework* are represented in the classroom of two disciplines: journalism and composition. But first, a bit of introduction into the mind-set of how these two disciplines relate to the general idea of information literacy is presented.

In the world of journalism, as well as the broader field of communications, reporters, editors, publishers, and writers in all media are *gatekeepers* of information; as journalists, they need to know the nature of the information they are handling and how to handle it. They need to know how to find sources, where to find sources, how to evaluate those sources, what to believe and not believe, how to read between the lines, and then how to use that information, ethically and for the greater good. As the *New York Times* so succinctly puts it, the news media is charged with bringing to the American people "all the news that's fit to print." American democracy depends on it.

A good journalist is not a cynic; a good reporter is a *skeptic*. Journalism students are asked to consider: How do you know what you know, why is this person telling you this information, what is not being said, who is not being heard? What is being left out, missed, ignored, or discounted? What is being "spun"? How significant are these facts or how relevant are they to the issue at hand? What purpose is being served? When considering such frames as "Information Creation as Process" as well as "Authority Is Constructed and Contextual," it is easily apparent that journalism students, as part of their education, are brought deep into some of the conceptual territories of information literacy as captured by the ACRL *Framework*; to be effective or even add value, further information literacy instruction will need to take this part of their education into account. This is clearly shared by the American Press Institute, which has stated: "The purpose of journalism is thus to provide citizens with the information they need to make the best possible decisions about their lives, their communities, their societies, and their governments" (Dean, 2017).

Similarly, to teach composition it is essential to teach students how to brainstorm, choose and narrow a topic, form research questions, find information to answer those questions, and then to evaluate and organize it. Students must learn how to integrate external information with their own writing and properly contextualize it. To write critically, students must be able to read critically and to recognize audience and purpose, hidden assumptions, and missing and faulty arguments, both in the texts they read and the texts they write. These are standard topics in teaching writing, as every significant textbook on composition reflects (figure 5.1). Again, as the information literacy frames are considered—for example, "Information Has Value," "Authority Is Constructed and Contextual," and "Information Creation as Process"—it is clear that writing students are being instructed in information literacy concepts.

College instructors are also gatekeepers, not only in the texts they choose for teaching, but in what they value or disregard in the classroom. Of course, they hope their students are learning the concepts and practices of the subject taught, but sometimes, at least, the students are learning more about fulfilling their instructor's expectations in order to get a good grade. Not that students are rhetorically conscious of this cultural process of education. Yet, irrefutably, from the student's perspective, classroom faculty are demonstrating implicitly to the class again and again throughout the life of a course how to approach information, how to deconstruct it, how to construct it, and how to organize it to make meaningful new information.

Librarians are gatekeepers as well. They construct, manage, and instruct in massive systems of information known as databases. Librarians select and deselect what information is to be stored or not stored. They choose, by the information products they purchase, the media for storage and, along with them, the means for access and retrieval.

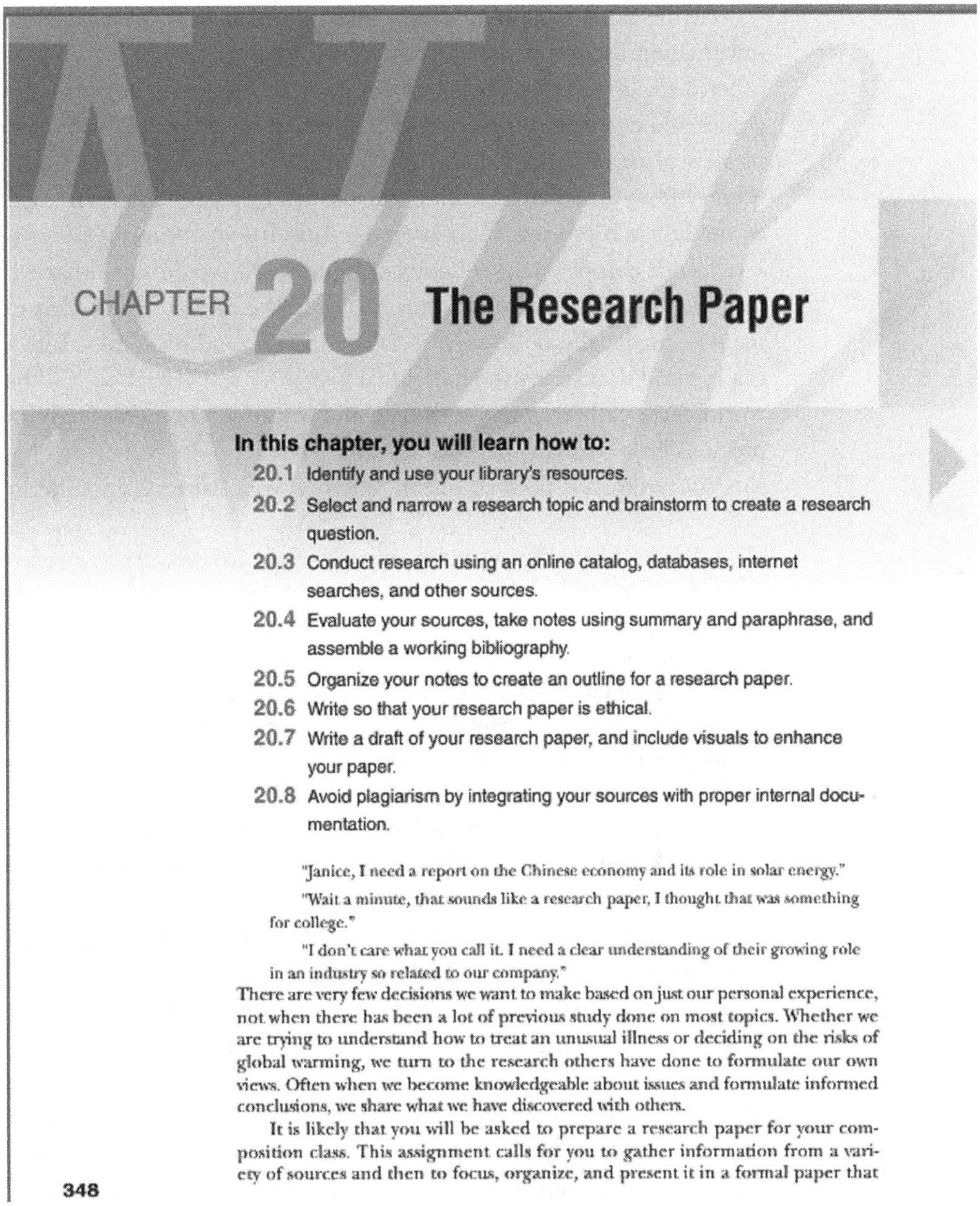

Figure 5.1. First page of a chapter on writing a research paper in *Strategies for Successful Writing*, a popular college composition textbook. *Reinking, James A., and Robert A. Von der Osten. 2013. Strategies for Successful Writing: A Rhetoric, Research Guide, Reader, and Handbook. 10th ed. Boston: Pearson. Used with permission.*

Despite the cultural and historical ramifications of librarians owning and practicing these responsibilities, studies have shown that faculty, for the most part and still today, perceive librarians as service providers and not as teachers or even as collaborators in teaching with discipline-specific faculty (Ducas and Michaud-Oystryck, 2004; Oberg, Schleiter, and Van Houten, 1989, as cited in Bury, 2011). Helping to reinforce these perceptions is the fact that many academic librarians do not hold faculty status. In addition, Heidi Julien and Lisa Given "point to misconceptions of IL [information literacy] roles on both sides [and] argue that librarians' predominantly negative characterizations of faculty behavior in the area of [information literacy] is less than constructive" (2003, as quoted by Bury, 2011).

At the same time that library and information science has been reconceptualizing information literacy to embrace its larger role in lifelong learning and critical thinking, other disciplines—notably composition—are also in the process of reformulating pedagogies and curriculum design to enfold the modern concept of information literacy and its new place in general education (Artman, Frisicaro, and Monge, 2010). Information literacy from a higher education perspective has been largely framed within the context of the research process. Only more recently has its meaning enlarged to denote a set of intellectual competencies—habits of mind, some would say—that enable the graduate to be a lifelong learner who can thus successfully negotiate all of life's information environments—financially, politically, socially, mentally, and physically. Information literacy thus is a life skill that serves the individual long after leaving school and being launched into a world chaotically teeming with data and information, increasingly from new media, and precious little that is issued from a library database. As Robert Monge and Erica Frisicaro-Pawlowski have pointed out in terms of workplace information literacy:

> [W]hile the concept of information literacy carries currency in academic discussions, there is no equivalent framework for capturing how information literacy is conceptualized, practiced, and collaboratively implemented in a workplace setting. It is therefore no surprise that there is a serious disconnect between information literacy in academic settings and in workplace settings, and this disconnect extends beyond the lack of a common language or framework to describe information literacy. It also entails a disconnect in prevailing practices. (2014: 63)

Library and information science long ago left behind the concept that information literacy is mostly bibliographic instruction and has embraced a new frontier for itself, as the new ACRL *Framework* well demonstrates. But discipline or classroom faculty, it should be argued, have made a different developmental journey. Faculty typically regard librarians as those who give bibliographic instruction (though few would know and use the term itself), and regard *themselves* as the ones responsible for investing students with many of the information literacy precepts embodied in the new ACRL *Framework*, though these faculty may name, contextualize, and describe them with different words. Nevertheless, Eleonora Dubicki (2013) has cited a number of studies showing the relative confusion and lack of agreement among faculty about what information literacy at the curricular or course level entails, how it should be handled, and who should do what. Indeed, a few might think that demands from their accrediting bodies to demonstrate information literacy instruction means that they must have more bibliographic instruction.

Clearly, librarians have the opportunity today to facilitate classroom instruction in information literacy, but just as clearly, along with understanding today's learning environment, librarians need to understand their faculty culture—both generally and specifically—to do so.

Two Examples: Information Literacy Contexts in Composition and Journalism

Composition

A first-year writing class in college takes a wide view of the reading and writing process. Primary learning outcomes include instructing students how to read and write critically.

Often at the college level, the first-year student has not thought much about writing or reading as critical processes that use specific strategies to both *construct* effective texts and *deconstruct* other authors' texts for a given purpose. Initially, they read and write superficially, unaware of the rhetorical forces at work and unschooled in strategies and methods for discerning credibility, expertise, or context, as well as audience and purpose. These intellectual habits are needed in order to understand and practice any of the information literacy frames. For example, in preparing written assignments, the students should come to experience the iterative nature of searching and learn to effectively evaluate the information found in order to develop more complex questions for research (important concepts in the frames "Searching as Strategic Exploration" and "Research as Inquiry").

The writing instructor leads and guides students through the planning and drafting of their writing assignments, which at the college level and not uncommonly at the secondary education level involves research. Students are instructed in how to break down and understand an assignment, then shown how to use that knowledge to zero in on an acceptable topic. They are guided in gathering appropriate information (thus engaging in frames such as "Authority Is Constructed and Contextual" as well as "Information Has Value") and in formulating a working thesis. Once they create a working thesis, they are helped to organize their information, perhaps discovering areas needing further research development or even new areas to explore (clearly concepts in the frames "Research as Inquiry" and "Searching as Strategic Exploration"). Along the way, students organize and reorganize their information, and then in preparation for writing their first drafts they create an outline. They often discover at this point that they need to refine their theses (concepts in the frames "Scholarship as Conversation" and "Information Creation as Process"). Once they have written a first draft, they go through the process of revision. When done properly, students treat their own writing as simply another text to be deconstructed. They test the thesis and examine the author's credibility and expertise. They evaluate the evidence used—is it appropriate for audience and purpose? Does it effectively support the thesis? Is it free of bias, relevant, complete? Are all claims supported (concepts in the frame "Authority Is Constructed and Contextual")? Is it appropriately contextualized—is enough background information included for clear understanding, are complex concepts adequately explained, are transitions between ideas adequate (concepts in the frames "Information Creation as Process" and "Information Has Value")? They will typically participate in peer review workshops or take their papers to the writing center (concepts in the frame "Scholarship as Conversation").

As the students' writing advances, they will experiment and practice various rhetorical strategies for the most effective communication ("Information Creation as Process" and "Information Has Value"). Is analysis needed? A demonstration of cause and effect? A comparison or description? Are claims made that aren't supported—or supported poorly? In turn, as their critical reading evolves, they become aware of these strategies in the texts they read ("Authority Is Constructed and Contextual").

Communications

The study of journalism, or more generally communications, expands the conversation about information literacy to all forms of communications—from mass media to visual media to social media. It includes interpersonal communications, nonverbal communications, and organizational communications. All information influences human behavior and human decision making, and different forms of communication—that is, the conveyance of information ("Information Creation as Process")—can dominate others. For example, communications research has shown that nonverbal communication is often more powerful than verbal—it's not what you say, it's how you say it (Adler, Rosenfeld, and Proctor, II, 2014). In the case of electronic communication, if a website looks terrific and is fun to navigate, people will tend to believe it is a credible site whether it is or not (van der Geest and van Dongelen, 2009). Communications research also shows that people tend to believe a message from a man over a woman, and a beautiful person over one less attractive (Adler, Rosenfeld, and Proctor, II, 2014).

Studies in journalism and communications also take into consideration the format of a message or item of information, whether a scholarly article in a peer-reviewed journal or a Twitter message ("Information Has Value," "Information Creation as Process," "Authority Is Constructed and Contextual"). "The medium is the message," Marshall McLuhan famously declared in his 1964 book, *Understanding Media: The Extensions of Man*. As he explains:

> The message of any medium or technology is the change of scale or pace or pattern that it introduces into human affairs. The railway did not introduce movement or transportation or wheel or road into human society, but it accelerated and enlarged the scale of previous human functions, creating totally new kinds of cities and new kinds of work and leisure. This happened whether the railway functioned in a tropical or northern environment, and is quite independent of the freight or content of the railway medium. (1964: 8)

Thus, for the student in communications studies, being information literate means understanding how the medium used to convey information influences that information and what that influence means in human affairs ("Information Creation as Process").

What Faculty Want to Do

Discipline or classroom faculty are driven by their student learning outcomes. These learning outcomes are scaffolded throughout the life of a discipline study. That is, as students advance from the beginning level to completion of a major, learning outcomes become more complex and critical, building on the successful attainment of subordinate-level outcomes. Thus, as student coursework becomes more analytical and intellectually dynamic, inherently *so should their use of information in their discipline*. Numerous studies have supported the faculty perception that students' information literacy skills improve as they advance in levels of education (Bury, 2011; Cannon, 1994, as cited in Dubicki, 2013; Gonzales, 2001; Leckie and Fullerton, 1999). As Dubicki has stated, "Faculty clearly perceive they are teaching students [information literacy] skills within course content" (2013: 111).

Thus, discipline-specific faculty are apt to think that information literacy is implicitly taught and implicitly measured by the successful completion of college courses in a discipline. And as these faculty diligently and faithfully teach to their learning outcomes, they are doing what they have been educated and hired to do, what they entered their professions to do. For these learning outcomes have been through the many layers of the curriculum planning process, through the approval processes explicitly dictated by departments, and through the approval process for accreditation both at the institution level and discipline level. Faculty cannot circumvent or supplant the standards of their discipline with those of any other, and often information literacy instruction is perceived as outside their discipline (Saunders, 2012). Therefore, helping faculty enfold information literacy instruction into their teaching requires demonstrating to them how they can include it within their discipline's learning outcomes. It's a bit like a sculptor revealing the art that exists within the block of stone.

What Faculty Don't Want to Do

Faculty don't want to teach library science—or be a student of library science. Librarians simply delivering unsolicited lectures or email links to LibGuides on information literacy most likely will not be met with enthusiasm or anticipation and most likely will be given little or no attention. And when it comes to preparing and teaching for their class, faculty usually don't want to collaborate, much less listen to instruction on how to teach in their course. Faculty typically work in isolation and are highly independent, with a well-developed sense of entitlement for their "academic freedom" (Hardesty, 1995, as cited in Gardner and White-Farnham, 2013). Working with a group of faculty to perform a common task has often been described as attempting to herd cats. Or, perhaps collaboration with faculty is more like racing rabbits (http://www.cbs.com/shows/amazing_race/episodes/77112/). Rabbits are perceived as mild-mannered and easy to get along with, non-aggressive, and even sweet. All of this is true. However, you cannot lead rabbits. You cannot *make* a rabbit race—that is, force it or command it to run a course and cross its finish line—by dragging it on a leash or prodding it. You must solicit its cooperation, entice it, and give it a reason to pursue the goal. Similarly, classroom faculty typically cannot be dragged or commanded to teach a course a certain way, to include elements or exclude others. Just as librarians are dedicated to their own field, discipline faculty are deeply invested in their disciplines and highly protective of the integrity of their courses. However, if they can be shown the relevancy of information literacy to their discipline, they are far more likely to come on board and, in fact, be curious about how they can include it. Librarians and classroom faculty need to collaborate first to determine what the information literacy needs are for the course or program, and then, *once the faculty acknowledges those needs*, work together to meet them.

What Their Concerns Are

Recent studies have shown that faculty are largely on board with information literacy goals (Nilsen, 2012; Weiner, 2014). They see the need, and they understand how information literacy competencies affect the quality of work of their students as well as how they impact graduates' future employability, especially in the professional studies. While faculty expect librarians to understand the research process, and absolutely rely on librarians to help access and retrieve information needed from library resources, discipline faculty see the other, more characteristically intellectual concerns of information literacy as within their domain as teachers. Classroom faculty concerns revolve around a number of pedagogical issues that must be addressed to teach their discipline and for their students to successfully learn. But they are unclear about how to teach the following within their discipline, and who should teach—or assess—these issues:

- How to discern the validity and relevance of information, based on a) argumentation and b) focus on an assignment problem, rather than slickness or quickness of presentation or ease of navigation, such as on a website

- How to synthesize information (not simply copy or repeat it)
- How to integrate source information, as opposed to placing it in text in a linear fashion
- How to practice Kuhlthau's "guided inquiry" (Kuhlthau, Maniotes, and Caspari, 2007, as cited in Dubicki, 2013: 109)
- How to read critically and analytically or have "comfort with literacy" (Dubicki, 2013: 109)
- How to collaborate (or work in a team) and how to discourse (or practice interactive interaction) to deepen students' learning and develop ideas
- How to maintain academic integrity—understanding when and how to give credit and under what circumstances credit is needed or not needed
- As an instructor, how to develop the practice of information literacy skills throughout a course or curriculum, teaching in a tiered way throughout the course of study.

The Impact on Library Instruction

It may be most practical to view the librarian's task of helping discipline faculty embed information literacy into their coursework as a task of working with an adult learner. Typically, adult learners (meaning "faculty members") are busy with their lives, their jobs and other important responsibilities, and time is a scarce commodity. Adult learners tend to have a fairly rigid expectation that the value and relevance of what is being taught should be immediately apparent, and they are routinely skeptical of an instructor's expertise and authority as well as the veracity of the content being taught. Adult learners may listen politely, but they will reserve judgment on the significance of what they are being told. While they are not averse to theoretical content, typically they are not patient with it just for its own sake. It is only valuable to them—and thus retained—if they are able to practically apply such knowledge within a reasonable amount of time. These attitudes are especially prevalent in the professional fields, where concepts of a liberal arts education are not commonly addressed. As the comparison of adult learners and child learners in figure 5.2 demonstrates, it may be far more effective for librarians to approach classroom faculty as adult learners.

At the same time, it's important to keep in mind how information literacy has changed, the new *Framework* being a prime example. Information literacy as a concept in education is defined far more broadly than simply library skills or even research skills. Its definition has evolved to include a range of intellectual competencies and problem-solving skills and, as such, it is embraced as an educational goal, one that has been harnessed to the goal of creating lifelong learners. Thus, as figure 5.3 suggests, in imagining information literacy as an intellectual competency needed to navigate a complex and oversaturated information environment, the perspective shifts from that of being a student completing assignments to that of an individual—to use a bit of ACRL *Framework* language—"negotiating and understanding the world" he or she must live in.

At any given moment, a person is either a receiver of information or a user, but the division is fluid, and shifts between the two functions (receiver/user) can be instantaneous. As an individual *receiving* information, he or she performs all the functions that make up the ring on the right side of figure 5.3—managing information by inquiring, accessing, searching, gathering, and organizing it. At some point, enough information is received (and managed or processed) and the receiver becomes the user, performing the activities making up the ring on the left side, and thus *creating* new information.

CHILDHOOD	ADULTHOOD
Most children perceive one of their major roles in life to be that of learner.	Adults perceive themselves to be doers-using previous learning to achieve success as workers, parents, etc.
Children actually perceive time differently than older people do; time seems to pass more quickly as we get older.	Adults are concerned about the effective use of time.
Children have a limited experience base.	Adults have a broad, rich experience base.
Children generally learn quickly.	Adults usually learn more slowly than children, but they learn just as well.
Children are open to new information and will readily adjust their views.	Adults are much more likely to reject or explain away new information that contradicts their beliefs.
Children's readiness to learn is linked to both academic development and biological development.	Adults' readiness to learn is more directly linked to needs related to their roles as workers, spouses, parents, etc.
Children learn (at least in part) because learning will be of use in the future.	Adults are more concerned about the immediate applicability of learning.
Children are often externally motivated (by the promise of good grades, praise from teachers and parents, etc.)	Adults are more often internally motivated (by the potential for feelings of worth, self-esteem, achievement, etc.)
Children have less-well-formed sets of expectations in terms of formal learning experiences. Their "filter" of past experience is smaller than that of adults.	Adults have well-formed expectations, which, unfortunately, are sometimes negative because they are based upon unpleasant past formal learning experiences.

Figure 5.2. Comparison of characteristics between child learners and adult learners. © *2011 Hopelink. Used with permission.*

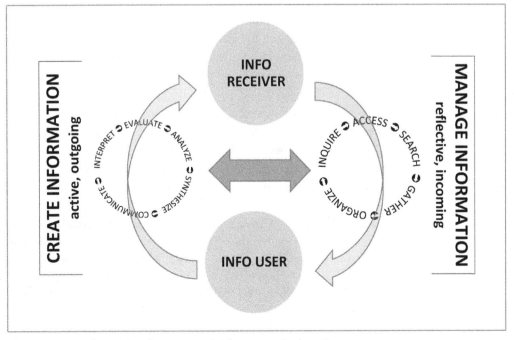

Figure 5.3. Information literacy model for general education.

But exercising the intellectual skills of information literacy is iterative, recursive, cyclic, and evolving; hence, the two-way arrow in the middle and the arrows right and left, as well as the arrows within those left and right rings, indicating that a person seamlessly moves between being a receiver and being a user, being active in creating information and being reflective in managing information.

The model is integrative, and so it is difficult, if not impossible, to sort the six frames on one side (Active) or the other (Reflective). There are elements of being reflective and being active in each frame. However, it can be argued that "Research as Inquiry," "Searching as Strategic Exploration," and "Information Has Value" are primarily *reflective* frames, and "Authority Is Constructed and Contextual," "Information Creation as a Process," and "Scholarship as a Conversation" are essentially *active* frames. Research is characterized by accessing, gathering, and inquiring (words from the ring on the right); searching is, too. One must make decisions about value to organize and to determine new things to access and gather. To understand authority, one must evaluate, analyze, and interpret (words used in the ring on the left in the model); to create information obviously is active; and in order to participate in scholarship, one must be actively communicating.

The model strongly illustrates that teaching information literacy is a shared world, a co-owned world. This has come to mean that for librarians, gaining access to the very people who need information literacy instruction—the students—has become today largely *indirect*. Practically speaking, there are not enough librarians, nor will there ever be, for them to get into every classroom across an institution to deliver this instruction themselves. To be effective, librarians need to work at the program level, helping shape curriculum, working with institutional policy makers, and interfacing with faculty and department heads as much as they do with individual students—perhaps even more so.

To help build these faculty-librarian collaborations in the disciplines, the library, if not the institution at large, should implement a marketing and public relations program that focuses on raising awareness for these newly framed information literacy concepts. Only their awareness will generate the sense of need essential for authentic collaboration. Students will go to librarians for help if their faculty are recommending that they do so. As Christina Nilsen has written (2012), librarians should focus first on creating and implementing mechanisms for building relationships with faculty rather than scheduling more in-class bibliographic instruction sessions. Likewise, students will take tutorials, investigate LibGuides, and attend library-sponsored workshops if *classroom faculty* are advising or even requiring them to do so. And they will only do so if they are informed and perceive the need.

To create discipline-specific content, librarians and discipline faculty can develop case studies and collect discipline-specific sample assignments, making a place on the library website for posting best practices for faculty. When planning online materials, librarians should gather input from faculty focus groups in order to plan and prepare the most effective online materials. Ideally, Monge and Frisicaro-Pawlowski have indicated that

> such collaborations will lead to the librarian being fully integrated into the learning community so as to support the efforts of the faculty in both the conception and execution of courses. In workplace language, teaching faculty in these collaborative communities serve as project architects or project managers. Librarians, in turn, serve as course design assistants and trainers—yet they may frequently also take on the role of fellow co-worker in assisting students. (2014: 68).

Writing centers and libraries need to collaborate in order to more closely target information literacy instruction to the current and specific needs of students coming to the writing center. Librarians should be invited or asked to participate or have input in student group sessions and ongoing writing center workshops. Librarians need to ask for any data kept by the writing center that pertains to information literacy (or collaborate with them to collect that data) so as to plan and adapt the information literacy instruction program and information literacy resources. Writing instructors and librarians need to collaborate so that librarians can become familiar with a great deal of writing instruction content that is historically used in writing centers and predates and overlaps with information literacy or library instruction, such as instruction on how to narrow a topic, how to evaluate sources, and how to cite these. Once familiar, librarians can more effectively focus on ways to assist and add value to what is already being done in the writing program.

Librarians need to be part of faculty governance to strengthen programs and create student learning outcomes that include measureable information literacy goals. Ideally, librarians should strive to create an information literacy credit-bearing course which, depending on the number of credits, could be repeated throughout the course of study. For example, plan a one-unit course for freshman, another at second-semester sophomore or first-semester junior, and a final capstone at the senior level. The instruction could be all online or hybrid (part online, part on-the-ground and face-to-face), and could include related content, such as critical thinking, to help satisfy more than one assessment or accreditation goal. Or, such a course could be positioned as a "lab" requirement for first-year seminars or freshman writing courses. Alternatively, librarians can create for-credit research courses at either the undergraduate or graduate level to include deeper information literacy instruction.

Finally, librarians need to collaborate with faculty development programs or any other pertinent institutional programs and initiatives to be a significant, visible, and ongoing resource in information literacy instruction across the curriculum.

Guidelines for Faculty-Friendly Collaboration

Librarians and classroom faculty need to embrace a higher education/general education/workplace model for information literacy instruction as it relates to in-class, discipline faculty–led, information literacy education. Faculty and academic departments are more responsive to those groups (such as accreditation bodies) and individuals who determine what they must do as educators and educational institutions. And faculty will shape their responses according to the expectations expressed by those determining groups and individuals. At the same time, particularly when looking at accrediting bodies, the level of development of expression on information literacy varies widely (see table 5.1). Some have much to say, while others do not even use the term "information literacy." Thus, in contexts where information literacy is not a significant issue, a library-based approach for an information literacy instruction program that reaches too far beyond conventional bibliographic instruction probably will not be met with much anticipation by its institution. Conversely, an institution that has been put on notice to answer to explicit information literacy requirements for accreditation will be eagerly receptive to collaboration from its librarians.

Table 5.1. Sampling of What Major Accrediting Bodies Say about Information Literacy

AGENCY	DEFINITION AND STANDARDS
Middle States Commission on Higher Education	From *Developing Research & Communication Skills: Guidelines for Information Literacy in the Curriculum*: The Middle States Commission on Higher Education, in the 2002 edition of *Characteristics of Excellence in Higher Education: Eligibility Requirements and Standards for Accreditation*, defines information literacy as "an intellectual framework for identifying, finding, understanding, evaluating, and using information. It includes determining the nature and extent of needed information; accessing information effectively and efficiently; evaluating critically information and its sources; incorporating selected information in the learner's knowledge base and value system; using information effectively to accomplish a specific purpose; understanding the economic, legal, and social issues surrounding the use of information and information technology; and observing laws, regulations, and institutional policies related to the access and use of information" (p. 32). From *Standards of Accreditation*: Standard III–Design and Delivery of the Student Learning Experience Criteria: An accredited institution possesses and demonstrates the following attributes or activities: 5.b. Offers a curriculum designed so that students acquire and demonstrate essential skills including at least oral and written communication, scientific and quantitative reasoning, critical analysis and reasoning, technological competency, and information literacy.
New England Association of Schools and Colleges (NEASC-CIHE: Commission on Institutions of Higher Education; NEASC-CTCI: Commission on Technical and Career Institutions)	From *Standards for Accreditation*: Standard 4: The Academic Program Assuring Academic Quality: 4.12 Expectations for student achievement, independent learning, information literacy, skills in inquiry, and critical judgment are appropriate to the subject matter and degree level and in keeping with generally accepted practice. Undergraduate Degree Programs: 4.15 Graduates successfully completing an undergraduate program demonstrate competence in written and oral communication in English; the ability for scientific and quantitative reasoning, for critical analysis and logical thinking; and the capability for continuing learning, including the skills of information literacy. They also demonstrate knowledge and understanding of scientific, historical, and social phenomena and a knowledge and appreciation of the aesthetic and ethical dimensions of humankind.
Northwest Commission on Colleges and Universities (NWCCU)	From *Standards for Accreditation*: Resources and Capacity Education Resources: 2.C.6. Faculty with teaching responsibilities, in partnership with library and information resources personnel, ensure that the use of library and information resources is integrated into the learning process. Library and Information Resources: 2.E.3. Consistent with its mission and core themes, the institution provides appropriate instruction and support for students, faculty, staff, administrators, and others (as appropriate) to enhance their efficiency and effectiveness in obtaining, evaluating, and using library and information resources that support its programs and services, wherever offered and however delivered.

AGENCY	DEFINITION AND STANDARDS
Higher Learning Commission (HLC; formerly, North Central Association of Colleges and Schools [NCA])	From the *Policy Book*: Criterion 2. Integrity: Ethical and Responsible Conduct: *The institution acts with integrity; its conduct is ethical and responsible.* Core Components: 2.E. The institution's policies and procedures call for responsible acquisition, discovery, and application of knowledge by its faculty, students, and staff. 2.E.1. The institution provides effective oversight and support services to ensure the integrity of research and scholarly practice conducted by its faculty, staff, and students. 2.E.2. Students are offered guidance in the ethical use of information resources. Criterion 3. Teaching and Learning: Quality, Resources, and Support: *The institution provides high quality education, wherever and however its offerings are delivered.* Core Components: 3.B. The institution demonstrates that the exercise of intellectual inquiry and the acquisition, application, and integration of broad learning and skills are integral to its educational programs. 3.B.3. Every degree program offered by the institution engages students in collecting, analyzing, and communicating information; in mastering modes of inquiry or creative work; and in developing skills adaptable to changing environments.
Southern Association of Colleges and Schools (SACS) Commission on Colleges	From *Principles of Accreditation*: Programs: 3.8 Library and Other Learning Resources 3.8.2 The institution ensures that users have access to regular and timely instruction in the use of the library and other learning/information resources. (Instruction of library use)
Western Association of Schools and Colleges (WASC-ACCJC: Accrediting Commission for Community and Junior Colleges; WASC-ACSCU: Accrediting Commission for Senior Colleges and Universities)	From the WASC-ACSCU Glossary (in the 2013 *Handbook of Accreditation*): According to the Association of College and Research Libraries, the ability to "recognize when information is needed and the ability to locate, evaluate, and use the needed information" for a wide range of purposes. An information-literate individual is able to determine the extent of information needed, access it, evaluate it and its sources, use the information effectively, and do so ethically and legally. From the 2013 *Handbook of Accreditation*: Standard 2: Achieving Educational Objectives through Core Functions Teaching and Learning: Criteria for Review 2.2a Undergraduate programs engage students in an integrated course of study of sufficient breadth and depth to prepare them for work, citizenship, and lifelong learning. These programs ensure the development of core competencies including, but not limited to, written and oral communication, quantitative reasoning, information literacy, and critical thinking.

Librarians need to be informed about how a discipline (e.g., biology, history) perceives and defines information literacy and how its department at their institution perceives and defines it. Again, particularly at those institutions needing to satisfy a higher demand for information literacy instruction, a good door-opening approach for librarians is to take the initiative to help a department or program explore what information literacy means in their field. Helping a department find resources or even preparing resources for their field and participating in focus groups or committees tasked with addressing the threading of information literacy instruction into coursework are two ways to build a culture of collaboration. Teaching faculty must articulate their own discipline-specific definitions of information literacy (Miller, 2010, as cited in Dubicki, 2013). Their context is their discipline and the courses they are teaching with their specific student learning outcomes; so, in order to make information literacy accessible to these faculty, it must be framed in language relevant to their discipline and course. Their rhetoric will guide librarians in their collaborations to create and sustain discipline-specific information literacy course content. Jennie Ver Steeg notes that

> library and course-integrated instruction are promoted through the power of relationships. G. Thompson, a professor of English literature at Earlham [College], stated that the success of bibliographic instruction is dependent on a process of "seduction," with the first steps taken by the librarian, adding that a shared interest is the best foundation for all collaborative teaching. (2000: 47)

Consider adding a faculty outreach librarian to the library program, making faculty outreach part of a librarian's job description, or embedding a librarian within a college. Susan Ariew has described the faculty outreach librarian as "someone who implements proactive outreach activities with faculty by setting up services such as electronic lists, email communications, faculty brown-bag luncheons, and timely newsletters" (2000: 65). However, her institution, Virginia Polytechnic Institute and State University, has used a slightly different model in its College Librarian program, in which a full-time librarian is housed in the college rather than the library. Being within the faculty's work environment increased the opportunities for collaboration and helped build the strong relationships between teaching faculty and libraries that were needed for robust collaboration.

Librarians and faculty can work on incremental change, construct collaborations as phased processes, and keep a history of these small accomplishments so that they can be celebrated or noted in library and department newsletters and other public relations communications. Nothing succeeds like success, so take your successes where you find them and promote them. Evaluate your successes and attempt to determine what is generalizable from them. But remain patient; let the success of one individual or one department help do the work of bringing in other faculty or departments.

Library subject liaisons should be informed or become familiar with their department's timelines in assigning classes to faculty each term and in performing curriculum and program review. They should contact new faculty and faculty teaching new courses in order to "get in on the ground floor" when syllabi and program changes are still in developmental stages. Faculty governance often works quite slowly and, after they have spent the time and effort to complete their work on an issue, faculty probably are not going to be open to revisiting it or modifying what they have. Practically speaking, faculty governance will have moved on and instructors are pressed to complete the next tasks; they usually won't feel they have time to go back and re-do or modify their courses. Library subject liaisons need to be proactive in becoming familiar with the language of curriculum development and other current educational issues in their liaison field, then take the time to create open-ended questions about what a department is doing. This will demonstrate the library's interest and willingness to walk alongside the department and individual classroom instructors.

Support a "just in time learning" model. This is "an electronic performance support system [to] provide specific information needed to complete a task . . . used while engaging in the activity on the job, and can be accessed whenever the worker needs the information . . . it involved short tutorials, tips, simulations, and other forms of digital support" (Monge and Frisicaro-Pawlowski, 2014: 64).

Librarians should be invited—or ask to be invited—to review the standard discipline assignments and help classroom faculty identify possible points of information literacy integration. Once identified, the teaching faculty can more easily determine the best ways to integrate information literacy elements into the assignment and will be far more likely to be invested and to follow through if they have made the decisions about what is feasible within their course.

Just as important as evaluating the culture of the various disciplines, do not neglect evaluating the culture of the library to identify its strengths for collaboration as well as its weaknesses. Be proactive in developing collaborative skills both in the library and in department programs, both in terms of personal development as well as staff development. Consider using a consultant or working with human resources or the faculty development office to properly assess staff or individuals, and develop appropriate training materials or venues. Instruments such as workshops, videos, and tutorials all can be done on campus, but there are also external resources that may be valuable and economically feasible. Do not simply require people to read material or attend workshops; perform due diligence to discern as intentionally and specifically as possible what is needed and to follow up with an assessment to determine effectiveness.

Classroom faculty and the institution itself need to foster a "culture of teaching" among librarians and address any training needs, particularly for librarians with no traditional classroom teaching experience. One way to do this is to utilize what Evergreen State College in Olympia, Washington, calls a "rotation program" within its coordinated studies program, which is "an interdisciplinary, team-based instructional model that allows a group of faculty and students to study a single topic for an extended period of time" (Walter, 2000: 55). The rotation program

> requires librarians to rotate onto a faculty team for one quarter out of every nine. . . . During the rotation, librarians are released from their normal duties and assume the responsibilities of a member of the classroom faculty for the collaborative guidance of a coordinated studies program. (2000: 57)

This, Scott Walter explains,

> allows librarians to bring their instructional skills into the "mainstream of the curriculum" [Hubbard, 1990, as cited in Walter, 2000], to further develop personal contacts with the classroom faculty, to more closely observe faculty methods of teaching, to gain a greater insight into faculty research interests, and to participate in the academic counseling and guidance of students outside the library setting. (2000: 57)

One advantage of this rotation model is that at Evergreen, it assured librarians' faculty status.

Review current discipline accreditation reports to help determine what the demand and expectation for further information literacy instruction is for that discipline and for direction in scaffolding information literacy instruction. Also, be mindful of timelines to get a sense of what can be accomplished within a specific situation. For example, once a discipline or institution completes an accreditation cycle and has just been awarded accreditation, say, for another nine years, those involved with that exhaustive work are not ready to ambitiously revisit their programs—or take time to work on changes not demanded by the accrediting body. They have just gone through a strenuous process and naturally will enter into a period of reflection and relative rest.

Librarians always need to be aware of and address the need for information literacy assessment with teaching faculty, doing it within their discipline at the department level, and working with administrative policies and programs to help craft appropriate and practical assessment vehicles for programs and courses. It is important for librarians to allow the institution or its agents to lead—while remaining proactive. Again, assessment methods and processes are discipline-specific. Some are highly specific and are more strictly governed by the requirements and recommendations of outside accrediting bodies, such as the National Council for Accreditation of Teacher Education (NCATE) and the Commission on Collegiate Nursing Education (CCNE). So, take the time to understand how assessment is done in the discipline and be aware of the timelines to help create information literacy instruction that is discipline-relevant, workable, and will deliver in a timely way the data needed for the next assessment cycle.

⊙ Key Points

This chapter has looked at information literacy as an issue in general education and from a classroom faculty perspective to guide both librarians and classroom faculty in becoming co-equal collaborators in implementing information literacy instruction as guided by the new ACRL *Framework*. It is important to note:

- Information literacy from a higher education perspective is framed first as part of the research process and, second and more recently, as part of a set of intellectual competencies essential for graduates to develop in order to be successful in life.
- Information literacy is well accepted in higher education, but there is relative confusion and lack of agreement among faculty about who teaches information literacy and how it is taught.
- Discipline faculty to varying degrees believe that information literacy skills are implicitly attained by students through their coursework, and that a separate information literacy instruction program from librarians can be resisted because it can be perceived as outside the domain of that faculty's department and course student learning outcomes.
- The teaching of information literacy aspects (beyond conventional librarian bibliographic instruction), such as how to read critically and analytically or how to synthesize and integrate information in writing, is viewed by educators as an issue within their purview but for the most part is not yet clearly defined.
- In future information literacy instruction, librarians' access to students' information literacy instruction will be much more indirect, working instead with faculty and institutional agents such as the writing center, faculty development office, and faculty governance bodies.
- Information literacy instruction increasingly requires librarians to assist discipline faculty in developing discipline-specific content that is integrated and consistent with and relevant to the discipline's student learning outcomes and accreditation needs.
- Successful librarian-faculty collaboration depends on librarians understanding and participating in the learning communities of teaching faculty, as well as understanding and working with department, program, and accrediting objectives, timelines, and educational issues.

Each institution has a unique culture or personality. In terms of implementing institutional change, what works wonderfully well in one environment could be disastrous in another. Given that the *Framework* is still new, the catalog of successful collaborations in implementing a cross-disciplinary program for information literacy instruction is still being built. Chapter 6 will offer tips for building such a *Framework* campus culture.

⦿ References

Adler, Ronald B., Lawrence B. Rosenfeld, and Russell F. Proctor, II. 2014. *Interplay: The Process of Interpersonal Communication*. 13th ed. Oxford, UK: Oxford University Press.

Ariew, Susan. 2000. "The Virginia Polytechnic Institute and State University: Collaboration through Faculty Outreach." In *The Collaborative Imperative: Librarians and Faculty Working Together in the Information Universe*, edited by Dick Raspa and Dane Ward, 64–71. Chicago: Association of College and Research Libraries.

Artman, Margaret, Erica Frisicaro-Pawlowski, and Robert Monge. 2010. "Not Just One Shot: Extending the Dialogue about Information Literacy in Composition Classes." *Composition Studies* 38, no. 2 (Fall): 93–109.

Bury, Sophie. 2011. "Faculty Attitudes, Perceptions and Experiences of Information Literacy: A Study across Multiple Disciplines at York University, Canada." *Journal of Information Literacy* 5, no. 1 (May): 45–64.

Cannon, A. 1994. "Faculty Survey on Library Research Instruction." *RQ* 33, no. 4: 524–41.

Dean, Walter. 2017. "What Is the Purpose of Journalism?" American Press Institute. https://www.americanpressinstitute.org/journalism-essentials/what-is-journalism/purpose-journalism/.

Dubicki, Eleonora. 2013. "Faculty Perceptions of Students' Information Literacy Skills Competencies." *Journal of Information Literacy* 7, no. 2 (December): 97–125.

Ducas, A. M., and N. Michaud-Oystryck. 2004. "Toward a New Venture: Building Partnerships with Faculty." *College & Research Libraries* 65, no. 4 (July): 334–48.

Gardner, Carolyn Caffey, and Jamie White-Farnham. 2013. "'She Has a Vocabulary I Just Don't Have': Faculty Culture and Information Literacy Collaboration." *Collaborative Librarianship* 5, no. 4: 235–42.

Gonzales, Rhonda. 2001. "Opinions and Experiences of University Faculty Regarding Library Research Instruction: Results of a Web-Based Survey at the University of Southern Colorado." *Research Strategies* 18, no. 3: 191–201.

Hardesty, Larry. 1995. "Faculty Culture and Bibliographic Instruction." *Library Trends* 44, no. 2: 339–67.

Julien, Heidi, and Lisa M. Given. 2003. "Faculty-Librarian Relationships in the Information Literacy Context: A Content Analysis of Librarians' Expressed Attitudes and Experiences." *Canadian Journal of Information and Library Science* 27, no. 3: 65–87.

Kuhlthau, C., L. K. Maniotes, and A. K. Caspari. 2007. *Guided Inquiry: Learning in the 21st Century*. Westport, CT: Libraries Unlimited.

Leckie, G., and A. Fullerton. 1999. "Information Literacy in Science and Engineering Undergraduate Education: Faculty Attitudes and Pedagogical Practices." *College & Research Libraries* 60, no. 1 (January): 9–29.

McLuhan, Marshall. 1964–1994. *Understanding Media: The Extensions of Man*. Cambridge, MA: MIT Press.

Miller, I. 2010. "Turning the Tables: A Faculty-Centered Approach to Integrating Information Literacy." *Reference Services Review* 38, no. 4: 657–62.

Monge, Robert, and Erica Frisicaro-Pawlowski. 2014. "Redefining Information Literacy to Prepare Students for the 21st Century Workforce." *Innovative Higher Education* 39, no. 1: 59–73.

Nilsen, Christina. 2012. "Faculty Perceptions of Librarian-Led Information Literacy Instruction in Postsecondary Education." Paper presented at the 78th annual World Library and Information Congress of IFLA, Helsinki, Finland.

Oberg, L. R., M. Schleiter, and M. Van Houten. 1989. "Faculty Perceptions of Librarians at Albion College: Status, Role, Contribution, and Contacts." *College & Research Libraries* 50, no. 2 (March): 215–30.

Reinking, James A., and Robert A. Von der Osten. 2013. *Strategies for Successful Writing: A Rhetoric, Research Guide, Reader, and Handbook.* 10th ed. Boston: Pearson.

Saunders, Laura. 2012. "Faculty Perspectives on Information Literacy as a Student Learning Outcome." *Journal of Academic Librarianship* 38, no. 4: 226–36.

van der Geest, Thea, and Raymond van Dongelen. 2009. "What Is Beautiful Is Useful: Visual Appeal and Expected Information Quality." In *Professional Communication Conference, IEEE International, Waikiki, Hawaii*, 1–5. http://ieeexplore.ieee.org/abstract/document/5208678/.

Ver Steeg, Jennie. 2000. "Earlham College: Collaboration through Course-Integrated Instruction." In *The Collaborative Imperative: Librarians and Faculty Working Together in the Information Universe*, edited by Dick Raspa and Dane Ward, 41–50. Chicago: Association of College and Research Libraries.

Walter, Scott. 2000. "The Evergreen State College: Collaboration through Faculty Rotation." In *The Collaborative Imperative: Librarians and Faculty Working Together in the Information Universe*, edited by Dick Raspa and Dane Ward, 54–60. Chicago: Association of College and Research Libraries.

Weiner, Sharon A. 2014. "Who Teaches Information Literacy Competencies? Report of a Study of Faculty." *College Teaching* 62, no. 1: 5–12.

⑥ Further Reading

DaCosta, J. W. 2010. "Is There an Information Literacy Skills Gap to Be Bridged? An Examination of Faculty Perceptions and Activities Relating to Information Literacy in the United States and England." *College & Research Libraries* 71, no. 3 (May): 203–21.

McGuiness, Claire. 2006. "What Faculty Think: Exploring the Barriers to Information Literacy Development in Undergraduate Education." *Journal of Academic Librarianship* 32, no. 6 (November): 573–82.

Probert, Elizabeth. 2009. "Information Literacy Skills: Teacher Understandings and Practice." *Computers & Education* 53, no. 1: 24–33.

Saunders, Laura. 2007. "Regional Accreditation Organizations' Treatment of Information Literacy: Definitions, Outcomes and Assessment." *Journal of Academic Librarianship* 33, no. 3: 317–26.

Tips for Creating a *Framework* Campus Culture

CHANGE IS CONSTANT. Just go to any yard sale in your neighborhood and gaze at the progression of popular recording media and the devices on which to play them: LP (long playing) 33 1⁄3 records, 8-track tapes, cassette tapes, CDs, DVDs, collectable USB flash drives, and iPods of various sizes. And so change has taken 15 years to birth another set of suggested information literacy guidelines not only for the profession of academic librarianship but also for the professorate, a profound inclusion. Not unlike other events of change, the *Standards* to *Framework* journey looks to be disruptive, unpleasant, or maybe even a little scary. This chapter will take a look at three tips, each providing step-by-step guidance that can be used to take first steps toward introducing and implementing the *Framework* to help librarians, classroom faculty, and administrators begin a journey with less unpleasantness and scariness.

In this chapter, a path toward creating an information literacy *Framework* campus culture starts with an immersive technique in Tip #1, introducing librarians, students, faculty, and perhaps administrators to the "what" of information literacy today. Moving on, Tip #2 explains how to teach the *Framework* to a group of classroom faculty in the context of a discipline-specific faculty meeting. Next, continuing to look at approaches to implementing the *Framework* model on campus, Tip #3 first takes a curricular, or a macro, view of the initiative, and then demonstrates how the six frames can address an evidence-based look at a disturbing trend in student research behaviors through a micro view of implementing the frames. Addressing misguided research behaviors of students is mission critical, because it means either graduating somewhat shallow-thinking, distracted, information-illiterate new alumni or launching out women and men who are thoughtful, deeper-processing, and information-literate people, equipped to be what employers are really expecting of the next-generation workforce.

◎ Tip #1: Teaching the Fundamentals of the *Framework* to *Standards* Advocates

The fundamentals. They are time-tested, basic, and often ignored. One path to creating a sustainable culture of information literacy on campus is to teach the fundamentals to those already familiar with the older 2000 *Standards*—the frontline experts. Legendary coach Vince Lombardi began each pro football season with his "This is a football" speech, a winning playbook reminder. Tip #1 is about how to win over your campus by first teaching "This is information literacy" to those on campus who are already information literacy champions.

Step 1: Fundamentals of Information Literacy (Talking Points)

Imagine you are an information literacy librarian or faculty member addressing a group of other information-literate, like-minded librarians and faculty. They know and have even practiced the former 2000 *Standards* in classrooms and other settings. Your goal is to introduce the new game rules of information literacy. You step up to the front of the room and write "2015 *Framework for Information Literacy*" on the board and say:

> The *Framework for Information Literacy for Higher Education*, adopted by the academic library profession in 2015, has a forward-thinking definition. Understanding the fundamentals and the few parts that make up the new *Framework* will equip you to be a more effective ambassador on campus for the new information literacy. The benefits to learners who become information literate through the *Framework* include (a) making better information choices, (b) finding information resources more efficiently, (c) using information sources more effectively, (d) preventing plagiarism mistakes, and (e) preparing them for a job market that is expecting higher levels of competency in information literacy. The definition of the *Framework for Information Literacy for Higher Education* is listed at the top of your handout. It's in an outline form for easier understanding. It is followed by a list of the six frames of the *Framework* and, to the left of the list, an image that can serve as a metaphor to illustrate the six frames and their interaction with one another. Take the next few minutes to individually work through the three exercises on page 1 of your handout. Look up when you're finished so I know when we can review your answers.

Note that this two-page handout, "*Framework for Information Literacy*: Fundamentals Handout," can be freely copied. It is found on pages 101–102 as well as on the book's website: https://implementingtheinformationliteracyframework.wordpress.com/ or https://tinyurl.com/ya6h4vyq under chapter 6. The two-page handout is available as both a PDF version (to be used as is) and as a Word version (to be changed to fit the need).

FRAMEWORK FOR INFORMATION LITERACY: FUNDAMENTALS HANDOUT

Exercise 1: In the definition of the *Framework for Information Literacy for Higher Education* (2015) circle occurrences of the word *information* and underline up to four important concepts.

Information literacy is the set of integrated abilities encompassing

> 1) the reflective discovery of information,
> 2) the understanding of
> > a) how information is produced and
> > b) valued, and
> 3) the use of information in
> > a) creating new knowledge and
> > b) participating ethically in communities of learning.

Source: Association of College & Research Libraries. 2015. *Framework for Information Literacy for Higher Education*. http://www.ala.org/acrl/standards/ilframework.

Exercise 2: Alphabetize the following frame titles of the *Framework* placing 1–6 in the blanks.

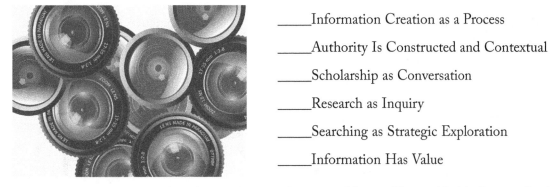

_____Information Creation as a Process

_____Authority Is Constructed and Contextual

_____Scholarship as Conversation

_____Research as Inquiry

_____Searching as Strategic Exploration

_____Information Has Value

Source: Image from Pixabay released under Creative Commons CC0-1.0 Universal Public Domain Dedication.

Exercise 3: How might the above image be a metaphor for the six frames? Write below.

Exercise 4: Circle the words *experts* and *novice learners* as found in the following frame's description.
Frame: Research as Inquiry
Research is iterative and depends upon asking increasingly complex or new questions whose answers in turn develop additional questions or lines of inquiry in any field.

Experts see inquiry as a process that focuses on problems or questions in a discipline or between disciplines that are open or unresolved. Experts recognize the collaborative effort within a discipline to extend the knowledge in that field. Many times, this process includes points of disagreement where debate and dialogue work to deepen the conversations around knowledge. This process of inquiry extends beyond the academic world to the community at large, and the process of inquiry may focus upon personal, professional, or societal needs. The spectrum of inquiry ranges from asking simple questions that depend upon basic recapitulation of knowledge to increasingly sophisticated abilities to refine research questions, use more advanced research methods, and explore more diverse disciplinary perspectives. Novice learners acquire strategic perspectives on inquiry and a greater repertoire of investigative methods.

Exercise 5: Fill in the blank letters as instructed during the presentation.
Knowledge Practices = **M__ __ __ G__ __ __ __**
Learners who are developing their information literate abilities

- formulate questions for research based on information gaps or on reexamination of existing, possibly conflicting, information
- determine an appropriate scope of investigation
- deal with complex research by breaking complex questions into simple ones, limiting the scope of investigations
- use various research methods, based on need, circumstance, and type of inquiry
- monitor gathered information and assess for gaps or weaknesses
- organize information in meaningful ways
- synthesize ideas gathered from multiple sources
- draw reasonable conclusions based on the analysis and interpretation of information.

Dispositions = **H__ __ __ __ G__ __ __ __**
Learners who are developing their information literate abilities

- consider research as open-ended exploration and engagement with information
- appreciate that a question may appear to be simple but still disruptive and important to research
- value intellectual curiosity in developing questions and learning new investigative methods
- maintain an open mind and a critical stance
- value persistence, adaptability, and flexibility and recognize that ambiguity can benefit the research process
- seek multiple perspectives during information gathering and assessment
- seek appropriate help when needed
- follow ethical and legal guidelines in gathering and using information
- demonstrate intellectual humility (i.e., recognize their own intellectual or experiential limitations).

As you might guess, this set of exercises can also be made into a PowerPoint, a Prezi, or a voiceover video tutorial presentation. The idea is to introduce the fundamentals of information literacy by examining the characteristics of the 2015 *Framework* as instructed in the "*Framework for Information Literacy*: Fundamentals Handout."

Step 2: Exercise Answers and More Fundamentals (Continued Talking Points)

When individuals are mostly finished with page 1, you continue:

> OK, what number did you get for the term *information*? Four? That is correct. The term *information* is repeated four times throughout the short 39-word description, at a ratio of 1:10. This means that for every 10 words, 1 is the term *information* which, only for the sake of observation, makes the term *information* more prevalent in the *Framework's* description than it was in the older 2000 *Standards* definition, which had 1 occurrence for every 14 words. Now, what words did you find in the outline that expressed some important ideas?

At this point, it might be helpful to write these words on a whiteboard or computer projection screen and use the following information for the ensuing discussion/lecture as talking points. For words given that are not included in the list, go ahead and write them out, but focus on the four sets of words selected as talking points below. These terms are presented in the order they are found in the *Framework* outline definition (exercise 1 in the handout).

Integrated Abilities

As a discussion/lecture talking point, you continue:

> The main parts of the *Framework* are six so-called frames or core ideas. It's useful to understand that the frames can stand alone OR can overlap with one another, similar to a single or overlapping view through different-colored camera lenses, as shown in the image to the left of the list of the six frames. The lens metaphor can help illustrate the *integrated abilities* of information literacy, which gives different perspectives while looking through one or more of the lenses. The idea of *integrated abilities* also provides a viewpoint that is different from a linear process (1–2–3–4–5) and, with such a perspective, the concept of information literacy can be viewed as more like the Internet, with its unlimited serendipitous discoveries. Information literacy is less like the idea that "one size fits all" to get the best results—always do A before B—and more like "sizes are unlimited" to get the best results—consider doing A before B, B before A, and also think outside the box. *Integrated abilities* can also refer to the multiple, overlapping skills needed to become information literate.

Reflective Discovery

As a discussion/lecture talking point, you continue:

> Shallow thinking can come from an unexamined life. The value of deeper thinking is realized through the practice of *reflective discovery*. Information literacy definitely includes the finding and accessing of high-quality information sources for an academic

assignment, but it is also much, much more. Purposeful, thoughtful reflection is an integral part of the *Framework* and can be expressed through such practices as journaling, face-to-face discussions, and engaging in social networking applications.

New Knowledge

As a discussion/lecture talking point, you continue:

Information literacy is certainly about a process of discovering information sources that strengthen student skills and about preventing unreliable, if not false, conclusions. But it is more than helping students create better assignments and increasing their competencies in finding, assessing, and using information appropriately. Using information literacy is the vehicle for creating *new knowledge*. This means all learners have the capacity to produce *new knowledge*.

Communities of Learning

As a discussion/lecture talking point, you continue:

Information literacy can be practiced alone, in self-study. But surprising synergy abounds when individuals are contributing to ongoing *communities of learning*. This concept can be expressed in face-to-face discussions and in unlimited forms in networking environments.

Step 3: Common Parts of the *Framework's* Six Frames

You, as the host continue:

Let's take a look at the common parts of the six frames. On page 2 of the handout there is a copy of one of the frames, "Research as Inquiry." As an alternative to this part of the handout, you can go online right now and search the Internet for the words *information literacy framework* and click on the link *Framework for Information Literacy for Higher Education*. This will bring up the *Framework* document, which includes an introduction and the current six frames. Just scroll down a little until you see the word "Frames" in a bold heading. Before I continue, take a minute to do exercise 4 at the top of page 2.

Wait until you see that participants have finished the exercise, and continue:

The *Framework* is made alive in its six frames or core ideas or, if you will, six colored overlapping camera lenses as found in the image for exercise 2. The six frames are arranged alphabetically, and so there is no intentional sequence or priority to teaching or learning them. This is one reason why the handout included exercise 2 on page 1—to familiarize you with the alphabetical order of the frames and to show that the order is not intended to be a ranking of some kind, from most important to least important. All frames are of equal standing.

Each frame has five parts. Looking at the frame on page 2 as an example, the first part is the title: "Research as Inquiry." The second part is a brief description of the frame. In this case: "Research is iterative and depends upon asking increasingly complex or new questions whose answers in turn develop additional questions or lines of inquiry in any field." The third part is a longer, more detailed understanding of the frame from the insights of *experts* and the perspective of *novice learners*.

So, for exercise 4, how many times did the word *expert* occur? Two? Yes, that's correct. And for *novice*? One? Yes, that's right. The handout instructed you to highlight this feature because the terms *expert* and *novice learners* occur this way throughout all six frames. It demonstrates that all information literacy learners fall somewhere on the two ends of a spectrum—*novice learner* on one side and *expert* on the other.

Let's look at the fourth part of a frame; it's a list of goals for the frame called *Knowledge Practices*. *Knowledge Practices* are information literacy competencies for that frame. It may be more useful to think of *Knowledge Practices* as a list of *mind goals* for learning. On page 2 of the handout, go ahead and write the words *mind goals* in the blank next to *Knowledge Practices* to help remind you what this list means. These *Knowledge Practices* answer the question, "Does the learner in this frame example conduct research with a deeper, thoughtful process of inquiry?" And finally, the fifth part of each frame is a second list of goals, labeled *Dispositions*. They represent affective preferences toward learning something. Think of *Dispositions* as a list of *heart* or *attitude* goals for learning. Write the words *heart goals* or the words *attitude goals* in the blank next to *Dispositions* to remind you what the list means. *Dispositions* answer the question, "Does the learner show that he or she in this frame example formulates questions for research based on information gaps?" Putting the words *mind goals* next to *Knowledge Practices* and the terms *heart goals* next to *Dispositions* for each of the frames will help you remember the important difference between the two lists and assist you in working with the frames as you move forward.

> Think of *Knowledge Practices* as a list of *mind goals* or *knowledge goals* for learning. Think of *Dispositions* as a list of *heart goals* or *attitude goals* for learning.

The *Framework*'s six frames include a total of 45 *Knowledge Practices* (mind goals) and 38 *Dispositions* (heart goals) for learning. Although neither the frames nor their *Knowledge Practices* and *Dispositions* were developed as learning outcomes, they were designed to be flexible enough to assist in tailoring your existing campus learning outcomes into information literacy learning outcomes as one way to embed information literacy principles into the campus culture toward a culture of information literacy. Examples of learning outcomes for each frame will be provided in chapters 8 and 9.

⑥ Tip #2: How to Introduce Classroom Faculty to Information Literacy

Classroom faculty risk losing much of the benefits of information literacy because they may not have a clear working knowledge of the basics as found in the *Framework* in order to more competently engage with their students. The *Framework* has a set of new information literacy terms and concepts that are different from past expressions, namely the 2000 *Standards*. Those involved in campus-wide integration of information literacy (students, librarians, classroom faculty, and administrators) should be knowledgeable about the current vocabulary and be able to explain and use them with others in the campus community. Among other reasons, the new terms and core concepts found in the *Framework*'s introductory paragraphs and six frames are critical for students and faculty to work more effectively with new and future information approaches. Those approaches are found in workplace and day-to-day life contexts such as consumerism (buying the right product), health care, finances, and civic engagement. This new information literacy mind-set empowers learners to retrieve and evaluate information from non-library sources such as mass media, popular culture, the Internet, and network environments. In addition, the *Framework* builds critical intellectual skill sets that employers are expecting and often have found lacking in college and university graduates (Raish and Rimland, 2016; Wiebe, 2015/2016).

For the following example, it is assumed that the librarian liaison overseeing the library needs of the biology and chemistry department has been tasked with introducing information literacy to this group of discipline-specific classroom faculty. However, in the context of the *Framework* model, a non-librarian resource person, such as from general education leadership or a faculty development representative, could also fulfill this presenter role. The provost has announced that all undergraduate programs are to move forward with the 2015 Information Literacy *Framework* in order to gather data for an upcoming accreditation report and site visit. The following steps, set in the context of addressing a discipline-specific faculty meeting, suggest one way to familiarize individuals with terms and principles found in the *Framework* and its six frames.

Step 1: The Invitation

If the librarian liaison has little to no relationship with the academic chair of the department, there are at least four ways to begin. First, if the department's faculty meet, say, monthly, arrange for the librarian to give a 15- to 20-minute presentation at a faculty meeting. If the librarian has been given an information literacy initiative, he or she can start by sending an email to the department chair with the information literacy requirement from the provost included in the message. If there is a positive and timely response, great; that's one way. If the chair does not respond in a reasonable time, a more proactive approach could be taken. During the librarian's next department visit, say to drop off book catalogs for faculty to mark up for collection development, have a conversation with the department secretary about getting on the next faculty meeting's agenda. If during the conversation the librarian learns that another faculty member organizes the meetings, go with that, which is the third way. If the structure of faculty meetings allows for guests to make comments at some point, that would be a fourth way. Eventually the librarian can get the needed 15 to 20 minutes at a faculty meeting.

Step 2: Before the Faculty Meeting

To prepare for the department meeting, the librarian should visit the department's website and become familiar with each faculty member's name. To create a handout for the meeting, first go to the full text of the *Framework* document (on the Internet, search for information literacy framework). Next, copy all six frames beginning with "Authority Is Constructed and Contextual" and ending with the last bullet of the sixth frame, ending in "to complete the information task." Paste all six frames into a new document. Adjust the size and separation between each frame so one frame appears on each page. As a second page of the handout, create a rubric. The *Framework for Information Literacy* "Six Frames Rubric: First-Year Undergraduate," found on page 107, is given to use as is or to adapt to specific department needs. The rubric can be freely copied. Print off all six frames so they are on one side of a page and make enough so that each faculty member will have two pieces of paper: one with one of the six frames on it and the other with the rubric. If possible, discuss ahead of time with the chair whether one or more of the frames are likely to be less relevant for this discipline and leave that material out of the presentation.

FRAMEWORK FOR INFORMATION LITERACY'S SIX FRAMES RUBRIC: FIRST-YEAR UNDERGRADUATE

Name: _____ Date: _____

Category of Points	Accomplished	Proficient	Developing	Novice
Name:	Yes: 4			No: 0
Authority Is Constructed and Contextual	Accesses adequate number of sources that are the most authoritative	Accesses adequate number of sources but these are not the most authoritative	Accesses sources that are mildly authoritative but not adequate in number	Accesses sources but these are not adequate in number nor authoritative
Score:	12–15	8–11	4–7	0–3
Information Creation as a Process	Uses information from a large range of formats	Uses information from more than one format/source	Uses information from one format/ source	Uses information from no legitimate format
Score:	12–15	8–11	4–7	0–3
Information Has Value	Provides accurate attribution to all resources	Provides accurate attribution to most resources	Provides accurate attribution to a few resources	Provides accurate attribution to no resources
Score:	12–15	8–11	4–7	0–3
Research as Inquiry	Research question shows complexity and good organization	Research question shows some complexity and some organization	Research question shows little complexity and little organization	Research question shows no complexity and no organization
Score:	12–15	8–11	4–7	0–3
Scholarship as Conversation	A literature review includes multiple diverse perspectives	A literature review includes more than one diverse perspective	A literature review includes at least one diverse perspective	A literature review has no diverse perspectives
Score:	12–15	8–11	4–7	0–3
Searching as Strategic Exploration	Description of searching process demonstrates broad and deep finding techniques	Description of searching process demonstrates narrow and shallow finding techniques	Description of search process demonstrates some finding techniques	Description of search process demonstrates no finding techniques
Score:	12–15	8–11	4–7	0–3
Total Score: /100				
Comments:				

Step 3: At the Faculty Meeting

The librarian should arrive on time, early if possible. Be dressed for success. Put the handouts in the hands of every attendee, along with a 3 × 5-inch index card. If permitted, before the meeting begins, write all six frame titles on a whiteboard in alphabetical order (as they are listed in the *Framework*). The meeting moderator should be provided with a brief written introduction of the librarian. Here is an example:

> Next on the agenda a faculty librarian is here to share some thoughts about information literacy as it relates to biology and chemistry. Please welcome Rhett Sarch, who is the librarian for the Department of Biology and Chemistry.

The librarian should thank the moderator and then share:

> Provost Karen Miller has announced the need to integrate information literacy on campus and to gather information literacy data for next year's accreditation report and site visit. I'm here this afternoon to help you begin that process with an introduction to information literacy. I have tailored some of my comments to the fields of biology and chemistry.
>
> Here at our school we are using a definition of information literacy created by the Association of College & Research Libraries, which consists of six so-called frames. Each frame represents core concepts that learners master on their journey to becoming information literate. All six of the frames have been passed out, one frame per handout. On page 2 of your handout is a rubric that I'll talk about in a moment. So, some of you will have the same frame, and all of you have the same rubric. Let's look at the page with your frame on it.
>
> Each frame has five parts. The first is its title. I have one of the six as an example up on the screen, "Information Creation as a Process." As you look at your handout, that may be your title, or you may have one of the other five frames I've listed on the whiteboard. The second part of each frame is a brief description. The third part is a longer, more detailed understanding of the frame from the insights of experts and the perspective of novice learners. The last two parts of each frame include two lists. The first list is called *Knowledge Practices*. *Knowledge Practices* are information literacy competencies for that frame. It may be more useful to think of *Knowledge Practices* as a list of *mind goals* or *knowledge goals* for learning. So, next to the term *Knowledge Practices* you may find it useful to write the words *mind goals* or the words *knowledge goals* as a reminder of what this list means. These *mind goals*, if you will, answer the question (let's use my frame's second bulleted mind goal as an example): "Does the learner assess the fit between an information product's creation process and a particular information need?"
>
> The second of the two lists is labeled *Dispositions*. *Dispositions* represent affective preferences toward learning something related to that frame. Think of *Dispositions* as a list of *heart* or *attitude* goals for learning for that frame. So, next to the term *Dispositions* it may be useful to write the words *heart goals* or the words *attitude goals* as a way to remember what this second list means. *Heart goals*, if you will, answer the question (again let's use my frame's second bulleted heart goal as an example), "Does the learner value the process of matching an information need with an appropriate product?"
>
> On the second page of your handout is the "*Framework for Information Literacy* Rubric: First-Year Undergraduate," created by campus classroom faculty and librarians last term and used to score first-year student papers. This information literacy data is entered into a shared Google Sheet, which is used in the information literacy part of the next year's accreditation report.

A note about rubrics: Rubrics are certainly one way to assess student work. This example, and others like it in the book and from the Internet, can form the basis of a working instrument for an ad hoc librarian/classroom faculty committee in order to create campus-specific, discipline-specific, information literacy learner outcomes and rubrics. The goal of the group would be to come up with learner outcomes and one or more rubrics that might be a good fit across one grade level of one campus academic discipline, or more than one discipline, or maybe all of them, as in the handout "*Framework for Information Literacy* Rubric: First-Year Undergraduate" (p. 107).

You continue:

> Let me finish my time with you by illustrating an example of information literacy from one of your biology syllabi assignments using one of the frames of the *Framework*, as well as demonstrating one way to measure information literacy learner outcomes using the rubric found on page 2 of your handout. A first-year biology syllabus instructs students to do a self-assessment exercise looking through the lens of the frame "Information Creation as a Process" by collaborating with two other classmates in such a way that each adds a *Wikipedia* entry for a newly discovered species of mammal. A link and some instructions are included for finding the frame "Information Creation as a Process." The professor provides a list of new species reported by Sci-News.com that have not been added to *Wikipedia*. The three students meet online using something like Padlet (an online bulletin board) to record their group and individual progress on three things: first, deciding on their three species; second, showing images, videos, documents about their species; and third, helping one another to get their species entry into *Wikipedia*. During the assignment, students self-assess, using Padlet, by describing their information literacy experiences, thoughts, and emotions as seen through the lens of the frame "Information Creation as a Process."
>
> Each student's assignment is accessed using the "*Framework for Information Literacy* Rubric: First Year Undergraduate," which was also included in the formal assignment. There is access to all Padlet posts where students regularly reflected on their progress, as well as links to their individual new species' write-ups in *Wikipedia*. In both Padlet and the *Wikipedia* entry, students were required to include resource citations. Student 1 found four sources for her species in two newsletters, a CNN news video report, and an institutional repository article by a graduate assistant who was on the field expedition that found the species. The professor awarded student 1 the *Accomplished* score as found in the rubric. The second student found two sources for his species that included an image originating from a blog about similar species, and the same image was used on a webpage with a detailed caption describing the species' differences compared to similar species. Student 2 received the *Proficient* score from the rubric for their grade. The third student only found one small newspaper article about his species. Consequently, student 3 received the *Developing* score from the rubric. The professor found that students 2 and 3 missed at least two sources for their species that would have made it possible for them to be awarded the *Accomplished* category. These three sets of grade categories are converted into standardized numbers and, along with appropriate confidential pieces of student narratives from Padlet, these numbers and others like them are added as data into a shared Google Sheet, which itself is used in drafting any information literacy statements for accreditation reports.

As the presenter you conclude:

> Thank you for allowing me to share a few things about information literacy along with an example in place within your department. In light of our campus information literacy

initiative, I'd like to offer myself as a resource or consultant, if you will, to help each of you implement information literacy into one or more of your course assignments. On the 3 × 5 card that was passed out, could you take a moment and put down your name, along with a date and time that we could meet in your office in the next two weeks for an hour to discuss how to work on this together. At this time, I'll be happy to take any questions. If not, thanks again for letting me share something that is important to all of us, integrating information literacy into our campus culture.

⊚ Tip #3: Implementing an Information Literacy Approach on Campus

Any approach to creating a campus culture of information-literate learners based on the *Framework for Information Literacy for Higher Education* will take time. There are a few elements when trying to move forward with a new initiative that can help to smooth the process. Those features include a) supportive administration and faculty, b) exemplary relationships between librarians and faculty, c) an institutional strategic plan with already clear information literacy commitments and the flexibility to add *Framework* language, d) a boilerplate statement in all syllabi affirming information literacy learning outcomes, and e) a librarian team on the same page when it comes to information literacy instruction. The following steps are suggested as guidelines to be used where such helpful elements are not strong or are missing altogether.

Step 1: Study the Document

One way that individuals can see progress in implementing the *Framework* on campus as a new guideline is to do two things: first, study the information literacy *Framework* document itself, and second, know your campus culture. It's helpful to have some broad understandings about the *Framework* document as a guide. It may be useful to approach the concepts in one or more of the six frames of the *Framework* for select general education and freshmen (beginning) writing classes, specifically for core assignments as well as for early courses for adult learner programs and master's and doctoral programs. It will also be helpful to view the conceptually based six frames of the *Framework* as quite appropriate for intensive writing courses, challenging cognitive assignments, or work leading up to a capstone, a master's thesis, or a doctoral dissertation. The *Framework for Information Literacy for Higher Education* is a versatile instrument. Also, the framers recommend other student experiences for implementing the document, such as co-curricular activities, including "courses with service learning or community engagement projects" (Jacobson and Gibson, 2015: 104).

Step 2: Know Your Campus Culture at the Macro Level

No two higher education or K–12 campuses are alike. Each embodies a culture with both explicit and implicit aspects. The wise classroom faculty and librarian who set about to change attitudes on campus regarding information literacy will know the campus culture. They know the explicit protocols for change. For example, information literacy instruction will usually take the form of a proposal through (often) slow-moving governance councils and, perhaps, hesitant curriculum centers on campus. However, the prudent school or academic librarian and classroom instructor will also know the implicit channels of what would be most effective for reinventing (or inventing for the first time) an information literacy program. They will know about the curriculum structure, for example, of the writing-intensive courses that all students must experience, and the "sweet spots" for embedding information literacy instruction as guided by the six frames. In a well-thought-out, long-term instruction plan, a classroom information literacy program could start with a one-shot introductory *Framework* session in all first-year beginning writing classes with an intentional focus on two of the frames, "Searching as Strategic Exploration" and "Information Has Value." This could be followed by an information literacy *Framework* workshop for upper-division, first-level writing-intensive courses with a focus on the frames "Authority Is Constructed and Contextual" as well as "Research as Inquiry." Finally, one or more deeper *Framework* conceptual sessions with senior capstone projects could potentially unleash the full experiences found in the frames "Scholarship as Conversation" and "Information Creation as a Process." At this kind of curriculum architecture level, the choices for successful mapping of an information literacy plan depends on knowing both the implicit and the explicit paths within your campus culture. The placing of one or more of the six frames in your curriculum structure may be similar to the above example, or very different.

Step 3: Know Your Campus Culture at the Micro Level

Step 2 illustrated how to move closer toward information literacy campus integration at the macro level (curriculum architecture). Now here's a look at what might be considered the micro level of implementing a campus culture of information literacy. This is first-responder activity in which the librarian and classroom faculty engage students during information literacy conversations at the library reference desk, in the faculty member's office, during one-shot classroom instruction sessions, and especially during a librarian- and/or faculty-taught information literacy course. To conduct information literacy instruction effectively, it is critical to understand the behaviors, specifically the research behaviors, of students. It will come as no surprise that seeking the help of a reference librarian, searching databases for peer-reviewed articles, or spending time critically evaluating sources of information are not first on our students' agendas when they begin their information-searching journey. Kate Lawrence (2015), vice president of user research for EBSCO Information Services, found the following 11 things about undergraduate students' research preferences. Students are:

- framing their school work much like their multitasking, long-list lives—by interest, by priority, and by *return on investment*
- motivated by *efficiency*
- waiting "until the *last 20 percent* of the assignment period to start and finish the work" (2015: 90)
- first, using *Google* ("it's my oxygen"; "Google anticipates my every need") (2015: 90)
- second, using *Wikipedia* (they know it's not 100 percent trustworthy; students read the first paragraph for a summary, for keywords, and for key people; they are willing to risk a small amount of inaccuracy for the sake of *efficiency*)
- third, using the *professor's recommendations* (having done the first and second steps, they are now ready for the scholarly challenges)
- seeking three important feelings during the process: *confidence, confidence, confidence* (Google's drop-down topical suggestions and auto-complete search-box structure at the top of the results list reduces student *anxiety* and heightens their immediate *confidence*)

- *scanning* results after a search, *scanning* titles, and *scanning* abstracts, but not taking the time for deeper reading
- opening the full text of a document if they think it *might* be useful, then going to the next document and opening its full text, and another, and another, and another full text, until maybe *30 screens* are open on one computer—and keeping them open on that computer until the *assignment is finished!*
- weeding the 30 screens by deeper *scanning* to answer "yes" or "no" to the question, "Is this one to be added to my paper?" without detailed reading—and nothing beyond the first page (apparently, students were taught this approach by teachers when preparing for standardized testing in high school and use the same approach in college research because it is *efficient*)
- seeking a trusted, close-by "*expert*" peer when stuck rather than librarians, because it's more *efficient*.

If librarians and faculty are honest, there is a gut feeling that these kinds of student research behaviors are more the norm than not, even after students attend carefully prepared information literacy instruction. Is it the goal of an information literacy program to change these behaviors? Or are there information literacy skills and concepts that speak to these students' research behaviors?

Step 4: Adjust to Student Research Behaviors; Well, Sort Of

With disturbing findings like those listed in Step 3, librarians and classroom teaching colleagues may find themselves griping about the information literacy incompetence of the current generation of students. Should educators give up and conclude that if they can't beat them, join them? Before that happens, consider trying these 10 information literacy responses to the above student research behaviors, each one found in the *Framework for Information Literacy*.

Librarians and classroom instructors can:

- ease students' *anxiety* and raise their *confidence* through guiding them toward the principles found in the frame "Research as Inquiry," by breaking *complex* parts of their assignment into *simpler* ones, by leading the student to tap into their own *intellectual curiosity* for one engaging topic, and by helping the student discern an appropriate *scope of investigation* by realigning unrealistic priorities so that learning and research get reasonable investments of time.
- apply the frame "Searching as Strategic Exploration" to students living in a land of *efficiency* in class instruction, in tutorials, in chat reference; demonstrating unambiguous *searching strategies* and *efficient access* to useful lists of results that are topic-specific, saving the student time.
- show students how to live out the frame "Information Creation as a Process" to lower research *anxiety* and build *confidence* by encouraging a process that starts with *Google* and then *Wikipedia* to take notes on their topic (Did I just type what I think I typed?), followed by a quick introduction to Google Scholar, which links to *relevant full-text articles* found both in the library's proprietary databases and freely on the Internet, resources that are saved to the students' Google Drive for later access in order to write that paper before their 10:00 a.m. class in three days.

- coach students (before they begin searching during that *last 20 percent* of the assignment period) how to apply the frame "Authority Is Constructed and Contextual" so that in addition to *scanning* titles and abstracts, they also are *scanning* keywords and subject headings, dates, and author's credentials before deciding "yes" or "no" to adding yet another full-text article to the already 30 other promising articles open in separate browser windows on their computer.
- carefully admonish students to follow the frame "Information Has Value" by directing them to *efficient* antiplagiarism tools like Purdue University's online writing lab, the citation links found in the library's databases, and Google Scholar, but also showing them how to use the citation manuals (APA, MLA, Chicago, etc.), both in print and online.
- provide students with credibility insights and tools, based on the frame "Authority Is Constructed and Contextual," to help students *discern a source's authority* (such as for a set of results from a Google search, a *Wikipedia* entry, or that group of 30 articles chosen from a quick scan of titles and abstracts). To become information literate, a student needs to think deeply about how authority is created, who is empowered, who is disempowered, and how authority changes based on the context of a given resource over time.
- widen the narrow and underdeveloped perspective students may have of products of information, based on the frame "Information Creation as a Process," with the knowledge that all resource products (websites, scholarly books, articles from a results list, blogs, tweets) had paths to their creation; understanding this creation path means students would use higher order thinking when resolving their information need (such as lightly *scanning* an article and deciding "yes" or "no" on using it in their capstone project).
- encourage students to *scan* results more carefully, as described in the frame "Research as Inquiry," in order to ask such questions as "What problems are left unanswered?" "Which sources seem to contradict one another and why?" and "How can I take a very complex interdisciplinary issue that I'm finding in my sources and break it down into simpler parts that I can address in my project?"
- share with learners the parallels between how they live their non-academic lives and the pleasure of scholarship, as found in the frame "Scholarship as Conversation," because, like communities of scholars, students deeply enjoy smart, engaging *conversations on topics of interest* (for scholars, it's reading literature reviews; for students, it may be re-tweeting celebrity gossip on Twitter—think Kim Kardashian). Learners also love *disseminating interesting findings* to their larger public (for scholars, it's getting published in a prestigious journal; for students, it's posting their latest selfie on Instagram) and maintaining "sustained discourse with new insights and discoveries occurring over time," which is the definition of "Scholarship as Conversation" (for scholars, it's attending yet another favorite annual conference in their discipline and talking with poster session presenters; for students, it's hanging out at the local Pizzology Craft Pizza & Pub with friends who have a *common interest* in Pokémon Go).
- share time-saving search strategies, as described in the frame "Searching as Strategic Exploration," in order to decrease student *anxiety*, and boost *confidence* while improving *efficiency*, by skipping Google and *Wikipedia* and going straight to Google Scholar to capitalize on its many *efficient* features (friendly interface,

quick-to-learn advanced features, one-click, all-in-title searching, deep full-text access, "cited by" links to access more recent like articles, three lines of word-relevant full-text snippets) to assist with students' *scanning* behavior.

These suggested, so-called micro-level ideas can go a long way toward beginning or continuing a campus movement of higher levels of information literacy competency in students and scholars. These practical, thoughtful actions can be used in library reference desk transactions, in classroom instruction, during student interactions with faculty outside the classroom, and in online tutorial experiences.

Key Points

Chapter 6 has been about first steps for beginning or continuing to change a campus toward a more information-literate culture. The ideas include a) starting with the fundamentals of information literacy with campus information literacy advocates, b) getting familiar with the terms and concepts found in the *Framework*, and c) seeing how the *Framework*'s six frames can address students' research behaviors. The following summarizes these ideas.

- The first tip takes a fundamentals approach to introducing the *Framework for Information Literacy* in a fun, interactive way to those librarians and faculty who know about and have worked with the former 2000 information literacy *Standards*.
- The second tip reviews five important parts of the *Framework*'s frames that are useful in moving a campus forward in today's information literacy movement, done in the context of a 15- to 20-minute, discipline-specific faculty meeting.
- The third tip provides a series of useful practices in four areas: (a) getting to know the *Framework* document, (b) moving an agenda of information literacy on your campus at both the curricular (or macro) level and the student (or micro) level, (c) understanding 11 common research behaviors practiced by students, and (d) seeing how the *Framework*'s frames can address these research behaviors in surprising ways.

In Chapter 7 you will learn about what academic librarians and classroom faculty have been doing with regard to implementing information literacy since the *Framework*'s initial adoption in February 2015. These examples begin with a *Framework*-friendly online course, followed by four practical step-by-step strategies worth considering when implementing *Framework* plans on any campus. The chapter finishes with six "thoughts" from the co-chairs of the originating task force that created the *Framework for Information Literacy for Higher Education*—about what they had in mind for implementing the *Framework*.

References

Jacobson, Trudi E., and Craig Gibson. 2015. "First Thoughts on Implementing the Framework for Information Literacy." *Communications in Information Literacy* 9, no. 2 (September): 102–10.
Lawrence, Kate. 2015. "Today's College Students: Skimmers, Scanners and Efficiency-Seekers." *Information Services & Use* 35, no. 1/2 (January): 89–93.

Raish, Victoria, and Emily Rimland. 2016. "Employer Perceptions of Critical Information Literacy Skills and Digital Badges." *College & Research Libraries* 71, no. 1 (January): 87–113.

Wiebe, Todd J. 2015/2016. "The Information Literacy Imperative in Higher Education." *Liberal Education* 101, no. 4/102, no. 1 (Fall/Winter): 52–57.

⑨ Further Reading

Mackey, Thomas P., and Trudi E. Jacobson. 2011. "Reframing Information Literacy as a Metaliteracy." *College & Research Libraries* 72, no. 1 (January): 62–78.

Mackey, Thomas P., and Trudi E. Jacobson. 2014. *Metaliteracy: Reinventing Information Literacy to Empower Learners*. Chicago: American Library Association.

Meyer, Jan H. F., Ray Land, and Caroline Baillie. 2010. "Editors' Preface." In *Threshold Concepts and Transformational Learning*, edited by Jan H. F. Meyer, Ray Land, and Caroline Baillie, ix–xlii. Rotterdam, Netherlands: Sense Publishers.

Moniz, Richard, Joe Eshleman, Jo Henry, Howard Slutzky, and Lisa Moniz. 2015. *The Mindful Librarian: Connecting the Practice of Mindfulness to Librarianship*. Waltham, MA: Chandos Publishing.

Salomon, G. 1994. "To Be or Not to Be (Mindful)?" Paper presented to the American Educational Research Association Meetings, New Orleans, LA.

CHAPTER 7

Practical *Framework* Inroads

IN THIS CHAPTER

▷ A *Framework*-centered online course strategy

▷ Four proven *Framework*-friendly strategies

▷ Six "thoughts" from the framers of the *Framework*

SINCE THE 2015 ADOPTION OF the new *Framework* by the Association of College & Research Libraries, librarians and other educators have taken multiple approaches toward the use and practice of the *Framework*. In ACRL President Ann Campion Riley's helpful January 15, 2016, *ACRL Insider* column, a number of *Framework*-related issues were discussed. One of them was that

> some [librarians] recognize the value of the *Framework* but believe it pairs well with a set of standards for purposes of assessment. We understand that some of you . . . are making inroads in new ways of assessment which are promising in terms of disciplinary and institutional alignment and collaborations. (Riley, 2016)

Taking this cue from Riley, and based on published examples of information literacy on U.S. campuses since early 2015, this chapter offers practical step-by-step cases on how the *Framework* can be implemented to help academic librarians and classroom faculty make relevant, initial *Framework* inroads on any campus.

A *Framework*-Centered Online Course Strategy

Introduction: Using the *Framework* in an Online Course on Information Literacy

As Riley reported, some institutions guided by librarians' initiatives have been using the 2015 *Framework* in teaching experiences toward helping students become more information literate on their campuses. A one-shot, 60-minute expression is one thing, but using the *Framework* and its six frames in a for-credit, asynchronous, online course on information literacy is something novel. Because this example was implemented during a time when both the 2000 *Standards* and 2015 *Framework* were in use, these suggested steps originally were intended to implement a two-document online information literacy course. Betsy Reichart and Christina Elvidge's 2015 article, "Information Literacy in the Changing Landscape of Distance Learning," provided the inspiration for the following plan.

How to Develop a *Framework*-Centered Online Course: A Step-by-Step Plan for Using the *Framework* in an Online Course on Information Literacy

Step 1: Plan before the Plan

Librarians and/or classroom faculty involved in a course's initial or ongoing development can take a critical look at the *Framework* and write out a course strategic plan connecting components of the *Framework* document with a few reasonably similar institutional mission statements such as a school's strategic plan, its mission, "what we believe" statements, motto, or vision statements. It can be strategic to use similar language found in these intuitional statements within the plan. Examples of words might be *student success, lifelong learners, attrition prevention, equipping leaders, pursuing excellence, feeding intellectual curiosity*, and *providing service learning opportunities*. This exercise will not only inform you about what is mission critical where you are employed but will acquaint you with the unique strengths and any complementary parts of the *Framework*. Do not skip this step. Plan before the plan.

Step 2: Co-Equals—Classroom Faculty and Librarian

The preference for information literacy course design and instruction is a collaboration between a classroom faculty member and a librarian. It certainly could be one librarian or a team of librarians. And it could be one or more teaching faculty. But these scenarios of librarians acting alone or teaching faculty acting alone miss the point of a *Framework*-centered course. Practicing information literacy with the *Framework* requires faculty and librarians working in collaboration, not separately on assigned tasks, but operating as *co-equal* collaborators, deeply sharing in planning, creating, and delivering content. Information literacy cannot be achieved by librarians alone but by a co-equal, collaborative experience with fellow classroom faculty.

Step 3: Content—The Classic Skills

Students will experience the course's online content through the six *Framework* frames. One metaphor used to describe the frames is as if they were six different-colored camera lenses that can easily overlap one another, illustrating a similar interaction among the six frames (see figure 7.1 for an image for this metaphor). This requires familiarizing students with the six frames, their definitions, and corresponding *Knowledge Practices* and *Dispositions*. The entire *Framework* document is easily found by searching the Internet for the words "information literacy framework."

In studying the *Framework*, you can find connections back to the more skills-based *Standards* of 2000 in each of the six frames. Students will still need to recognize when information is needed and be able to locate, evaluate, and incorporate what's found into

Figure 7.1. A metaphor for the *Framework*—six independent, and yet potentially overlapping, different-colored camera lenses. © *Pixabay, image from https://pixabay.com/ released under Creative Commons CC0 1.0 Universal Public Domain Dedication. Used with permission.*

their knowledge base and effectively use the needed information (ACRL, 2000). In the context of the online course, these more prescriptive skills (locate, evaluate, etc.) can be covered in lessons over the course of each week, perhaps one skill per lesson.

The following are suggested concepts for the skills-based elements of the course and the corresponding frame.

- effective online searching ("Searching as Strategic Exploration")
- critical resource assessment ("Authority Is Constructed and Contextual")
- intellectual growth ("Scholarship as Conversation")
- academic integrity expectations ("Information Has Value")
- consequences for integrity violations ("Information Has Value")
- precision and accuracy of citation style ("Information Has Value")

Information literacy skills are kept basic, and students are continually engaged with hands-on, sometimes small-team exercises. Weekly quizzes and/or short written assignments help assess learning outcomes achieved by individual students and provide aggregate data for accreditation reports. Finally, within a *Framework*-based course, there are intentional links among additional student learning outcomes, the university's strategic plan statements, and regional accreditation expectations for information literacy.

Step 4: Content—Metacognitive Reflection

Continuing with the same theme in step 3 (skills), step 4, in light of the pedagogy of the online course, is about students learning certain skills as a core part of their information literacy journey and is also about reviewing what they are learning using *metacognitive* reflection. Thomas Mackey and Trudi Jacobson define a *metacognitive* approach to information literacy as moving "beyond rudimentary skills development and [preparing] students to dig deeper and assess their own learning" (2014: 13). This idea of deeper student self-reflection is essential to the *Framework* and can be accomplished through student journaling, blogs, threaded discussions, or using the newest social media network. As the course progresses, students are required to find expressions in one or more of the six frames' *Knowledge Practices* and *Dispositions* that they can reject, affirm, or grow into as they regularly engage in the reflection parts of the course.

For example, a nine-week, three-unit, online course called Information Literacy Basics includes weekly threaded discussions. Students contribute to the discussion board (threaded discussions) in three ways: a) an initial response, b) a reply to at least one other student's post, and c) a response to the original issue using one of the six frames' *Knowledge Practices* or *Dispositions* expressed as a personal reflection.

One discussion prompt to a threaded discussion could be, "For the three peer-reviewed articles you found for your topic this week, explain how you felt during your searching process. What best ideas did you discover that you'd like to share with others?"

A student's initial response might be:

I followed the video instructions on how to use the database for my topic, but found few of the 315 articles of any use. I then used the LibGuide alternative instructions and was able to rewrite my search string using subject headings. I wish I'd done that first. It would have saved me an hour. This second batch of articles was much better, but I still need to decide among 15 for my three final choices.

And for the student's frame response part of their reflection:

My experience seemed to be best matched with the "Searching as Strategic Exploration" frame, particularly the second *Disposition*, "understand that first attempts at searching do not always produce adequate results." To be honest, I almost dropped this course because of the frustration I felt doing the first search assignment. At my high school I always seemed to get something good just searching the Internet, so I thought: What's the big deal about using databases? I decided not to give up trying it the way the librarian showed us in class. What really made the difference was the LibGuide and some of the other students' ideas on how to get better articles. I surprised myself when it worked. I'm not saying I'm any kind of expert, but I felt so much better using subject headings with field indicators where I brought up a few really great articles. But I know I have a way to go and can't be tempted to use Google all the time.

Four Proven *Framework*-Friendly Strategies

Strategy #1 Introduction: *Framework* Lite, Using the Popular Mnemonic C.R.A.P.

Referring again to ACRL President Riley's comments at the beginning of the chapter, some academic librarians took information literacy as defined in the *Framework* and made "inroads in new ways of assessment which are promising" (Riley, 2016). One of those inroads was taking a popular instruction technique used for the 2000 *Standards* and applying it to the *Framework*.

Although some have shied away from the humorous, if not crass, acrostic C.R.A.P. technique, librarians have reported consistent success when using the mnemonic as a way for undergrads to recall most of the *Framework*'s core concepts (LeBlanc and Quintiliano, 2015). In order to fit within the four-letter acrostic, the six frames are collapsed into four. It becomes useful, then, to refer to this technique as "*Framework* Lite." Robert LeBlanc and Barbara Quintiliano's 2015 article "Recycling C.R.A.P.: Reframing a Popular Research Mnemonic for Library Instruction" was used in coming up with the following steps.

How to Develop Strategy #1: A Step-by-Step Plan for Using the Mnemonic C.R.A.P. (a.k.a. the *Framework* Lite Exercise)

Step 1: Setting the Stage

This exercise can be used to start a one-shot library instruction session, or as the first of multiple sessions on information literacy, or within a subject course. Begin by walking up to the front of the room and writing on the whiteboard or computer screen vertically, top to bottom, in large letters: C–R–A–P, with room enough to the right of each letter to write the words later that each letter represents (Conversation, Revision, Authority, and Property, written in each of the next four steps). Step back a little and while looking at the letters, shout "C. . . . R. . . . A. . . . P." and then face the class and in a normal teaching voice say,

> This is an acrostic for four library information literacy concepts I want to talk about today. Let's shout out the letters together three times as our information literacy yell! Ready, go:
>
> C. . . . R. . . . A. . . . P.
> C. . . . R. . . . A. . . . P.
> C. . . . R. . . . A. . . . P.!

Of course, exactly how to introduce the letters depends on the class and the instructor's own comfort level. Nevertheless, the exercise is meant to be an unexpected fun experience with an uncharacteristically shouting librarian or classroom instructor, not to mention the word CRAP. Students will not easily forget this information literacy instruction session. As has been explained, the lack of a six-word acrostic indicates that some of the six frames will be collapsed under one of the four terms. The ideas of all six frames are retained, but four of the frames are collapsed into two of the terms, as shown in figure 7.2. It may be more helpful and more memorable to label this introduction to information literacy as the *Framework* Lite exercise.

Step 2: Conversation

Explain, "The C. in the acrostic stands for Conversation." Write *Conversation* next to C. Ask the class, "Help me list ways we have scholarly conversations with others about ideas." At this point, broad ideas from the class would include: books, articles in journals, face-to-face or online classroom discussions among students, listening to and asking questions of the instructor in class, and communicating via social media. Continue, "For all of us to participate in the scholarship of conversation, you need to know how to find ideas of others." Refer to some of the ideas students just gave (books, journal articles,

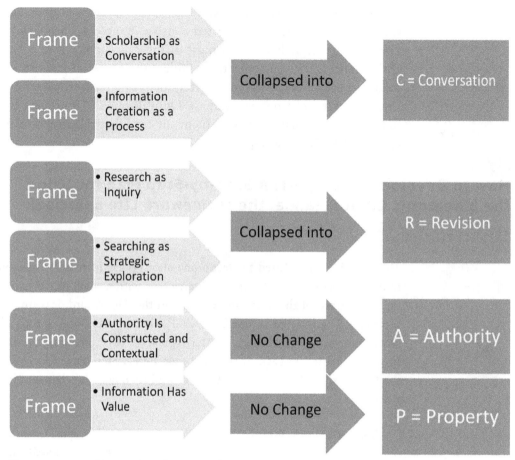

Figure 7.2. Collapse of six frames into four terms for the C.R.A.P. exercise (a.k.a. *Framework Lite* exercise).

newspaper stories, or social media) and demonstrate a finding skill using that resource with a proprietary library database. Or, perhaps, show how to locate scholarly books about the course's subject matter and how students can join in the conversation by reading others' ideas and reflecting on what they find.

Do the same for demonstrating how to find scholarly articles about a favorite topic for a student assignment. And show how to find a social media thread about a controversial topic. Conversation is the single term used to represent the two frames "Scholarship as Conversation" and "Information Creation as a Process" as illustrated in figure 7.2. More discussion prompts and ideas on Conversation can be found in both frames' *Knowledge Practices* and *Dispositions*. Although not the intent of this chapter, the librarian or classroom instructor could use the *Framework* Lite exercise to springboard into the many rich areas of information literacy found in the six frames. However, introducing the six frames using the *Framework* Lite exercise is certainly not a complete understanding of the six frames. More step-by-step ideas to teach each frame are presented in chapters 8 and 9.

Step 3: Revision

Explain, "The R. in the acrostic stands for Revision." Write *Revision* next to the R. "Revision means the research process is ongoing, a constant *re-visioning* of your search, and hence the term *re-search*. Let's take a topic and see how that works." Ask for a topic from the students (in a one-shot library instruction session or information literacy course) or use one relevant to their course's subject matter. Show how to access an appropriate database for the topic, perhaps begin a search using keywords, then continue explaining the revision necessary using a truncation symbol, and then limit the quantity of results by using quotation marks around two or more search terms that need to stay together as a phrase. Continue to show revision by narrowing, using limiters like date and language, as well as by using the Boolean operator AND along with different field indicators (author, title, subject heading, etc.). Other topics that could be covered under the Revision step in research include how to revise an idea for a topic toward a workable thesis, the steps required for a research paper, the process of looking at results to give reasons why specific documents or articles would be useful for a topic (timely, relevant, prominent, scholarly, peer-reviewed, and discipline-specific criteria), and why other documents might not work (too old, not scholarly, not the correct topic). Revision is the term used to represent the frames "Research as Inquiry" as well as "Searching as Strategic Exploration," as shown in figure 7.2.

Step 4: Authority

Next explain, "The A. in the acrostic represents the word Authority." Write *Authority* next to A. and continue:

On the surface, authority deals with a resource's credentials. For example, let's say on the left side of an imaginary horizontal line are popular magazines like *People* or *Sports Illustrated*. Somewhere in the middle are those sources neither popular nor scholarly but significant, such as renowned special-interest publications such as *Psychology Today* and *Scientific American*. On the right side of this scale are scholarly, peer-reviewed journals like the *Journal of the American Medical Association* or the *Journal of Higher Education*. Other important resources that might not fit on this line as popular or scholarly are trade publications that every profession has, like *Computer World* or *Advertising Age*.

If time allows, you can share another perspective:

Authority also determines which of three categories information can fit in: primary, secondary, or tertiary. Primary authority is the raw source of information, like personal letters, an autobiography, or original research in journal articles. Secondary authority is a mashup of primary sources, like most books, such as one covering the Revolutionary War based on, say, personal letters and war memos, or most journal articles (unless it's original research or written at the time of an event), or textbooks. The third or tertiary authority is highly refined information, such as entries in an encyclopedia or a dictionary, topical bibliographies, or an almanac.

Authority is the word used in the acrostic to represent the single frame "Authority Is Constructed and Contextual," as demonstrated in figure 7.2.

Step 5: Property

Finish with, "Finally, the fourth letter P. represents the word Property." Write the word *Property* next to the letter P. and continue:

The idea of Property, in its most practical way, is expressed in what you do throughout and at the end of many of your written papers, which are the in-text citations and the references you list at the end. Because most of the sources you will be using for your assignments are someone's intellectual property, you will need to know how to properly give credit; that is, how to cite it correctly. In this course, you will be using the APA style. You must learn to master this skill (accurate citation), or you risk turning in something that is not really your work but someone else's and then being accused of plagiarizing (stealing) another's ideas (property). Consequences for that behavior can get you expelled from this campus.

If there is time, walk through the details of proper citation for an online scholarly article and also for a book. Next, show one or more examples of proper in-text citation. Finally, as time allows, an example of paraphrasing can be demonstrated.

Obviously, there is much more that could be covered under Property or in another session led by the librarian or classroom instructor. This includes such topics as understanding when common knowledge is not cited or when student synthesis of a topic or original thoughts are not cited. But for the *Framework* Lite exercise, additional content is at the discretion of the instructor. Finally, as was the case with the other three terms, the word Property is used in the acrostic to represent the single frame "Information Has Value," as described in figure 7.2.

At the very end of this segment of instruction, close with:

So let's all repeat our information literacy yell: C. stands for Conversation, R. stands for Revision, A. stands for Authority, and P. stands for Property.

C.... R.... A.... P.

C.... R.... A.... P.

C.... R.... A.... P.!

Strategies #2, #3, and #4 Introduction: Using the *Framework* with Guided Group Discussions, Online Discussion Boards, and Web 2.0 Technologies

One thing that is clear in comparing the older *Standards* with the new *Framework* is the shift from primarily skills-based learning to metaliteracy-based learning and discovery. What this means is an enlarged focus on students being not only consumers of information, but also creators of new information. It also means a major addition to measuring student success by nationally recognized standards and competencies—measuring student success by their increasingly deeper levels of engagement with core concepts (found in the six frames), and by students assessing their own learning process.

It makes sense that, until recently, most information literacy work and study have been done in synchronous, face-to-face environments—that is to say, the classroom. But the online education explosion compels the new directions of information literacy to be fully immersed in web-based expressions, including social media. These next three strategies and their steps move in that direction, starting with a traditional classroom example, moving on to seeing how the technique looks in an online experience, and finishing with integrating information literacy into students' Web 2.0 social media experiences.

Certainly, a classroom faculty member alone could employ all three of the following *Framework* techniques, one in brick and mortar, the other two using the growing online environment as a vehicle for progressing through course material, including information literacy. One indication of a successful *co-equal* collaboration between a librarian and classroom instructor is how they might share in teaching the following three experiences. With this in mind, "instructor" is meant to be either a librarian or a faculty member in the context of an information literacy course or an information literacy focus in a traditional disciplinary class. Melissa Anderson's uses of the *Framework*, as found in her 2015 article, "Rethinking Assessment: Information Literacy Instruction and the ACRL *Framework*," helped provide guidance for the following steps in strategies #3, #4, and #5.

How to Develop Strategy #2: A Step-by-Step Plan for Using the *Framework* with a Face-to-Face Guided Group Discussion

Step 1: Creating the Guided Groups

Break the class into small groups (three to five students each) with one student facilitating each group using instructor-designed prompts for the classroom topic of that session's lesson plan.

Step 2.1 (The First of Three Alternatives): Classroom Instructor Does Assessment

The instructor goes around to each group and takes notes, capturing what learning is taking place and observing student behaviors. After class, notes are coded by common words, synonyms, and phrases to reveal possible themes in learning. Take the coded data and evaluate it with a qualitative method such as one used in a focus group. In addition, begin to interpret the data using one or more of the *Framework*'s *Knowledge Practices* or *Dispositions* that best lends itself to (or fits) the topic. The purpose of using the *Framework* is to find the direction of student responses in one or more of the frames. Then, using that frame's *Knowledge Practices* or *Dispositions*, facilitate deeper learning in the class moving forward. Be ready to discover unexpected new perspectives on topics (as groups have the capacity to do). The following are two examples.

1. With the lens of "Authority Is Constructed and Contextual" on the topic of discussion, the instructor a) lists the types of authority described by the students during their discussion, b) identifies what indicators of authority students are using, if any, c) if authorities are named, notes whether there is a sense of agreement, disagreement, or neutral, and d) sees how students are participating in a community of practice.
2. With the lens of "Information Has Value" on the topic of discussion, what dimension of information value do students seem to reflect: information as a commodity, information as a means of education, information as a means of influence, information as entertainment, information as self-expression, or information as a means of negotiating and understanding the world? Is information discussed in a way that marginalizes populations or exposes gaps between the information privileged and the information underprivileged?

Step 2.2 (The Second of Three Alternatives): Students Do Assessment with Discussion Audits

After the guided discussion, have students create *discussion audits*, which are brief reflections on the discussion through answering the following types of questions:

- What disagreements or tensions, if any, did you notice?
- If there were long moments of silence, what do you think was going on during that time?

- What was brought out in the discussion that you think people agreed on?
- What was brought up that seemed to be misunderstood? (Brookfield and Preskill, 2005)

Step 2.3 (The Third of Three Alternatives): Students Do Assessment with Discussion Logs

After the guided discussion, instruct students to create *discussion logs*, which are like *discussion audits* but shorter. Students would write brief answers to the following types of questions:

- What did you learn during the discussion that you did not know before?
- What one thing can you do now that you couldn't do before the discussion?
- Based on the discussion, if you were put in a situation to teach something to another person, what would that be? (Brookfield and Preskill, 2005)

How to Develop Strategy #3: A Step-by-Step Plan for Using the *Framework* in an Online Discussion Board (Threaded Discussions)

Step 1: Find an Appropriate Discussion Board

If you are not already using a learning management system (Edmodo, Moodle, Blackboard, etc.), which likely has a discussion board or a threaded discussion feature, then this is the time to find an appropriate discussion board (threaded discussion) that best fits the type of students, the class content, and/or the topic in this exercise. For suggestions, go to http://www.quertime.com/article/15-best-online-forum-platforms-software-free-and-paid/.

Step 2: Determine Groups and Set Ground Rules

Unlike a face-to-face guided group discussion as described in strategy #3, step 1, all students in a course using a discussion board (threaded discussions) could participate as one group. But just as easily there could be multiple groups, with or without the need for an accountability student-facilitator per group. Provide simple, clear ground rules.

For example, in a multi-week, online course that starts, say, Sundays at midnight, all students must post a response to the question or topic by Wednesday at midnight. All students must comment on at least one other person's post before Saturday at midnight. At some point, posts can no longer be made (at the end of the week, at the end of a week and one day, two weeks, or whatever works best) but past discussions are accessible throughout the course as possible reference points for students and instructor. This is so everyone is contributing to the same topics during the same span of time. Grade on quality of post content, not necessarily length (such as three points given per weekly discussions: one point for making an initial post, one point for commenting on another's post, and one point for quality). As a ground rule, disrespect will not be tolerated (or simply refer to rules set out in the syllabus).

Step 3: Real-Time Evaluation of Student Learning

The instructor should maintain regular viewings of online contributions and quickly contact students who miss the first deadline. An instructor's evaluation of students' threaded responses using the *Framework* for guidance can occur during or after the close of a weekly discussion. So, what does it mean to use the *Framework* to assess student responses? One of the purposes of the *Framework* is to use one or more frame definitions, *Knowledge Practices*, and/or *Dispositions* to generally determine students' understanding and direction regarding class content. Once a frame-defined understanding or direction is determined, the instructor can then use that frame's definition, *Knowledge Practices*, and *Dispositions* to facilitate deeper student learning. Here are two examples of assessment during an online response exercise:

1. Online discussion boards require every student's conscious participation. In that type of rich contribution, students are expressing their individual authoritative voice with peers, which fits well with the frame "Authority Is Constructed and Contextual." In the instructor's online threaded responses, this learning connection can be pointed out and then covered in depth by the instructor using this frame's *Knowledge Practices* and *Dispositions* as guides.

2. As one student's response becomes a significant thread, the instructor can direct all students to respond to that thread. In a similar way, if students' responses seem to be getting off track, the instructor can facilitate the discussion back to the original intended direction or can change the focus of the discussion altogether. This easily fits the frame "Scholarship as Conversation." The instructor can bring out points covered in this frame's *Knowledge Practices* and *Dispositions*. This includes suggesting to students that (a) their discussions can be approached in scholarly ways, (b) highly engaging conversations don't need to conclude at the week's end, and (c) they should see themselves not only as *users* of scholarship but also as *makers* of it and other new forms of information.

Step 4: Ex-Post Evaluation of Student Learning: Online Discussion Board

After the time frame of responses is finished (a week, a week and one day, etc.), the threads can be used for content analysis. Based on findings such as recurring themes or half-built ideas, in a future week the instructor can intentionally go deeper, starting with previous learning and using one or more frame's *Knowledge Practices* or *Dispositions*. Here are two examples of an ex-post evaluation:

1. Five students demonstrated qualities of authoritative leadership during one week's posts. Without naming the five students, in a future online discussion the instructor will describe those qualities of authoritative leadership in the context of a frame. The instructor also can determine gaps or superficial attempts expressed by the students. This information can help facilitate deeper experiences based on a frame's *Knowledge Practices* and *Dispositions*. For the frame "Authority Is Constructed and Contextual," students can be challenged to express their own types of authority, to examine the liabilities and advantages in those authorities, and to reflect on where they think they will find themselves in light of the information ecosystem in three years, five years, and ten years.

2. Review the problems or questions that remained unanswered from the contributions of the previous week in light of the frame "Research as Inquiry." In a sociology class, for instance, the classroom instructor can ask students to take one common social problem brought up and unanswered fully from the previous week's discussion and have them suggest how it could be broken down into simpler, manageable

parts. Direct students to think of solutions to these smaller parts by having them quickly review the literature on the issue and then propose ways that have yet to be tried or discovered. Encourage students to go deeper as they become the makers of new knowledge as they answer real problems.

How to Develop Strategy #4: A Step-by-Step Plan for Using the *Framework* with Social Media Platforms

Step 1: Find an Appropriate Social Media Platform

Choose one Web 2.0 social media platform that most students in class are familiar with (Facebook, blogging, Twitter) or try one that's less known (3D immersive environments like Second Life). For more ideas, conduct an Internet search for the most popular social media (or networking) sites.

Step 2: Determine One or Multiple Groups and Set Ground Rules

Demonstrate in a face-to-face class session (or with an online instructor video, for example) how everyone gets started using the chosen platform. Team up possible technology strugglers with students who could help. As discussed in the online discussion boards above, create clear and simple directions, especially the time when blog responses, Facebook conversations, or tweets (for example) need to be started and ended.

Step 3: Evaluate Student Learning Using a Social Media Platform

In light of the *Framework*, the purposes of using social media are to a) provide a place where students have conversations, b) allow a place to assess students' understandings of course content and learning outcomes, and c) offer a place for students to grow deeper in their learning, facilitated by a classroom instructor. These assessments can occur during or after an exercise. The following are suggested exercises.

- Assessment *during* a social media interaction: Students are randomly paired, and each pair will do the following five things as an information literacy assignment. These instructions represent five of the six information literacy competency *standards* for higher education approved by the ACRL Board in 2000. Throughout the assignment, pairs of students communicate using the social media platform to:
  - Determine the nature and extent of information needed on a topic related to the class.
  - Access needed information effectively and efficiently.
  - Evaluate information and its sources critically.
  - Use information effectively to create a 10-item annotated bibliography on the topic: half a page summarizing the content of each resource and the other half for personal reflections, either as one joint student narrative or two individual reflections.
  - Demonstrate an understanding of the economic, legal, and social issues surrounding the use of information; access and use information ethically and legally.

As students are using the social media, the instructor has access to their communications. Using the lens of the frame "Searching as Strategic Exploration," the faculty member notes students' intuitive applications of any *Knowledge Practices* or *Dispositions*. As the process continues, suggest an appropriate item from this frame that could help each pair of students deepen their understanding of the process at hand. If another frame works better, use it.

- Assessment *after* a social media interaction: Students are randomly paired, and pairs are instructed to create an annotated bibliography with 10 resources on their topic. Annotated bibliographies are rich artifacts that can be assessed in at least two ways. Assess the annotations using a quantitative method by measuring the citations against a required style (e.g., APA, MLA, or Chicago) and the stated instructions. Each citation begins with, say, 10 points. Points are taken off for style inconsistencies such as not italicizing a journal or book title or for incomplete information such as a missing volume number for an article or page numbers for a book chapter. Additional point reductions would come from such errors as incorrect web links, insufficient information to retrieve a source, or incorrect formatting for the chosen style (for example, mixing elements of APA and MLA).

How does that look? Let's say the annotations by a student pair in a Facebook context fall into five peer-reviewed scholarly articles and five discipline-specific trade journal articles. The students' annotations indicated that they understood the distinction between the two types of resources. Here the instructor could craft comments using the lens of the frame "Authority Is Constructed and Contextual" by first agreeing with the students about the uniqueness of the two types of resources based on authority. The instructor could then go to a deeper level of learning by encouraging the students to keep an open mind while continuing with their assignment, which requires writing and presenting about their topic, especially when they find these authorities giving conflicting perspectives. This is the first bullet under this frame's *Dispositions*: "develop and maintain an open mind when encountering varied and sometimes conflicting perspectives" (ACRL, 2015: 6).

Step 4: Ex-Post Evaluation of Student Learning: Social Media Platform

An ex-post assessment of this assignment done in the context of social media is conducted after the close of student work. Through the lens of a frame, for example "Scholarship as Conversation," student learning and engagement can continue to be deepened. In light of this frame, let's say the instructor perceives that the student pair clearly think their topic can be covered by just one source, with the rest of the nine sources pretty much agreeing with the main source and these nine sources in agreement among themselves. The instructor can then suggest that discourse on a topic can change direction significantly in the context of competing perspectives. The instructor can then encourage the two students to more critically evaluate the ideas of others on their topic, others who may be contributing to the conversation in another information environment and certainly outside the one school of thought the students have already discovered. These attempts at deeper ideas come from the fourth bullet of this frame's *Knowledge Practices*: "critically evaluate contributions made by others in participatory information environments" (ACRL, 2015: 11). As part of the next step in this assignment, students would change the settings in their social media tool to include the entire class, and not just a partner and the instructor.

Step 5: Ex-Post Evaluation of Student Learning: Students Present Their Learning

Continuing in the social media context, have each pair of students create a summary presentation of their work in four parts. They would: a) present an illustration or case study of their topic findings, b) summarize the literature review, c) share any shortcomings, and d) explain how their process and product could lead to contributing to new knowledge. This could be a written narrative or more creative alternatives (student-created video, voiceover animation). After all presentations are posted and complete, individual students are then required, in the social media environment, to engage in "conversation" with at least one other pair of their choice, perhaps based partly on the summary presentation of that pair's topic and partly on the pair's annotated bibliography. The following is one example of a pair's four-part presentation.

> Team A did an annotated bibliography on the gender differences in college students as it related to same-sex friendship and the concept of well-being. a) They illustrated their findings by videotaping two 30-second scenarios. One scenario showed two women becoming disgruntled with their same-sex friendship, which did not affect their well-being. The other scenario showed two men becoming displeased with their friendship, which negatively affected their well-being. b) The students summarized their literature review by focusing on one primary article published in 2011 that had over 80 references and, based on Google Scholar, was cited by 14 other articles. This single article was the sole source for their final list of all 10 resources (coming from the 80 references and the 14 citing articles). c) The two-student team explained that shortcomings of the 10 articles included very small populations that were studied, that the populations were mostly self-selected, and that the results of the studies were not generalizable. d) The two students thought that what they had learned during the process, as well as the product, could lead to a presentation in another class where they would describe possible new knowledge from their literature review.

Step 6: Ex-Post Evaluation of Student Learning: The Power of Peer Evaluation

Students as class peers can provide thoughtful, critical reflections on student pairs' contributions, as well as encourage dissemination of any perceived new knowledge each pair may have discovered. Examples of student-peer evaluation might include: a) remarking on an important resource in their 10 sources, b) praising a well-done presentation, c) recommending a next direction for their work, such as submitting an article proposal to a trade magazine editor, d) suggesting the students present their findings at a local conference, and e) encouraging the students to rewrite their annotation as a book review (if a book was included in their 10 sources) and post the review on Amazon.com.

⊚ Six "Thoughts" from the Framers of the *Framework*

About a year after the *Framework for Information Literacy for Higher Education* had been accepted by the ACRL, the co-chairs for the *Framework*'s almost two-year task force published an article on their thoughts about how the *Framework* and the frames could be implemented. Trudi Jacobson and Craig Gibson are to be commended for their continued professional vision and unrelenting years of work on the *Framework*, including their informative article, "First Thoughts on Implementing the Framework for Information Literacy" (2015), which assisted in the following thoughts.

Thought 1: The Larger Scope of the *Framework*

The *Framework* was designed to work not only with the obvious traditional curricular situations, but also co-curricular situations. That means information literacy would gradually be embedded in courses and assignments dealing with service learning, campus initiatives in the surrounding community, academic clubs, faculty/student research, and study-abroad experiences.

Thought 2: The Student as Information Producer

One reoccurring theme toward implementing the *Framework* is how students are perceived in terms of their own scholarship production. It is assumed that students would not only be consumers of information but also producers of information—that is to say, new knowledge. This discovery of new knowledge could take place in collaboration with other students, even other students outside their own university and abroad internationally.

Thought 3: The Relationship between Librarian and Classroom Faculty

The *Framework*—or any alternative future direction in information literacy—will have very little effect unless classroom faculty are in ongoing professional relationships with librarians and are carrying out their own faculty *Framework* responsibilities in curriculum development and classroom implementation. This is not the librarian showing up for one-shot library instruction sessions after receiving a request from the faculty member. It means the librarian and faculty are co-equal collaborators, implementing the *Framework* largely based on a relationship with one another.

Thought 4: Framework Words versus Core Strategies

Using the exact words found in the six frames is less important than being faithful to the following three core strategies for implementing the *Framework*:

1. Allow students to engage with the *Framework*'s "big ideas."
2. Create regular opportunities for students to self-reflect critically on their own learning of these "big ideas."
3. Provide students occasions to exercise creativity in the information ecosystem, such as social media, multimedia, and web-based digital expressions.

Thought 5: Develop Learning Outcomes

It is true that the *Knowledge Practices* (described as actions and behaviors), the *Dispositions* (characterized by attitudes, beliefs, and values), and the definitions of the six frames are not learning outcomes. Rather than a long list of nationally recognized learning outcomes, these three parts of each of the six frames offer librarians and classroom faculty ideas for writing localized, institutionally relevant, information literacy learning outcomes.

Learning outcomes for information literacy can now be developed along a disciplinary focus, or librarians and faculty can take their current campus information literacy outcomes based on the 2000 *Standards* and revise or modify them based on the *Framework*. Finally, the *Knowledge Practices* and *Dispositions* of the six frames are meant to augment student learning outcomes rather than replace them, allowing learners to more clearly engage and understand discipline-centered information as well as concepts implicit in the frames' titles: authority, information value, research, searching, information process, and scholarship.

Thought 6: Measure Student Learning over Time

Assessing student information literacy skill competencies (such as doing a set of steps to find something useful) is important, but measures only part of student progress. As new or revised information literacy learning outcomes are written based on the *Knowledge Practices* and *Dispositions* of the *Framework*, librarians and classroom faculty will have larger, richer conversations about information literacy and student successes over time, along with the rest of the academy.

Some of the suggested information literacy assessment methods fall under action research and pedagogical research. More specifically, the following qualitative techniques could be used in assessing student learning progress in all areas of the curriculum, including information literacy: (a) conversations captured in threaded discussion in learning management systems, (b) textual analysis of e-portfolios, (c) pop quizzes, one-minute papers, or concept information maps showing suggested relationships between concepts, and (d) analysis of social media embedded in instruction, such as blogs, Second Life, Twitter, and Facebook. As is true of any classroom assessment, using these methods can reveal gaps in learning outcomes so that timely curricular changes can be made.

Key Points

Chapter 7 has been about what academic librarians and classroom faculty were doing with the 2015 *Framework* during its first year of application and beyond. In this chapter, these practices included a *Framework*-friendly online course and four practical step-by-step strategies. Finally, six "thoughts" on how to implement the *Framework* as published by the co-chairs of the originating task force for the *Framework for Information Literacy for Higher Education* were presented. The following summarizes what was learned:

- The chapter began with suggestions for using the 2015 *Framework* in a for-credit online course on information literacy, where the classroom instructor and the librarian work as *co-equal* collaborators. The content of the course included classic *Standards* skills as well as *Framework* metacognitive reflection by students.
- Strategy #1 uses a proven information literacy instruction mnemonic known as C.R.A.P. and adapts it to the *Framework*. The idea is labeled *Framework* Lite because the six frames are collapsed to four with the four-letter acrostic: C = Conversation, R = Revision, A = Authority, and P = Property.
- Strategy #2 provides a plan for using the *Framework* within a face-to-face guided group discussion. Here students break into small groups, each led by a student with instructor-designed prompts. The strategy concludes with offering three ways to assess learning: by instructor coding, by student discussion audits, and by student discussion logs.
- Strategy #3 offers another group discussion method. Here the *Framework* is used within an online discussion board where the instructor assesses student learning in a real-time evaluation approach and in an ex-post evaluation approach.

- Strategy #4 also offers a group discussion method. This time the *Framework* is practiced within a social media platform where the instructor assesses in a real-time evaluation approach and in an ex-post evaluation approach of student learning (as in strategy #3).
- The final section of the chapter provided a summary of six "thoughts" for implementing the *Framework* as proposed by the co-chairs of the original task force that submitted the final report to the ACRL board in January 2015.

In chapter 8 you will learn tips for the first three frames of the *Framework*, including suggested learning outcomes, assignment handouts, and rubrics handouts for "Authority Is Constructed and Contextual," "Information Creation as a Process," and "Information Has Value."

References

ACRL (Association of College & Research Libraries). 2000. *Information Literacy Competency Standards for Higher Education*. American Library Association. http://www.ala.org/acrl/standards/informationliteracycompetency.

ACRL (Association of College & Research Libraries). 2015. *Framework for Information Literacy for Higher Education*. American Library Association. http://www.ala.org/acrl/standards/ilframework.

Anderson, Melissa J. 2015. "Rethinking Assessment: Information Literacy Instruction and the ACRL *Framework*." *SJSU* [San Jose State University] *School of Information Student Research Journal* [alternative title: *iSchool Student Research Journal*] 5, no. 2. http://scholarworks.sjsu.edu/slissrj/vol5/iss2/3.

Brookfield, Stephen, and Stephen Preskill. 2005. *Discussion as a Way of Teaching: Tools and Techniques for Democratic Classrooms*. San Francisco: Jossey-Bass.

Jacobson, Trudi E., and Craig Gibson. 2015. "First Thoughts on Implementing the Framework for Information Literacy." *Communications in Information Literacy* 9, no. 2 (September): 102–10. Some steps in this chapter were derived in part from the original.

LeBlanc, Robert E., and Barbara Quintiliano. 2015. "Recycling C.R.A.P.: Reframing a Popular Research Mnemonic for Library Instruction." *Pennsylvania Libraries: Research & Practice* 3, no. 2 (Fall): 115–21. Used under Creative Commons CC BY, http://creativecommons.org/licenses/by/4.0/. Some steps in this chapter were derived in part from the original.

Mackey, Thomas P., and Trudi E. Jacobson. 2014. *Metaliteracy: Reinventing Information Literacy to Empower Learners*. Chicago: American Library Association.

Reichart, Betsy, and Christina Elvidge. 2015. "Information Literacy in the Changing Landscape of Distance Learning." *Pennsylvania Libraries: Research & Practice* 3, no. 2 (Fall): 144–55. Used under Creative Commons CC BY, http://creativecommons.org/licenses/by/4.0/. Some steps in this chapter were derived in part from the original.

Riley, Ann Campion. 2016. "Update from the ACRL Board of Directors on the Framework for Information Literacy for Higher Education." *ACRL Insider* (blog), January 15. http://www.acrl.ala.org/acrlinsider/archives/11232.

Further Reading

Archer, Alyssa, Joe Eshleman, Mandi Goodsett, Nicole Tekulve, and Karen Tercho. 2015. "ACRL's Framework for Information Literacy in Practice." *Library Instruction Roundtable News* 38, no. 2 (December): 8–11.

Bravender, Patricia, Hazel McClure, and Gayle Schaub, eds. 2015. *Teaching Information Literacy Threshold Concepts: Lesson Plans for Librarians.* Chicago: Association of College and Research Libraries.

Dempsey, Paula R., and Heather Jagman. 2016. "'I Felt like Such a Freshman': First-Year Students Crossing the Library Threshold." *portal: Libraries and the Academy* 16, no. 1 (January–March): 89–107.

Oakleaf, Megan. 2014. "Metrics: A Roadmap for Assessing Student Learning Using the New Framework for Information Literacy for Higher Education." *Journal of Academic Librarianship* 40, no. 5: 510–14.

Valenza, Joyce Kasman, and Wendy Steadman Stephens. 2015. "Challenging Channels: School Librarians and Evolving Literacies." *Journal of Media Literacy* 9, no. 3/4: 28–38.

Teaching Information Literacy

First Three Frames of the *Framework*

IN THIS CHAPTER

▷ Information literacy teaching aids for the first three frames of the *Framework*:

- Frame distinctions
- Sample SLOs for a frame's *Knowledge Practices* and *Dispositions*
- Sample assignment handouts
- A sample rubric handout for each assignment

▷ Teaching the Frame "Authority Is Constructed and Contextual"

▷ Teaching the Frame "Information Creation as a Process"

▷ Teaching the Frame "Information Has Value"

THE TASK IMAGINED BY the Association of College & Research Libraries for the *Framework for Information Literacy for Higher Education* is daunting. The objective is simple: ideally, librarians and classroom faculty at their respective colleges and universities together engage every student in a process so that on graduation day, each student has the practical tools to successfully practice information literacy skills as well as the intellectual capacity to think conceptually as an information-literate person. This chapter offers practical teaching aids and strategies to help librarians and classroom faculty accomplish this challenge with the first three *Framework* frames:

- Authority Is Constructed and Contextual
- Information Creation as a Process
- Information Has Value

The last three frames of the *Framework*, "Research as Inquiry," "Scholarship as Conversation," and "Searching as Strategic Exploration," will be addressed in the next chapter.

◎ Four Information Literacy Teaching Aids for the First Three Frames

The following descriptions explain four ready-to-use teaching aids that can effectively communicate the principles found in the six frames of the 2015 *Framework for Information Literacy for Higher Education* (see table 8.1). The teaching aids are designed to assist the librarian and the classroom faculty member as they collaborate, teach, and assess information literacy in their specific roles and settings. The four aids, applied to each of this chapter's three frames, are:

- Frame distinctions (a figure illustrating each frame's unique characteristics)
- Sample *Knowledge Practices* student learning outcomes (SLOs) and sample *Dispositions* SLOs (compiled in a separate table for each frame)
- Sample assignment handouts for each frame
- A sample rubric handout for each assignment.

It's important to note that the use of both the *Knowledge Practices* and the *Dispositions* found in each frame is core to the ACRL information literacy *Framework* model. The *Framework* document defines *Knowledge Practices* as "proficiencies or abilities that learn-

Table 8.1. The Four Teaching Aids with Short Descriptions

TEACHING AID	SHORT DESCRIPTION	FIGURE/TABLES/HANDOUTS
1. *Distinctions* Diagram	Brief set of terms and concepts unique to a frame	Figure 8.1 is a diagram of the distinctions of the first three frames
2. Student Learning Outcomes (SLOs) Table	Suggested student learning outcomes (SLOs) adapted from a frame's *Knowledge Practices* and *Dispositions*	Tables 8.2, 8.3, and 8.4 contain four columns; the first and third columns list sample SLOs mapped to each frame's *Knowledge Practices* and *Dispositions*
3. Assignment Handout (one page)	Sample assignment handout adapted from the *Knowledge Practices* or *Dispositions* of each frame and one of its suggested SLOs, designed to help engage students in that frame's concepts	Assignment handouts are ready to use or adapt as needed
4. Rubric Handout (one or more pages)	A sample rubric handout used with its corresponding assignment handout to facilitate student accountability, grading, course evaluation, and information literacy data for institutional reporting	Rubric handouts are ready to use or adapt as needed

ers develop as a result of their comprehending a threshold concept," and a *Disposition* is "a tendency to act or think in a particular way . . . a cluster of preferences, attitudes, and intentions, as well as a set of capabilities that allow the preferences to become realized in a particular way" (ACRL, 2015).

A More In-Depth Description of Each Frame's Distinctions

Figure 8.1 shows a set of terms and ideas derived from a frame's two-paragraph description (as found in the *Framework* document). These frame summaries are intended to help the busy instructor more quickly and easily grasp the core concepts or "big ideas" found throughout the frames. In addition to the diagram for these three frames' distinctions, each presentation of a frame in this chapter begins with a summary of that frame's terms and ideas, plus a brief contrast in perspectives between expert learners and novice learners.

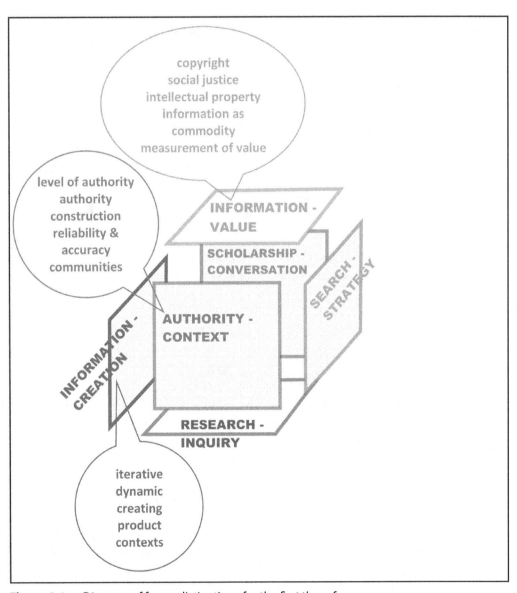

Figure 8.1.   Diagram of frame distinctions for the first three frames.

A More In-Depth Description of the Sample SLOs for a Frame's *Knowledge Practices* and *Dispositions*

The suggested student learning outcomes for each frame are presented in a four-column table (columns 1 and 3) and are adapted from each frame's *Knowledge Practices* (column 2) and its *Dispositions* (column 4). These SLO statements can be used by the librarian and/or faculty member unaltered, or adapted so as to teach and assess information literacy in whatever ways are considered useful. These are particularly useful for establishing a student learning outcome for an assignment and its corresponding rubric.

A More In-Depth Description of the Sample Assignment Handouts

The sample assignment handouts provided for each frame are ready to use or can be adapted as needed, on the ground or online, and are designed to engage students in that frame's information literacy's concepts. Each of the three sample assignment handouts is grounded by at least one information literacy SLO from a *Knowledge Practice* or a *Disposition* of the frame at hand where students demonstrate reaching threshold levels for that SLO through competent completion of the assignment. Also, copies of assignment handouts for this chapter are available in both PDF and Word versions on the book's website, https://implementingtheinformationliteracyframework.wordpress.com/ or https://tinyurl.com/ya6h4vyq, under chapter 8.

A More In-Depth Description of the Sample Rubric Handouts

The sample rubrics are ready to use or can be adapted as needed and are assessment tools created to measure the corresponding sample assignment for each frame. Each rubric handout directly follows its respective assignment handout. The rubric is used to facilitate student accountability, grading, assignment assessment, and information literacy data for institutional reports and for information literacy student experiences based on the *Framework* model. Copies of the chapter's rubric handouts (in PDF and Word versions) are available on the book's website (https://implementingtheinformationliteracyframework .wordpress.com/ or https://tinyurl.com/ya6h4vyq), under chapter 8.

Strategies for Using the Teaching Aids

Before setting the stage for some approaches for implementing information literacy strategies, it's important to note that the four descriptions above correlate with the four information literacy teaching aids for the last three frames of the *Framework*, "Research as Inquiry," "Scholarship as Conversation," and "Searching as Strategic Exploration," covered in the next chapter.

Strategies for using these four teaching aids can be implemented in a number of ways. In order to help visualize different approaches to trying these teaching aids, each frame's four teaching aids are demonstrated by two scenarios. The first scenario describes how a librarian and/or faculty member might prepare to teach a particular frame as guided by the *Framework* model. The second scenario represents the dialog between the same librarian and faculty as they continue to collaborate on how to implement the teaching of the frame by modifying an existing syllabus assignment or creating a new one and then creating an accompanying rubric. The two-part scenarios for each of the three frames

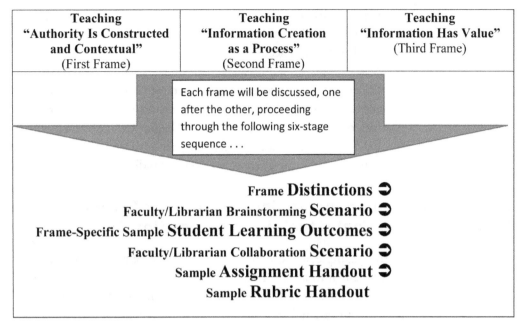

Teaching "Authority Is Constructed and Contextual" (First Frame)	Teaching "Information Creation as a Process" (Second Frame)	Teaching "Information Has Value" (Third Frame)

Each frame will be discussed, one after the other, proceeding through the following six-stage sequence . . .

Frame **Distinctions** ⮌

Faculty/Librarian Brainstorming **Scenario** ⮌

Frame-Specific Sample **Student Learning Outcomes** ⮌

Faculty/Librarian Collaboration **Scenario** ⮌

Sample **Assignment Handout** ⮌

Sample **Rubric Handout**

Figure 8.2. Structure for the rest of chapter 8.

covered in this chapter also set the backstories for each sample assignment handout and corresponding sample rubric handout.

What follows are the aforementioned four teaching aids applied to the first three frames of the *Framework*: "Authority Is Constructed and Contextual," "Information Creation as a Process," and "Information Has Value" (see figure 8.2). As mentioned, chapter 9 will cover the last three frames ("Research as Inquiry," "Scholarship as Conversation," and "Searching as Strategic Exploration") with the same teaching aids for each frame.

Teaching the Frame "Authority Is Constructed and Contextual"

Distinctions Found in the Frame "Authority Is Constructed and Contextual"

Of the six frames, classroom faculty may notice that the first one, "Authority Is Constructed and Contextual" (ACRL, 2015), is most like the questioning and application of critical thinking to the authenticity of information, a common theme in higher education and *habits of mind* skills (Costa and Kallick, 2000). Librarians and some classroom faculty may also note the similarities between this frame's distinctions and the third competency from the now rescinded *2000 Standards*, which was "Evaluate Information and Its Sources Critically" (ACRL, 2000). For a detailed depiction of this and other similarities between the 2000 *Standards* and the 2015 *Framework*, see tables 2.2 and 2.3 in chapter 2 and appendix C, "Thematic Coding of the 2000 *Standards* as Found in the 2015 *Framework*."

Unique concepts expressed in this frame, "Authority Is Constructed and Contextual," include (see also figure 8.1):

- authority construction
- communities
- contexts

- information need
- level of authority
- reliability and accuracy.

Experts in the information literacy frame "Authority Is Constructed and Contextual" are viewed as informed skeptics when assessing authority, but open to new, unlikely views. Novices, on the other hand, may need to begin with the basics of this frame, such as publication-level understandings between peer-reviewed and non-peer-reviewed, or reliable versus unreliable authorities, as well understanding what constitutes author qualifications.

Faculty/Librarian Brainstorming Scenario for Teaching "Authority Is Constructed and Contextual" in a Composition Class

In this example, an academic librarian begins a process to adapt a current composition assignment into an information literacy student experience by contacting a classroom faculty member she's known over the years in one of her library faculty liaison areas, the department of English. And the instructor teaches three or four freshmen composition classes every year. In the librarian's initial contact, she explains that she'd like to meet with him to talk about information literacy and what ideas they can come up with together to possibly modify one assignment in his freshmen composition course to create a measurable information literacy element. The librarian provides, for his use, a copy of this book and a copy of the *Framework for Information Literacy for Higher Education* in advance of their meeting.

They meet the next week in his office. They start their time by sharing what each found in comparing the syllabus with the frame descriptions and their *Knowledge Practices* and *Dispositions* from the *Framework* document. Both had come to a decision that an assignment asking students to find three peer-reviewed, scholarly articles on their individual topics seemed to fit best with the frame "Authority Is Constructed and Contextual."

They then compare notes and find a few links between the freshmen composition assignment and this frame's description [words within quotation marks are from the *Framework* document]: Students need to understand that a) in the academic setting of composition, the "authority construction" of a peer-reviewed journal generally is considered more advanced and scholarly than that of a non-peer-reviewed article, b) "information need" is not just the three relevant articles but also each student reaching a certain threshold of critical thinking to effectively search and evaluate, and c) "information context" is not merely fulfilling an assignment for a freshmen composition class but also crossing intellectual thresholds to understand any authority, expertise, and credibility issue in any context, whether peer-reviewed or not (ACRL, 2015).

The librarian and class instructor then turn to the teaching aids for the frame "Authority Is Constructed and Contextual" in the book. They discover that their decision to use this frame is further strengthened by a number of common ideas between the assignment and the distinctions found in the frame "Authority Is Constructed and Contextual." In reviewing the frame's distinctions (see figure 8.1), they note the following common associations with the assignment and this frame: (a) students need to reach a certain threshold of critical thinking in order to determine if an article seems deficient in "reliability and accuracy," (b) students need to understand the "communities" that created the information as well as the "communities" in which the information *they* create will be used, and (c) students need to develop their own criteria for evaluating "reliability and accuracy" of authors and sources (ACRL, 2015). (The words in quotations are in figure 8.1 for the frame "Authority Is Constructed and Contextual.") The two colleagues agree that some of the concepts are slightly beyond a freshmen level and may be more appropriate for upperclassmen. With this in mind, the faculty member makes a note to himself to add a few pieces of explanation to his lecture as needed.

Creating an SLO for Teaching the Frame "Authority Is Constructed and Contextual"

The librarian and faculty next determine at least one SLO that will be the guiding foundation for both modifying the class assignment and for crafting a grading rubric for the assignment. To help with this process, they scan through this frame's sample SLOs for *Knowledge Practices* and *Dispositions* detailed in the book (see table 8.2).

They eventually agree on the frame's third *Knowledge Practice* SLO, "Identify known authorities (people, publications, etc.) in a specific topic and search for and identify any evidence that those authorities are questioned in their expert role or are validated in their expert role" (ACRL, 2015). Together they change the SLO slightly to work better with the modified assignment: "Information literacy learners are able to identify known authorities (people, publications, etc.) in any given topic and search for and identify evidence that questions their expertise and/or validates their expertise." The faculty member takes what he has learned to create a short assignment handout that still addresses the original assignment and incorporates the ideas in the chosen SLO. He and the librarian set a time to meet in a week to finalize the assignment and to look at the book's sample rubric as a possible grading tool.

Faculty/Librarian Collaboration Scenario for Teaching "Authority Is Constructed and Contextual" to Modify an Assignment and Build a Rubric

The same librarian and the composition class faculty meet up again, this time in one of the library's small group study rooms. The following conversation unfolds.

Librarian: Nice to see you again. How are your writing classes going?

Faculty: They're all going a little better than I expected. I'm making good use of the Writing Center for those that struggle. And that YouTube library tutorial you created last year is being used by about half the students. So, I have the sample assignment handout from the book and made some changes to make it a better fit for my class.

Librarian: Great! What are they?

Faculty: Well, I think it needs to start out with the student learning outcome at the top. That way students know the big picture and what they will likely be graded by. Let's see, that would be: "Student learning outcome: Information literacy learners are able to identify known authorities (people, publications, etc.) in any given topic and search for and identify evidence that questions their expertise and/or validates their expertise."

Librarian: Yes, that's an easy fix. What else?

Faculty: I see that the core of the assignment puts students in groups of two or three and then they work together through three research steps. But it doesn't give details.

Librarian: I noticed that, too. How about this: "In class, after students individually fill in their topic, they are instructed to work in their group to first, go to *Wikipedia*, and second, Google Scholar, then third, log in to one of our library databases, as they help one another with each other's topic at each step." Research has found that students typically

Table 8.2. The Frame "Authority Is Constructed and Contextual" Sample SLOs Adapted from Its *Knowledge Practices* and *Dispositions*

AUTHORITY IS CONSTRUCTED AND CONTEXTUAL			
KNOWLEDGE PRACTICES SLOS INFORMATION LITERACY LEARNERS ARE ABLE TO . . .	**KNOWLEDGE PRACTICES** INFORMATION LITERACY LEARNERS ARE ABLE TO . . .	**DISPOSITIONS SLOS** INFORMATION LITERACY LEARNERS ARE ABLE TO . . .	**DISPOSITIONS** INFORMATION LITERACY LEARNERS ARE ABLE TO . . .
1. Use criteria to discriminate among a range of scholarship authorities (trade magazine, popular blog, journal with a high impact number) in a given discipline, with explicit examples	Define different types of authority, such as subject expertise (e.g., scholarship), societal position (e.g., public office or title), or special experience (e.g., participating in a historic event)	1. In a literature review narrative, discuss a topic from the perspective of the most influential authorities, showing where they agree and where they disagree and why	Develop and maintain an open mind when encountering varied and sometimes conflicting perspectives
2. Determine criteria that can authenticate a source as being true, questionable, or false, and explain how those criteria might be used differently under different contexts	Use research tools and indicators of authority to determine the credibility of sources, understanding the elements that might temper this credibility	2. Discover and articulate criteria or factors that give an expert or organization the power and authority to speak into a particular controversy or topic, including unconventional ones (e.g., a recognized financial expert who doesn't have a finance degree)	Motivate themselves to find authoritative sources, recognizing that authority may be conferred or manifested in unexpected ways
3. Identify known authorities (people, publications, etc.) in any given topic and search for and identify evidence that questions their expertise and validates their expertise	Understand that many disciplines have acknowledged authorities in the sense of well-known scholars and publications that are widely considered "standard," and yet, even in those situations, some scholars would challenge the authority of those sources	3. Clearly identify their preconceived perspectives or biases on the topic at hand and recognize how their biases changed or didn't change after studying an issue	Develop awareness of the importance of assessing content with a skeptical stance and with a self-awareness of their own biases and worldview

4. On a scale of formal to informal, determine where on the scale influential sources (authors, organizations, schools of thought, publications) for a topic are positioned and demonstrate an understanding of the nature and impact of the channels by which those sources are delivered (print, online, social media, etc.)	Recognize that authoritative content may be packaged formally or informally and may include sources of all media types	4. Describe how information, including news, is traditionally gathered and communicated, and how that process differs for other newer technologies (blogs, social media), focusing on shared and diverse perspectives and gathered information's criteria for accuracy, evidence, and ethics	Question traditional notions of granting authority and recognize the value of diverse ideas and worldviews
5. Demonstrate evidence in assignments or other information products, their own authoritative voice when speaking into a particular subject and of their adherence to ethical standards such as accuracy, reliability, respect, and participation	Acknowledge that they are developing their own authoritative voices in a particular area and recognize the responsibilities this entails, including seeking accuracy and reliability, respecting intellectual property, and participating in communities of practice	5. Evaluate a current issue from a stance different from their own, discerning in the case of each side WHO is not being represented and WHAT is not being asked, and HOW valid supporting evidence is; effectively seek out alternative perspectives and reevaluate and adjust a stance based on new and valid evidence	Are conscious that maintaining these attitudes and actions requires frequent self-evaluation
6. Construct a timeline of events, publications, and names that contributed to a given current topic, showing how they interact with one another	Understand the increasingly social nature of the information ecosystem where authorities actively connect with one another and sources develop over time		

These *Knowledge Practices and Dispositions* originate from the frame "Authority Is Constructed and Contextual" in the *Framework for Information Literacy for Higher Education* (ACRL, 2015). Used with permission from the American Library Association.

start with *Wikipedia* and Google to gain general information about their topic before moving on to suggested library resources (Lawrence, 2015). How's that?

Faculty: Yes, that's much clearer. Also, in that book you gave me, one of the core ideas about the *Framework* is allowing students opportunities to reflect. I'd like to include a reflection component to the assignment.

Librarian: Yes, that's one of the recommendations of the *Framework* and I think that would be ideal. Do you have a threaded discussion site in mind?

Faculty: Sure, I think I'll use Padlet for discussions where they can post their reflections and general comments. It's free and I've used it with my other classes.

Librarian: Sounds good. Have you been able to look at the book's sample rubric? I noticed it works well with Bloom's Taxonomy: (1) Group—Understanding, find up to four authorities on student's topic from *Wikipedia*; (2) Group—Applying, finding two more additional insights using Google Scholar; and (3) Group—Creating, putting together citations in correct style. Does that work for your class?

Faculty: Yes, grading them as a group is fine; those in each group would get the same grade. With the added threaded discussions, I want to include individual students sharing clear ideas that relate to the frame and one more item for the rubric related to something about students reflecting on the assignment as a whole.

Librarian: OK, all you need to do is add those ideas to the rubric and you are ready to go.

Faculty: Great. I can't wait to try this out in class!

Creating the "Authority Is Constructed and Contextual" Assignment and Rubric

For the librarian and faculty's collaborative results in creating the assignment and rubric, see the two-page "'Authority Is Constructed and Contextual' Assignment Handout for a Composition Class" and the "'Authority Is Constructed and Contextual' Rubric Handout for a Composition Class." These teaching aids are designed to be used as is or can be adapted as needed for either online or on-the-ground instruction. Copies of the two-page assignment and rubric documents, in a PDF and a Word version, are available on the book's website (https://implementingtheinformationliteracyframework.wordpress.com/ or https://tinyurl.com/ya6h4vyq) under chapter 8.

"AUTHORITY IS CONSTRUCTED AND CONTEXTUAL"
ASSIGNMENT HANDOUT FOR A COMPOSITION CLASS

Name: _____ Group: _____ Date: _____

Student Learning Outcome: Information literacy learners are able to identify known authorities (people, publications, etc.) in any given topic and search for and identify evidence that questions their expertise and/or validates their expertise.

Exercise 1: Write your topic here _____
In a group of two or three, first, go to *Wikipedia* and together help search your topics. List up to four persons, theories, publications, etc., that appear to be authorities for *your* topic.

-
-
-

Second, as a group, go to Google Scholar (GS, scholar.google.com) and help each other search your topics. Tip: Use quotation marks around words needing to be together (examples: "dramatic irony" "feminist criticism"). Add to your GS search the last name of an apparent authority on your topic found in *Wikipedia*. List two things discovered as further insights on *your* topic.

-
-
-

Third, as a group, go to the library's main page. In the single search box type the same search used in GS (your topic plus the last name of an apparent authority). Narrow your search results by date, by English, and by peer-reviewed scholarly journals. In the citation style for the class (APA, MLA, Chicago, etc.) accurately list the citations from three articles you've found on your topic. Download the full text of each of the three articles on your computer. If you are unable to locate the full text of an article, contact a librarian for help.

-
-
-

Exercise 2: Sign up for Padlet (http://padlet.com). You can work alone or in a group.
Study the description for frame "Authority Is Constructed and Contextual" listed on this handout or go to https://tinyurl.com/frameworkauthority. Using this frame's description like a lens, evaluate the information you discovered in Exercise 1 by the following prompts using Padlet for your comments/reflections.

- Describe your process in Exercise 1. Include what your group found at each of the three steps and maybe how you felt about your progress or lack of progress on *your* topic.
- Look at the full text of the three articles found in Exercise 1. First, just read the literature review for each article, usually found at the article's beginning. Regarding your topic, analyze similarities and differences found by these possible authorities and post your findings in Padlet. Include common themes, earliest thoughts on the topic, chronological progress of the topic, and most current studies on the subject.
- Second, read/scan the full articles and look for evidence that any authorities on the topic are disputed; explain why. Include in your postings disputed theories or theorists, the less dominant schools of thought, controversies, and majority and minority opinions.
- In Padlet, comment on at least three other classmates' postings.

"AUTHORITY IS CONSTRUCTED AND CONTEXTUAL" ASSIGNMENT HANDOUT FOR A COMPOSITION CLASS (CONTINUED)

Information resources reflect their creators' expertise and credibility and are evaluated based on the information need and the context in which the information will be used. Authority is constructed in that various communities may recognize different types of authority. It is contextual in that the information need may help to determine the level of authority required.

Experts understand that authority is a type of influence recognized or exerted within a community. Experts view authority with an attitude of informed skepticism and an openness to new perspectives, additional voices, and changes in schools of thought. Experts understand the need to determine the validity of the information created by different authorities and to acknowledge biases that privilege some sources of authority over others, especially in terms of others' worldviews, gender, sexual orientation, and cultural orientations. An understanding of this concept enables novice learners to critically examine all evidence—be it a short blog post or a peer-reviewed conference proceeding—and to ask relevant questions about origins, context, and suitability for the current information need. Thus, novice learners come to respect the expertise that authority represents while remaining skeptical of the systems that have elevated that authority and the information created by it. Experts know how to seek authoritative voices but also recognize that unlikely voices can be authoritative, depending on need. Novice learners may need to rely on basic indicators of authority, such as type of publication or author credentials, where experts recognize schools of thought or discipline-specific paradigms.

"AUTHORITY IS CONSTRUCTED AND CONTEXTUAL"
RUBRIC HANDOUT FOR A COMPOSITION CLASS

Name: _____ Group: _____ Date: _____

Student Learning Outcome: Information literacy learners are able to identify known authorities (people, publications, etc.) in any given topic and search for and identify evidence that questions their expertise and validates their expertise.

Standards of Evaluation	Accomplished	Proficient	Developing	Novice
GROUP: UNDERSTANDING **Summarize person, theory, publication authorities**	Summarized four or more topic authorities	Strong in three topic authorities	Strong in two topic authorities	Strong in one or none
Score:	15–20	10–14	5–9	0–4
GROUP: APPLYING **Applying *Wikipedia* knowledge to identify more in Google Scholar**	Identified two or more insights into the topic that were strong	Strong in two of listed areas	Strong in one of listed areas	Strong in none of the listed areas
Score:	15–20	10–14	5–9	0–4
GROUP: CREATING **Creating three citations in the correct style**	Created three or more accurate citations in the correct style	Created two accurate citations	Created one accurate citation	Created none
Score:	15–20	10–14	5–9	0–4
INDIVIDUAL: CREATING POSTS IN PADLET **Number and quality**	More than three clear, thoughtful concepts found in frame	Three clear, thoughtful concepts found in frame	Less than three remarks about concepts found in frame	No remarks about concepts in frame
Score:	15–20	10–14	5–9	0–4
INDIVIDUAL: APPLYING **Reflective in Padlet**	Clearly stated one important part of the lesson	Stated one important part but not clearly	Stated minor importance	Missed stating any important parts
Score:	15–20	10–14	5–9	0–4
Total Score: /100				
Comments:				

⊚ Teaching the Frame "Information Creation as a Process"

Distinctions Found in the Frame "Information Creation as a Process"

Among the six frames, classroom faculty may notice that this frame, "Information Creation as a Process" (ACRL, 2015), is most like the *habits of mind* concepts of flexible thinking and open-mindedness to changing perspectives, which involves continuous learning and processing. Librarians and some classroom faculty may likely see similarities between this frame and the fourth competency in the 2000 *Standards* "Use Information Effectively to Accomplish a Specific Purpose" (ACRL, 2000). For a detailed depiction of this and other similarities between the *Standards* and the *Framework*, see tables 2.2 and 2.3 in chapter 2 as well as appendix C, "Thematic Coding of the 2000 *Standards* as Found in the 2015 *Framework*."

Unique concepts expressed in this frame, "Information Creation as a Process," include (see also figure 8.1):

- context-sensitive value
- creating
- dynamic
- information product
- iterative.

Experts on ideas found in "Information Creation as Process" look beyond possible formats of end products when selecting sources in the creation process and focus on underlying causes of the creation process to help them evaluate information usefulness. On the other hand, when novice learners begin to appreciate the creation process, it helps them better connect information needs with information products.

Faculty/Librarian Brainstorming Scenario Teaching "Information Creation as a Process" in an Advanced Mathematics Class

A classroom faculty member and the department's liaison librarian are reading parts of the book *Framework for Information Literacy for Higher Education* together and discussing it as their way to help implement information literacy within their campus culture. Here's a conversation over one of their regular book discussion lunch meetings.

Faculty: I read ahead in chapter 8 last night and a light bulb came on as I looked through the details for the information literacy frame "Information Creation as a Process" and its sample assignment.

Librarian: Sounds interesting. What are you thinking?

Faculty: One of the classes I teach next term is an advanced course in mathematics. As you know, I just wasn't sure information literacy would ever work for any of my courses, let alone this one. But reading the book, especially this part, has changed my mind.

Librarian: How so?

Faculty: Let's look at the assignment together—here, it's on this page [see the "'Information Creation as a Process' Assignment Handout for an Advanced Math Class" on page 153]. I like that it involves students creating their own rubric to evaluate parts of a scholarly article. In the past, I have had students read and report on articles but nothing this engaging or from an information literacy perspective.

   Librarian: Looks like the idea to create the rubric in the assignment comes from one of the sample *Disposition* student learning outcomes of that frame [see table 8.3]. I see that one exercise in the assignment has students writing three article citations in the correct style. Is that measured in the assignment's rubric? [See "Information Creation as a Process" Rubric Handout for an Advanced Math Class on page 154.]

   Faculty: Yes, it certainly is in the rubric and measured as a student group activity and not as individual effort.

   Librarian: Maybe this is something we could collaborate on for your class. If that's the direction you might go, would you be OK if I shared a few tips on searching strategies and correct citation style?

   Faculty: Yes, that's one reason we've been meeting all these weeks, to find ways to collaborate on teaching students information literacy in the classroom! But I want to make sure the rubric that goes with the assignment is clear enough for students to understand, for my grading, and that it provides some data for university accreditation reports. Let's work through this frame and its teaching aids a little deeper and come back next week to finish the rubric.

   Librarian: Works for me!

Creating an SLO for Teaching the Frame "Information Creation as Process"

As with the previous frame ("Authority Is Constructed and Contextual"), the librarian and faculty next need to create at least one SLO to help guide the modification of the class assignment and to craft a grading rubric. To do that, the two scanned through this frame's sample SLOs for *Knowledge Practices* and *Dispositions* detailed in the book (table 8.3).

Faculty/Librarian Collaboration Scenario for Teaching "Information Creation as Process" to Modify an Assignment and Build a Rubric

The same classroom faculty member and department librarian are meeting again over lunch to finalize a new information literacy experience that will be used in a modified advanced mathematics assignment. Let's pick up on their conversation.

   Faculty: Like you said, reading through the first two teaching aids does give some helpful scaffolding to the frame "Information Creation as a Process." Now let's focus on the last aid, the assignment and rubric.

   Librarian: Sure. I've printed off two copies of what we've done so far. Here's one for you.

   Faculty: Thanks. I'm glad there's a student example of a rubric in the assignment. It takes my older assignment of just summarizing three articles on a math topic to a much deeper critical thinking experience. [See "Information Creation as a Process" Assignment Handout for an Advanced Math Class on page 153.]

   Librarian: Speaking of rubrics, let's look at what we have so far in the rubric you'll use to grade students.

   Faculty: Yes, and I have some concerns about why half of the rubric score is focused on the citation style.

Table 8.3. The Frame "Information Creation as a Process" Sample SLOs Adapted from Its *Knowledge Practices* and *Dispositions*

INFORMATION CREATION AS A PROCESS			
KNOWLEDGE PRACTICES SLOS INFORMATION LITERACY LEARNERS ARE ABLE TO . . .	*KNOWLEDGE PRACTICES* INFORMATION LITERACY LEARNERS ARE ABLE TO . . .	*DISPOSITIONS SLOS* INFORMATION LITERACY LEARNERS ARE ABLE TO . . .	*DISPOSITIONS* INFORMATION LITERACY LEARNERS ARE ABLE TO . . .
1. In a comparison of information products (web-based, broadcast, print, etc.), identify and articulate the skills and resources needed in the creation processes of each as well as advantages and disadvantages of each	Articulate the capabilities and constraints of information developed through various creation processes	1. On a given topic, find and retrieve relevant information and, using a rubric, analyze the information based on the process authors took in creating: a) a literature review, b) a methodology, c) results, and d) a conclusion	Are inclined to seek out characteristics of information products that indicate the underlying creation process
2. For any given information need, identify the appropriate information product to meet that need in terms of a) efficiency, b) appropriateness, c) return on investment, and d) shortcomings	Assess the fit between an information product's creation process and a particular information need	2. For any problem, identify and articulate the appropriate steps to create an effective information product to help resolve it	Value the process of matching an information need with an appropriate product
3. For a given discipline, compare and explain similar and not-so-similar aspects of a conventional, older means of producing an end product versus a developing, new means of producing an end product	Articulate the traditional and emerging processes of information creation and dissemination in a particular discipline	3. Recognize and identify the range of formats or modes in the marketplace of ideas used for the creation of new information and articulate which formats are considered an expected or an unexpected source	Accept that the creation of information may begin initially through communicating in a range of formats or modes

4. Identify and describe the perceptions of information receivers of any given information product and, when creating these information, ethically manage these perceptions	Recognize that information may be perceived differently based on the format in which it is packaged	4. In a given discipline, recognize and articulate emerging ideas and points of controversy and reserve judgment until evidence is conclusive	Accept the ambiguity surrounding the potential value of information creation expressed in emerging formats or modes
5. List possible different perceptions found in a static, non-changing format versus a dynamic format, accurately assess the advantages and disadvantages for a given purpose	Recognize the implications of information formats that contain static or dynamic information	5. Identify and ethically utilize appropriate criteria for evaluating validity of information regardless of how information is created or presented; accurately assess validity of information received apart from format	Resist the tendency to equate format with the underlying creation process
6. Accurately assess credibility issues in the creation process of various types of information products and ethically manage these issues in information production	Monitor the value that is placed upon different types of information products in varying contexts	6. Proactively search for, choose, and use effectively and ethically appropriate methods of information dissemination for a given purpose and articulate the rationale for the choice	Understand that different methods of information dissemination with different purposes are available for their use
7. Based on current trends in a given discipline, identify, access, and ethically use emerging forms of information products	Transfer knowledge of capabilities and constraints to new types of information products		
8. Given any scenario with any perspective, anticipate and ethically manage the possible outcomes and messages that could be expressed that were (a) intended or expected, or (b) that were not intended or expected	Develop, in their own creation processes, an understanding that their choices impact the purposes for which the information product will be used and the message it conveys		

Librarian: Oh, that was my way of creating a place marker until a few more standards for evaluation are added. So far there are two group indicators, one for finding quality articles and one, as you've noted, for citation style. And a third one is measuring students' threaded discussion postings.

Faculty: Sure, that's fine. So, let's add something that grades their level of creating their own rubric with its four parts and detailed criteria. I like that the students' quality of posts is now graded. I don't think we do enough reflection in our program. Also, I'd like to add turning in the assignment on time. I don't know what it is, but that's become a problem lately.

Librarian: I wouldn't have thought to add timeliness. Since there are five criteria, are you going to give each 20 points?

Faculty: Hmm, 20 points seems like a lot for handing something in on time. But like I said, it's been such an issue. So, yes, for this first run, each criterion will have the same points. How do these scores help with data for other university assessment needs?

Librarian: That's easy. The librarians, in discussions with other faculty, have come up with our campus information literacy model as measuring only three pieces of data: group work for finding relevant resources, group work on creating correct citations, and individual work on quality postings. And your assignment rubric measures all three!

Faculty: That makes me feel better. Let's keep reading the book and meeting and see if another information literacy piece can be added to another class.

Librarian: I'm good with that. See you next week.

Finalizing the "Information Creation as Process" Assignment and Rubric

The faculty member and librarian will meet one more time to finalize the assignment and rubric handouts. See the results in the "Information Creation as a Process' Assignment Handout for an Advanced Math Class" and "'Information Creation as a Process' Rubric Handout for an Advanced Math Class." These teaching aids are designed to be used as is or adapted as needed for either online or on-the-ground instruction. Copies of the assignment and rubric documents, in a PDF and a Word version, are available on the book's website (https://implementingtheinformationliteracyframework.wordpress.com/ or https://tinyurl.com/ya6h4vyq) under chapter 8.

"INFORMATION CREATION AS A PROCESS"
ASSIGNMENT HANDOUT FOR AN ADVANCED MATH CLASS

Name: _____ Group: _____ Date: _____

Student Learning Outcome: Information literacy learners are able to, on a given topic, find and retrieve relevant information and, using a rubric, analyze the information based on the process authors took in creating: a) a literature review, b) a methodology, c) results, and d) a conclusion.

Assignment:

Exercise 1: Write your topic here _____
For all of exercise 1, in a group of two or three, help one another find three current, scholarly, full-text articles on your topic by typing your topics, one at a time, in the single search box found on the library's main web page or use a database suggested by the professor. Then help one another write three article citations in the correct style (APA, MLA, etc.) and add the citations below. Visit a librarian if full text does not appear available.

-
-
-

Exercise 2: On your own, create one rubric, like the example below, to analyze each of your article's *process in creating*: (a) literature review, (b) methodology, (c) results, and (d) conclusion. Create detailed criteria to measure these four parts under each column heading. For other ideas, search for *literature review rubrics* on the Internet.

Standards of Evaluation	Strongly Evident	Evident	Somewhat Evident	Not Evident
LITERATURE REVIEW Quality of process	Topic's background in-depth, high quality studies cited	Topic's background adequate, most studies cited are quality	Topic's background lacks important studies, some studies from non-scholarly sources	Background coverage questionable, low-quality studies cited
METHODOLOGY Quality of process	Research design logical and clear, instrument explained well	Research design is fine, instrument is OK	Research design has problems, instrument needs work	Research design not clear or logical, no instrument
RESULTS	Etc.			
CONCLUSION	Etc.			
Comments:				

Exercise 3: In threaded discussions, post a copy of your rubric and create at least three postings, sharing reflections on any part of this assignment. Hand in this form and your individual three rubric assessments.

"INFORMATION CREATION AS A PROCESS"
RUBRIC HANDOUT FOR AN ADVANCED MATH CLASS

Name: _____ Group: _____ Date: _____

Student Learning Outcome: Information literacy learners are able to, on a given topic, find and retrieve relevant information and, using a rubric, analyze the information based on the process authors took in creating: a) a literature review, b) a methodology, c) results, and d) a conclusion.

Standards of Evaluation	Accomplished	Proficient	Developing	Novice
GROUP: ANALYZING Three scholarly articles	Three a) topic relevant, b) current, c) scholarly	Lacking in one of the three articles in a), b), and c)	Lacking in two of the three articles in a), b), and c)	Lacking all three of the articles in a), b), and c)
Score:	15–20	10–14	5–9	0–4
GROUP: APPLYING Citations accuracy and completeness	All three citations were accurate and complete	Two of the three citations were accurate and complete	One of the three citations was accurate and complete	None of the three citations were accurate and complete
Score:	15–20	10–14	5–9	0–4
INDIVIDUAL: CREATING Level of creating one rubric with four parts and detailed criteria	Created a rubric with four parts and all column boxes with detailed descriptions	Rubric with three parts and filled in most column boxes with detailed descriptions	Rubric with two parts and filled in some column boxes with detailed descriptions	Rubric with one or no parts and most column boxes did not have detailed descriptions
Score:	15–20	10–14	5–9	0–4
INDIVIDUAL: CREATING POSTS IN THREADED DISCUSSIONS Number and quality	Posted rubric and more than two thoughtful reflections related to the assignment	Posted rubric and more than one thoughtful reflection related to the assignment	Posted rubric and only one thoughtful reflection related to the assignment	Posted no rubric and no reflections
Score:	15–20	10–14	5–9	0–4
INDIVIDUAL: Turned in full assignment in timely manner with thoughtful assessments	Handout completely filled out with one rubric assessing three articles, on time	Handout with one rubric thoughtfully assessing two articles OR handout with three articles but late	Handout with one rubric thoughtfully assessing one article, on time OR at least two articles assessed but late	Turned in late and nothing completely filled out
Score:	15–20	10–14	5–9	0–4
Total Score: /100				
Comments:				

Reproduced from *Implementing the Information Literacy Framework: A Practical Guide for Librarians* by Dave Harmeyer and Janice J. Baskin. © 2018 Rowman & Littlefield Publishers.

ⓖ Teaching the Frame "Information Has Value"

Distinctions Found in the Frame "Information Has Value"

Among the six frames, classroom faculty may notice that the frame "Information Has Value" (ACRL, 2015) is most like the higher education concepts of ethical decision-making, moral choices, social justice sensitivity, and plagiarism prevention. Librarians and some classroom faculty may likely see similarities between this frame and the fifth or last competency in the 2000 *Standards*: "Understand the economic, legal, and social issues surrounding the use of information, and access and use information ethically and legally" (ACRL, 2000). For a detailed depiction of this and other similarities between the *Standards* and the *Framework*, see tables 2.2 and 2.3 in chapter 2 as well as appendix C.

Unique concepts expressed in this frame, "Information Has Value," include (see also figure 8.1):

- copyright
- fair use
- information as commodity
- measurements of value
- social justice.

Experts on ideas found in "Information Has Value" understand that value can be controlled by power that marginalizes certain views and privileges others and recognize that responsible choices may include complying with practices or challenging them. Novice learners, on the other hand, may find it hard to understand why they must comply with copyright laws in a world of seemingly unlimited "free" information.

Faculty/Librarian Brainstorming Scenario for Teaching "Information Has Value" in a Culminating Project (e.g., Senior Capstone, Master's Thesis, or Dissertation)

The library's information literacy committee, comprised of classroom faculty, librarians, and an administrator, has been using the book *Framework for Information Literacy for Higher Education* to gain ideas for implementing a campus-wide information literacy program. The committee's strategy involves assessing information literacy at three levels of the curriculum: freshman seminars, discipline-specific writing II courses, and culminating projects like a capstone, master's thesis, or dissertation. The following is a conversation among the members during a meeting.

Committee Chair: Our three-year, cyclical information literacy program will be ending its second year in a few weeks and already we have enough Writing II course data to create benchmarks and a narrative. Now we need to plan for the third year of the cycle as we look to the fall. What are some ideas?

Psychology Faculty: I'd like to suggest we take all courses starting in the fall that cover the beginning of culminating projects, like capstones, theses, and dissertations, and take a random, statistically relevant sample of all and include one assignment in each project that measures one of the six frames. The large numbers of these classes don't justify measuring every one of them at this time.

Librarian 1: That sounds like a great idea and it would clearly measure one of the three curricular levels of our information literacy program, the students' final projects. I also think it's useful to measure one frame, perhaps adapting one of the sample assignments and its rubric mentioned in chapters 8 and 9 of the book.

Nursing Faculty: I've been looking over the six information literacy frames and the one for "Information Has Value" seems to be a good fit for our master's and doctoral students. I think it will motivate students at the onset to develop their topics and thesis statements at a deeper level than they typically do.

Librarian 2: And I think it would certainly be useful for undergraduate capstone seniors.

Business Faculty: I agree. A better senior capstone will also help them move on to graduate school.

Committee Chair: OK, great. Would anyone like to make a motion?

Psychology Faculty: I move that we take a sample of fall culminating project syllabi that cover how to select a topic and implement the sample assignment and rubric for the frame "Information Has Value" into those courses.

Librarian 2: I second.

Committee Chair: Any discussion? Hearing none, all those in favor of this motion say aye. [10 ayes were heard.] And noes? [None were heard.] Great, the motion passes unanimously. Thanks everyone, our next meeting is in two weeks. Let's all finish reading chapter 10 in the book. And I'll look into getting a list of all courses teaching capstones, theses, and dissertations. Meeting adjourned.

Creating an SLO for Teaching "Information Has Value"

Many weeks later as committee members worked through a selection of capstones, theses, and dissertation course syllabi, they followed a simple formula to come up with integration of information literacy into these courses. First, they had a list of the six frames and their definitions in front of them as they searched each syllabus for a component within one of the course assignments that would be a good fit with one of the six frames. Many saw the merits of "Information Has Value" fitting with what was common across all culminating experiences: the assignment of determining an appropriate topic. After additional collaboration among faculty members and librarians, the group decided to select the SLO from the frame's *Knowledge Practices*, "Demonstrate the difference between their ideas and those of others by citing others' intellectual property accurately and completely" (table 8.4).

Faculty/Librarian Collaboration Scenario for Teaching "Information Has Value" to Modify an Assignment and Build a Rubric

The campus-wide information literacy committee continued their discussion to finalize the implementation of an information literacy experience for students at the beginning of their culminating projects, including senior capstones, master's theses, and dissertations. We sit in on the finishing comments on the initiative.

Committee Chair: Lastly, there is a motion on the floor to make sure that the rubric contains explicit language that students are to include library-based subject headings in their deliverable, namely the concept map. Is there any further discussion?

Higher Education Faculty: Far be it from me to dispute our librarian colleagues, but the use of subject headings has passed its usefulness, what with the algorithms used in today's search engines.

Librarian 1: That may be true in part. I'd suggest you try your hand at doing what would be, in essence, a keyword search in any database with any common subject matter. Then compare those results with one that includes the use of subject headings after properly accessing the database's thesaurus. The difference, especially for culminating research, will trump keyword attempts.

Psychology Faculty: I agree for the graduate level, especially for dissertations, where the quality of the research is more critical. It could mean the difference between getting published or not. Can we amend it to limit it to graduate courses, when their information literacy levels are higher? I think underclassmen would feel overwhelmed. And librarians would be as well, since they are going to be the ones doing most of the instruction for undergraduate classes. Let's see how it goes at the graduate level.

Business Faculty: That sounds good to me. We can always revisit it later. I'd like to amend the motion to include subject headings for the rubrics for graduate students.

Psychology Faculty: I second that.

Committee Chair: Any further discussion? Any? Seeing none, we will now vote. Those in favor of including a subject heading component to the assignment and the rubric for graduate students, please say aye. [seven ayes] Those opposed? [two noes] The motion passes. Meeting adjourned.

Finalizing the "Information Has Value" Assignment and Rubric

The graduate faculty who teach culminating projects finalize their assignments and rubrics to include the subject heading component in their courses. See the results in the "'Information Has Value' Assignment Handout for a Culminating Project" as well as the "'Information Has Value' Rubric Handout for a Culminating Project." Copies of the assignment and rubric documents, in a PDF and a Word version, are available on the book's website (https://implementingtheinformationliteracyframework.wordpress.com/ or https://tinyurl.com/ya6h4vyq) under chapter 8.

Table 8.4. The Frame "Information Has Value" Sample SLOs Adapted from Its *Knowledge Practices* and *Dispositions*

		INFORMATION HAS VALUE	
KNOWLEDGE PRACTICES SLOS INFORMATION LITERACY LEARNERS ARE ABLE TO . . .	*KNOWLEDGE PRACTICES* INFORMATION LITERACY LEARNERS ARE ABLE TO . . .	*DISPOSITIONS SLOS* INFORMATION LITERACY LEARNERS ARE ABLE TO . . .	*DISPOSITIONS* INFORMATION LITERACY LEARNERS ARE ABLE TO . . .
1. Demonstrate the difference between their ideas and those of others by citing others' intellectual property accurately and completely	Give credit to the original ideas of others through proper attribution and citation	1. Demonstrate knowledge of and evidence of adherence to appropriate ethical standards for respecting the intellectual property of others	Respect the original ideas of others
2. Demonstrate knowledge of consequences of violating copyright or fair use in a given context and information format	Understand that intellectual property is a legal and social construct that varies by culture	2. For any significant idea, concept, or invention, discover the source of creation and create a timeline leading up to that invention, etc., including names, places, influential works that made it possible	Value the skills, time, and effort needed to produce knowledge
3. Articulate the purpose and distinguishing characteristics of copyright, fair use, open access, and public domain	Articulate the purpose and distinguishing characteristics of copyright, fair use, open access, and the public domain	3. Demonstrate through creating appropriate information product their participation in and contributions to a chosen discipline or interest	See themselves as contributors to the information marketplace rather than only consumers of it
4. In any given information context, identify and articulate any evidence that either marginalizes or privileges a group in light of production and dissemination of information; demonstrate effective and ethical use of information to minimize these effects	Understand how and why some individuals or groups of individuals may be underrepresented or systematically marginalized within the systems that produce and disseminate information	4. Accurately assess and describe their level of information privilege and demonstrate responsibility and fairness to all groups when using and producing information	Are inclined to examine their own information privilege

		**		**	
5. Articulate what "digital divide" means for their community, workplace, or information context generally, and propose ways to mitigate this situation	Recognize issues of access or lack of access to information sources	**		**	
6. Describe advantages and disadvantages of using any given publishing source; articulate a valid rationale for choosing a specific publishing source and context for delivery	Decide where and how their information is published	**		**	
7. Understand and describe the consequences of personal information being shared in any given online medium; understand and demonstrate appropriate safeguards when choosing to share online	Understand how the commodification (definition: to turn into a commodity; make commercial) of their personal information and online interactions affects the information they receive and the information they produce or disseminate online	**		**	
8. On a spectrum of "never/high risk to privacy" on one side and "always/low risk to privacy" on the other side, on that scale place all types of their personal information they would provide online and why (examples: name, address, credit card information, etc.)	Make informed choices regarding their online actions in full awareness of issues related to privacy and the commodification of personal information	**		**	

**These boxes are intentionally left blank because here are eight *Knowledge Practices*, but only four *Dispositions*.

These *Knowledge Practices* and *Dispositions* originate from the frame "Information Has Value" in the *Framework for Information Literacy for Higher Education* (ACRL, 2015). Used with permission from the American Library Association.

"INFORMATION HAS VALUE" ASSIGNMENT HANDOUT FOR A CULMINATING PROJECT

Name: _____ Group: _____ Date: _____

Student Learning Outcome: Information literacy learners are able to demonstrate the difference between *their* ideas and those of *others* by citing others' intellectual property accurately and completely.

Exercise 1: Write your topic here _____
For all of Exercise 1, in a group of three to five, each student explains his or her topic in one to two minutes. Determine what terms (one to four concepts) expresses your topic best, write it on a sticky Post-it note, and place it on a flat surface (wall, easel, poster board) in the center of what will be your concept map. For three to five minutes, the group brainstorms ideas that complement, narrow, broaden, or enrich your topic. As ideas come up, write them on other sticky notes and place these in proximity, logically to the topic. When done, take a picture on a phone, or hand copy the map on the back of this page. Repeat this process for each person. If helpful, change up your final map.

Exercise 2: Seek the help of a reference librarian. Find at least one appropriate database for your topic. Inside the database, a) click on the "Thesaurus" or "Subject Terms" link (usually top left), b) find your topic as its SUBJECT TERM/S, and c) see how other SUBJECT TERMS are related to it (broader terms, narrower terms, related terms, and used for). Add any relevant concepts to your concept map. In this database, search for your topic using the SUBJECT TERMS found in the thesaurus. Narrow results by date, scholarly, peer-reviewed, or other criteria. Find four relevant articles/sources. List them accurately in correct citation style (APA, MLA, or Chicago):

-
-
-
-

Exercise 3: Freehand or use an online tool (try bubbl.us) to create your concept map. Example:

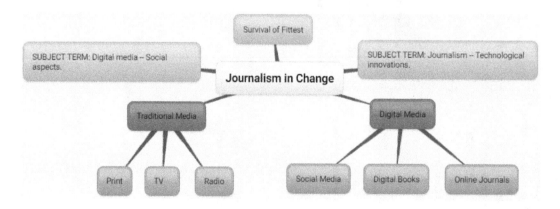

Exercise 4: In class threaded discussions, post a copy of your concept map and create at least three postings reflecting on any part of this assignment. Hand in this worksheet and concept map.

"INFORMATION HAS VALUE" RUBRIC HANDOUT FOR A CULMINATING PROJECT

Name: _____ Group: _____ Date: _____

Student Learning Outcome: Information literacy learners are able to demonstrate the difference between *their* ideas and those of *others* by citing others' intellectual property accurately and completely.

Standards of Evaluation	Accomplished	Proficient	Developing	Novice
GROUP: CREATING Group helped brainstorm useful ideas for the concept map	All concepts are a) topically relevant, b) current, c) scholarly	Lacking in one of the three categories: a), b), or c)	Lacking in two of the three categories: a), b), or c)	Lacking in all three categories: a), b), and c)
Score:	15–20	10–14	5–9	0–4
INDIVIDUAL: CREATING The student's concept map	Concept map: a) thoughtful, b) logical, c) at least one SUBJECT TERM	Lacking in one of the three categories: a), b), or c)	Lacking in two of the three categories: a), b), or c)	Lacking in all three categories: a), b), and c)
Score:	15–20	10–14	5–9	0–4
INDIVIDUAL: EVALUATING Finding and accessing 4 appropriate, quality articles/sources	All four articles appear to be a) topically relevant, b) current, and c) scholarly	Lacking in one of the three categories: a), b), or c)	Lacking in two of the three categories: a), b), or c)	Lacking in all three categories: a), b), and c)
Score:	15–20	10–14	5–9	0–4
INDIVIDUAL: CREATING Accurately and completely creating 4 citations in correct style	Created four or more accurate and complete citations in the correct style	Created three accurate and complete citations in the correct style	Created two accurate and complete citations in the correct style	Created none or one accurate and complete citation in the correct style
Score:	15–20	10–14	5–9	0–4
INDIVIDUAL: CREATING POSTS IN THREADED DISCUSSIONS Number and quality	Posted concept map and three or more clear, thoughtful reflections related to the assignment	Posted concept map and two clear, thoughtful reflections related to the assignment	Posted concept map and one clear, thoughtful reflection related to the assignment	Posted no concept map and no reflections
Score:	15–20	10–14	5–9	0–4
INDIVIDUAL: Turned in a complete and quality assignment in a timely manner	Turned in the handout completely filled out and a quality concept map on time	Turned in the handout and concept map lacking in nothing except lateness	Turned in the handout partly filled out and/or concept map lacking some quality but on time	Turned in late and nothing completely filled out
Score:	8–10	5–7	2–4	0–1
Total Score: /100				
Comments:				

Chapter 8 has been about practical teaching applications for the first three information literacy frames of the *Framework* model, including suggested learning outcomes, sample assignments, and corresponding sample rubrics for the information literacy frames "Authority Is Constructed and Contextual," "Information Creation as a Process," and "Information Has Value."

- Four teaching aids guide the discussion for each frame: a) a diagram illustrating its distinctions, b) a table of student learning outcomes derived from its *Knowledge Practices* and *Dispositions*, c) a sample assignment handout, and d) an accompanying sample rubric handout.
- Presented along with each frame's four teaching aids are two discipline-specific or curriculum-level librarian and classroom faculty scenarios that become the background for the frame's sample assignment and its sample rubric.
- The first scenario demonstrates a faculty/librarian brainstorming session with the goal of finding common ground between a syllabus assignment and a frame's descriptions, followed later by a faculty/librarian collaborating scenario with the goal of modifying an assignment and building a corresponding rubric.
- The first frame, "Authority Is Constructed and Contextual," is introduced conceptually as authenticating information, followed by a proposed student learning outcome that focuses on issues of authority and concludes with a sample assignment and its rubric intended for a first-year composition class in which students discover background articles on their topic and determine and utilize criteria for evaluating the validity of each article's content.
- The second frame, "Information Creation as a Process," is most like the *habits of mind* idea of flexibility and being open to new ideas through continuous learning, evaluating, and adapting to change. Its suggested student learning outcome concentrates on the social effects of the processes of information creation and ends with a sample assignment and its rubric designed for an advanced research course in mathematics where students create their own rubrics to evaluate the creation process of scholarly authors.
- The third frame, "Information Has Value," is distinguished conceptually as dealing with ethical decision making and social justice sensitivity; its suggested student learning outcome deals with copyright law and "digital divide" issues and concludes with a sample assignment and its rubric intended for master's or doctoral students, who in groups brainstorm ideas for thesis or dissertation concept maps and research questions.

Chapter 9 is essentially a continuation of chapter 8 and provides practical teaching applications for the last three information literacy frames of the *Framework* model, including suggested student learning outcomes, sample assignments, and sample rubrics for the frames "Research as Inquiry," "Scholarship as Conversation," and "Searching as Strategic Exploration."

References

ACRL (Association of College & Research Libraries). 2000. *Information Literacy Competency Standards for Higher Education*. American Library Association. http://www.ala.org/acrl/standards/informationliteracycompetency.

ACRL (Association of College & Research Libraries). 2015. *Framework for Information Literacy for Higher Education*. American Library Association. http://www.ala.org/acrl/standards/ilframework.

Costa, Arthur L., and Bena Kallick. 2000. "Habits of Mind." Adapted from *Habits of Mind: A Developmental Series*. Alexandria, VA: Association for Supervision and Curriculum Development. http://www.chsvt.org/wdp/Habits_of_Mind.pdf.

Lawrence, Kate. 2015. "Today's College Students: Skimmers, Scanners and Efficiency-Seekers." *Information Services & Use* 35, no. 1/2 (January): 89–93.

Further Reading

Astin, Alexander W., Trudy W. Banta, K. Patricia Cross, Elaine El-Khawas, Peter T. Ewell, and Pat Hutchings, et al. 1992. "American Association for Higher Education (AAHE) Principles of Good Practice for Assessing Student Learning." National Institute for Learning Outcomes Assessment (NILOA). http://www.learningoutcomesassessment.org/PrinciplesofAssessment.html.

Banta, Trudy W., Jon P. Lund, Karen E. Black, and Frances W. Oblander. 1996. "Assessment: It Starts with What Matters Most." In *Assessment in Practice: Putting Principles to Work on College Campuses*, edited by Trudy W. Banta, Jon P. Lund, Karen E. Black, and Frances W. Oblander, 3–9. San Francisco: Jossey-Bass.

Dempsey, Megan E., Heather Dalal, Lynee R. Dokus, Leslin H. Charles, and Davida Scharf. 2015. "Continuing the Conversation: Questions about the Framework." *Communications in Information Literacy* 9, no. 2 (April–June): 164–75. http://dx.doi.org/doi:10.7282/T36975JZ.

Jacobson, Trudi E., and Craig Gibson. 2015. "First Thoughts on Implementing the *Framework for Information Literacy*." *Communications in Information Literacy* 9, no. 2 (April–June): 102–10.

Kraft, Amanda, and Aleck F. Williams, Jr. 2016. "#Shelfies Are Encouraged: Simple, Engaging Library Instruction with Hashtags." *College & Research Libraries News* 77, no. 1 (January): 10–13. http://crln.acrl.org/index.php/crlnews/article/view/9425/10637.

Milczarski, Vivian, and Amanda Maynard. 2015. "Improving Information Literacy Skills for Psychology Majors: The Development of a Case Study Technique." *College & Undergraduate Libraries* 22, no. 1 (January–March): 35–44.

Teaching Information Literacy

Last Three Frames of the *Framework*

CHAPTER 9 IS THE continuation of what was started in chapter 8—a series of practical teaching aids and strategies to help librarians and classroom faculty fulfill the daunting task of teaching information literacy using the *Framework for Information Literacy for Higher Education*. That task's objective is simple: Ideally, librarians and classroom faculty at their respective colleges and universities together engage every student in a process so that, on graduation day, each student has the tools to successfully practice information literacy skills and the intellectual capacity to think conceptually as an information-literate person. This chapter offers practical teaching aids and strategies to help librarians and classroom faculty accomplish this challenge with the last three *Framework* frames:

- Research as Inquiry
- Scholarship as Conversation
- Searching as Strategic Exploration

The first three frames of the *Framework*, "Authority Is Constructed and Contextual," "Information Creation as a Process," and "Information Has Value," were addressed in chapter 8.

⦾ Four Information Literacy Teaching Aids for the Last Three Frames

The following descriptions explain four ready-to-use teaching aids to effectively communicate the principles found in each frame of the *Framework for Information Literacy for Higher Education* (table 9.1). The four teaching aids are designed to assist the librarian and the classroom faculty member as they collaborate, teach, and assess information literacy in their specific roles and settings. The four teaching aids, applied toward each of this chapter's three frames, are:

- Frame distinctions (a figure illustrating each frame's unique characteristics)
- Sample *Knowledge Practices* student learning outcomes (SLOs) and sample *Dispositions* SLOs (compiled in a separate table for each frame)
- A sample assignment handout for each frame
- A sample rubric for each assignment.

Table 9.1. The Four Teaching Aids with Short Descriptions

TEACHING AID	SHORT DESCRIPTION	FIGURE/TABLES/ HANDOUTS
1. *Distinctions* Diagram	Brief set of terms and concepts unique to a frame	Figure 9.1 is a diagram of the distinctions of the last three frames
2. Student Learning Outcomes (SLOs) Table	Suggested student learning outcomes (SLOs) adapted from a frame's *Knowledge Practices* and *Dispositions*	Tables 9.2, 9.3, and 9.4 contain four columns; the first and third columns list sample SLOs mapped to each frame's *Knowledge Practices* and *Dispositions*
3. Assignment Handout (one page)	Sample assignment handout adapted from the *Knowledge Practices* or *Dispositions* of each frame and one of its suggested SLOs, designed to help engage students in that frame's concepts	Assignment handouts are ready to use or adapt as needed
4. Rubric Handout (one or more pages)	A sample rubric handout used with its corresponding assignment handout to facilitate student accountability, grading, course evaluation, and information literacy data for institutional reporting	Rubric handouts are ready to use or adapt as needed

It's important to note that the use of both the *Knowledge Practices* and the *Dispositions* found in each frame is core to the ACRL information literacy *Framework* model. The *Framework* document defines *Knowledge Practices* as "proficiencies or abilities that learners develop as a result of their comprehending a threshold concept," and a *Disposition* is "a tendency to act or think in a particular way . . . a cluster of preferences, attitudes, and intentions, as well as a set of capabilities that allow the preferences to become realized in a particular way" (ACRL, 2015).

A More In-Depth Description of Each Frame's Distinctions

Figure 9.1 shows a set of terms and ideas derived from a frame's two-paragraph description (as found in the *Framework* document). These summaries are intended to help the busy instructor more quickly and easily grasp the core concepts or "big ideas" found throughout the frames. In addition to the diagram for these three frames' distinctions, each presentation of a frame in this chapter begins with a summary of that frame's terms and ideas plus a brief contrast in perspectives between expert and novice learners.

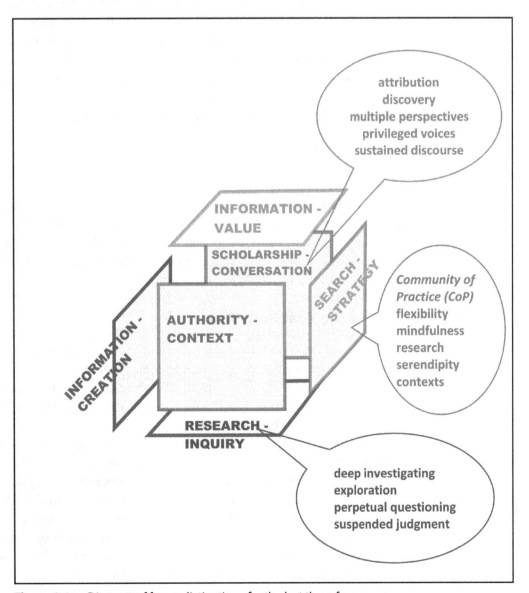

Figure 9.1. Diagram of frame distinctions for the last three frames.

A More In-Depth Description of the Sample SLOs for a Frame's *Knowledge Practices* and *Dispositions*

The suggested SLOs for each of the last three frames are presented in columns 1 and 3 of a four-column table and are adapted from each frame's *Knowledge Practices* (column 2) and its *Dispositions* (column 4). These SLO statements can be used by the librarian and/or faculty member unaltered or adapted so as to teach and assess information literacy in whatever ways are considered useful. These suggested SLOs are particularly useful in establishing an information literacy-related student learning outcome for an assignment and its corresponding rubric.

A More In-Depth Description of the Sample Assignment Handouts

Sample assignment handouts are ready to use or can be adapted as needed, on the ground or online, and are designed to engage students in that frame's information literacy concepts. Each sample assignment handout is grounded by at least one information literacy SLO from a *Knowledge Practice* or a *Disposition* of the frame at hand, where students demonstrate reaching threshold levels for that SLO through competent completion of the assignment. Also, copies of assignment handouts for this chapter are available in both PDF and Word versions on the book's website (https://implementingtheinformationliteracy framework.wordpress.com/ or https://tinyurl.com/ya6h4vyq) under chapter 9.

A More In-Depth Description of the Sample Rubric Handouts

The rubrics are ready-to-use or adapt-as-needed assessment tools that have been created to assess the corresponding sample assignment for each frame. Each sample rubric handout follows its respective assignment handout and is used to facilitate student accountability, grading, assignment assessment, and information literacy data for institutional reports and for information literacy student experiences based on the *Framework* model. Copies of the chapter's rubric handouts (in PDF and Word versions) are available on the book's website (https://implementingtheinformationliteracyframework.wordpress.com/ or https://tinyurl.com/ya6h4vyq) under chapter 9.

Strategies for Using the Teaching Aids

Before setting the stage for approaches to implementing information literacy strategies, it's important to note that the detailed descriptions above correlate to the four information literacy teaching aids used with the first three frames of the *Framework*: "Authority Is Constructed and Contextual," "Information Creation as a Process," and "Information Has Value" covered in chapter 8.

Strategies for using these four teaching aids can be implemented in a number of ways. Two scenarios help to visualize different approaches to trying these teaching aids. The first scenario describes how a librarian and/or faculty member might brainstorm to prepare to teach a particular frame as guided by the *Framework* model. The second scenario represents the dialog between the same librarian and faculty as they collaborate on how to implement the teaching of the frame by modifying an existing syllabus assignment or by creating a new one and then creating an accompanying rubric. The two scenarios for each of the three frames covered in this chapter also set the backstories to each of the sample assignment handouts and their corresponding sample rubric handouts.

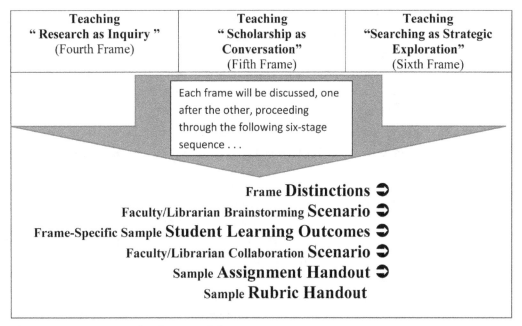

Teaching "Research as Inquiry" (Fourth Frame)	Teaching "Scholarship as Conversation" (Fifth Frame)	Teaching "Searching as Strategic Exploration" (Sixth Frame)

Each frame will be discussed, one after the other, proceeding through the following six-stage sequence . . .

Frame **Distinctions** ⮎
Faculty/Librarian Brainstorming **Scenario** ⮎
Frame-Specific Sample **Student Learning Outcomes** ⮎
Faculty/Librarian Collaboration **Scenario** ⮎
Sample **Assignment Handout** ⮎
Sample **Rubric Handout**

Figure 9.2. Structure for the rest of chapter 9.

What follows are the aforementioned four teaching aids applied to each of the last three frames of the *Framework*, namely "Research as Inquiry," "Scholarship as Conversation," and "Searching as Strategic Exploration" (figure 9.2). As mentioned, chapter 8 covers the first three frames ("Authority Is Constructed and Contextual," "Information Creation as a Process," and "Information Has Value") with the same teaching aids for each frame.

Teaching the Frame "Research as Inquiry"

Distinctions Found in the Frame "Research as Inquiry"

Among the six frames, classroom faculty may notice that the fourth, "Research as Inquiry" (ACRL, 2015), is most like higher education ideals of sincere listening and thoughtful questioning, where disagreements lead to new questions for new answers, all wrapped up in qualities of humility and wonderment. Librarians and some faculty will likely see similarities between this frame and the first competency in the now rescinded 2000 *Standards*, which was "Determine the Extent of Information Needed," as well as the third competency, "Evaluate Information and Its Sources Critically" (ACRL, 2000). For a detailed depiction of this and other similarities between the *Standards* and the *Framework*, see tables 2.2 and 2.3 in chapter 2, as well as appendix C, "Thematic Coding of the 2000 *Standards* as Found in the 2015 *Framework*."

Unique concepts expressed in the frame "Research as Inquiry" include the following (see also figure 9.1):

- deep investigating
- exploration
- perpetual questioning
- suspended judgment.

Experts who are familiar with the concepts found in the frame "Research as Inquiry" are attracted to difficult, unresolved problem-questions and can easily see value in discipline-specific collaboration because it extends new knowledge in that field. Novice learners, on the other hand, will begin to succeed as they become more efficient at questioning and gain increasingly sophisticated tools of inquiry.

Faculty/Librarian Brainstorming Scenario for Teaching "Research as Inquiry" in a Bible and Religious Studies Lower Division Class

A librarian has been teaching one-shot library instruction classes for the Department of Biblical and Religious Studies (DBRS) for 10 years. He and his fellow librarians are working toward a more collaborative approach with faculty to implement the new ACRL *Framework*-based information literacy (IL) initiative on campus in response to ongoing accreditation needs. The director of the DBRS released all the current Old Testament undergraduate syllabi to her department's librarian. Working together, the two chose Exploring Genesis as the course to begin an IL student experience, and it was one of the classes for which the librarian had taught library instruction for most of its sections. All undergraduate DBRS majors take the course before their junior year; therefore, a relatively large number of students would be engaged with an IL experience. Because the Genesis course had two dozen sections taught through the DBRS, with one-third of the sections taught by adjuncts, the director and the librarian decided to introduce the IL idea in this course and get feedback from faculty at a late Saturday afternoon wine and cheese get-together at a favorite off-campus hangout. A meeting request explained that the get-together had been set up to discuss a proposal to add an information literacy component to an existing assignment in Exploring Genesis. The time and location were selected to accommodate adjunct faculty. Of the 22 meeting requests sent, 16 faculty responded they were coming—half of them adjuncts—as well as the department's associate dean. The following is the conversation between the DBRS director, the librarian, and 16 classroom faculty.

Department Director: If you don't mind, let's go ahead and get started on our agenda. I want to say thanks to each one of you for taking time from your Saturday afternoon to join me in some refreshments and a chance to address a need to add information literacy into our curriculum. As some of you know, this time and location was chosen so that many of our adjuncts could also join us. I want to acknowledge the associate dean who is here to listen and take our recommendations back to the curriculum committee.

Associate Dean: No problem. Thanks for the refreshments!

Department Director: Most of you know our department librarian. He has taught the library component in all your classes at one time or another in the past few years. He and I have met a couple of times and we've decided on several items to save us time in today's meeting. I'll let him take it from here as he has some important things to say about the campus initiative to implement information literacy into the curriculum. Go ahead ...

Librarian: Great. OK, thanks, Director. Nice to see so many familiar faces. So, as most of you know, I've been teaching the library section in all your Exploring Genesis classes for a while. While I will always continue to meet with your students, the director and I are suggesting something different. We are implementing a process in which an information literacy component is integrated into one of your existing course assignments. Please, go ahead and take a handout I brought for each of you called "Research as Inquiry." The title refers to one of six frames from the *Framework for Information Literacy for Higher Education*, a guideline of new academic library standards for information literacy. On your handout [note: reproduced here in table 9.2] from a recent *Framework* book, I've copied a summary of the "Research as Inquiry" frame to help us be more familiar with this information literacy concept. Following this summary is a two-column chart of suggested student learning outcomes related to two categories called *Knowledge Practices* and *Dispositions* found in the frame "Research as Inquiry." I also have a copy of the Genesis syllabus up on the screen. Our job this afternoon is simple: Take one of the assignments in the syllabus and see how we can modify it to fulfill one of these student learning outcomes. Once that's done, your director and I will collaborate to modify an assignment for that outcome and a rubric for grading. Oh, I see a question?

Faculty Member 1: So, your "Research as Inquiry" handout is one of six such information literacy topics? Why are we only looking at this one?

Librarian: Well, yes, it's one of six topics or "frames" of a larger *Framework* document on information literacy. And so, while the director and I were looking over the assignments in the Genesis course, this frame seemed to be the best fit for most of the assignments.

Faculty Member 2: OK, sure, that makes sense. Once we decide tonight and you work out a new information literacy assignment with the director, could it be sent to all the professors who teach Genesis for their input?

Director: Yes, of course!

Librarian: Yes, that's a given I hadn't mentioned. Your feedback is needed, not only to help fulfill an institutional information literacy outcome, but to give our students an information literacy experience that will add to their college learning.

Faculty Member 3: How about we look at the second assignment in the course: Cultural Context Assignment, where students relate a Genesis passage to its historical-cultural context.

Librarian: OK, how do the rest of you feel about this?

Faculty Member 2: That depends on the information literacy learning outcome.

Librarian: Yes, let's look at the two-column section of the handout and I'll scroll my screen to that assignment in the syllabus. The right side of the columns are sample student learning outcomes.

Creating an SLO for Teaching "Research as Inquiry"

After some time and discussion, the group lands on the *Knowledge Practice* #7 student learning outcome: "Locate, access, evaluate, and synthesize new information from diverse sources, from multiple perspectives, and multiple media, both formal and informal; effectively compare and contrast their accuracy and relevancy" (see table 9.2). The group discussed whether this outcome would meet the original intent of the assignment. The librarian continued:

Librarian: OK, now let's take a vote. All in favor of this information literacy frame and its student learning outcome to modify this assignment, say "Aye."

All Faculty: Aye!

Librarian: A unanimous vote. It passes. Thanks, everyone. After this outcome is adapted for the current assignment and a rubric is drafted, these will be sent on to all of you who teach a section of the course for your input. After that, we'll send it to the associate dean, who will take it to the curriculum committee for their approval.

Associate Dean: Thanks, but the curriculum committee's approval isn't needed. The lead faculty will look at the final draft of the new handout and rubric and work with the

Table 9.2. The Frame "Research as Inquiry" Sample SLOs Adapted from Its *Knowledge Practices* and *Dispositions*

	RESEARCH AS INQUIRY		
KNOWLEDGE PRACTICES SLOS INFORMATION LITERACY LEARNERS ARE ABLE TO . . .	*KNOWLEDGE PRACTICES* INFORMATION LITERACY LEARNERS ARE ABLE TO . . .	*DISPOSITIONS SLOS* INFORMATION LITERACY LEARNERS ARE ABLE TO . . .	*DISPOSITIONS* INFORMATION LITERACY LEARNERS ARE ABLE TO . . .
1. Identify and articulate gaps on a topic and propose research questions to address the gaps. Identify and articulate points of differences and points of agreement in conflicting information and propose questions to deconstruct these differences and similarities	Formulate questions for research based on information gaps or on reexamination of existing, possibly conflicting, information	1. Demonstrate an open-ended, engaging attitude of research and discovery	Consider research as open-ended exploration and engagement with information
2. Describe the conceptual and concrete boundaries for an inquiry	Determine an appropriate scope of investigation	2. Respond to the most mundane queries by investigating their value and deconstructing their troublesome aspects	Appreciate that a question may appear to be simple but still disruptive and important to research
3. Break down complicated issues into their simpler components and effectively focus an investigation with adequately narrowed and well-defined research questions	Deal with complex research by breaking complex questions into simple ones, limiting the scope of investigations	3. Demonstrate intellectual curiosity in yourself and discern it in others as first steps toward developing new questions and in discovering new approaches to a problem	Value intellectual curiosity in developing questions and learning new investigative methods
4. Accurately determine and effectively implement one or more appropriate qualitative and/or quantitative methods for a study	Use various research methods, based on need, circumstance, and type of inquiry	4. Engage and practice open-mindedness and curiosity while exercising a healthy skepticism as well as accountability	Maintain an open mind and a critical stance

5. Demonstrate habits of persistence, adaptability, and flexibility, acknowledge vagueness and ambiguity as part of the research process	Value persistence, adaptability, and flexibility and recognize that ambiguity can benefit the research process	Monitor gathered information and assess for gaps or weaknesses	On any given data, identify and describe unusual patterns, missing information, outliers, and weaknesses in methods used to gather the data
6. Demonstrate the understanding of multiple perspectives throughout the process of finding and assessing information	Seek multiple perspectives during information gathering and assessment	Organize information in meaningful ways	For any given information, reorganize it in one or more ways to better interpret and analyze the information or to devise one or more meaningful presentations for information
7. When needed, seek help from library professionals and information experts	Seek appropriate help when needed	Synthesize ideas gathered from multiple sources	Locate, access, evaluate, and synthesize new information from diverse sources, from multiple perspectives, and multiple media, both formal and informal; effectively compare and contrast their accuracy and relevancy
8a. Recognize when attribution is needed and create complete and accurate citations 8b. Seek out, find, and follow ethical standards when using information	Follow ethical and legal guidelines in gathering and using information	Draw reasonable conclusions based on the analysis and interpretation of information	In order to present a useful and meaningful summary of information, articulate well-reasoned conclusions in a systematic analysis and demonstrate a clear understanding of the details and qualifiers
9. Acknowledge and express self-awareness and intellectual humility when confronted with experiential and intellectual limitations	Demonstrate intellectual humility (i.e., recognize their own intellectual or experiential limitations)		[blank]

These *Knowledge Practices* and *Dispositions* originate from the frame "Research as Inquiry" in the *Framework for Information Literacy for Higher Education* (ACRL, 2015). Used with permission from the American Library Association.

rest of us to implement the change. Something like this does not need any other vetting. Your help has been invaluable. Thanks for leading our discussion.

Librarian: Sure thing. Again, thanks everyone. We are dismissed. Have a few snacks on your way out.

Faculty/Librarian Collaboration Scenario for Teaching "Research as Inquiry"

A week later, the lead faculty for the Exploring Genesis course and the librarian meet in the faculty's office. Following is their conversation.

Librarian: Hard to believe I've been coming to your Genesis classes for 10 years. Where does the time go?

Department Director: Yes, seems like just last year we started working together. I think the meeting on Saturday went pretty well. I can't remember the last time that many of us got together in one place. Now, remind me what we're doing with the class again; I've been pretty swamped.

Librarian: No problem. Can you pull up a copy of the syllabus on your computer? OK, scroll down to the Cultural Context Assignment. Good. Now it says, students will take one of 25 key passages from Genesis and prepare a slide presentation of the passage's historical-cultural context before the professor covers it in class.

Department Director: That's been a favorite of mine; it gets students engaged in the context of those areas and helps with the learning level.

Librarian: As you know, I usually come in before the first presentation to explain how students find sources for their project. Now let's combine my part and the assignment description and change it into an information literacy learning experience. Here, I've put together a handout to see what you think.

Department Director: OK, hmmm, this is a different approach, but looks like it covers the SLO for this assignment. I see you have the information literacy SLO we chose last weekend at the top of the page; I like that.

Librarian: Yes, and I've taken a rubric from a similar assignment in another class and sketched out an idea for something to measure this information literacy outcome.

Department Director: Great, thanks, your help saves me time. This assignment looks fine for a start, but let me make a few adjustments.

Librarian: Sure, go ahead . . .

The two talk through the content of both the assignment and the rubric and make changes as they go along until they are both satisfied. View the results in the "'Research as Inquiry' Assignment Handout for a Genesis Class" and "'Research as Inquiry' Rubric Handout for a Genesis Class." These teaching aids are designed to be used as is or adapted as needed for either online or on-the-ground instruction. Copies of both the assignment and rubric documents, in a PDF and a Word version, are available for use on the book's website (https://implementingtheinformationliteracyframework.wordpress.com/ or https://tinyurl.com/ya6h4vyq) under chapter 9.

"RESEARCH AS INQUIRY" ASSIGNMENT HANDOUT FOR A GENESIS CLASS

Name: _____ Group: _____ Date: _____

Student Learning Outcome: Information literacy learners are able to locate, access, evaluate, and synthesize new information from diverse sources, from multiple perspectives, and from multiple media, both formal and informal; effectively compare and contrast their accuracy and relevancy.

Assignment: Find at least two books, two peer-reviewed articles, and two non-academic Internet sources on a given topic and reorganize the content into a literature review following the Turabian citation style.

Exercise 1: Write your Bible passage here: _____
In a group of two or three, after choosing a group name, watch this 3 ½ minute review of how to search the Religion database using the Scripture feature at https://www.youtube.com/watch?v=CzNsulA8498. Together, help one another find a minimum of two peer-reviewed articles that relate to your individual passages' historical-cultural context and help one another write your citations in Turabian style.

-
-

Exercise 2: With your group, go to the library's online catalog and together find at least two books that cover your Genesis passage and its historical-cultural context. This can be a Bible commentary or a book/e-book on the historical-cultural context of a topic. Help one another write Turabian style citations below.

-
-

Exercise 3: Again, with your group, use Google to search for the words historical (or cultural) background of the book of Genesis [chapter of your passages] plus non-academic Internet sources. Help each other list at least two sources in Turabian style, plus a minimum of five reasons why this source is credible, such as authorship, timeliness, balance, accuracy, relevancy, etc.

-
  - Credibility strengths:
-
  - Credibility strengths:

Exercise 4: As an individual, reorganize the content found in exercises 1–3 as a written literature review of three or four pages in Turabian style. Follow the Turabian/Chicago sample paper found in Purdue University's Online Writing Lab at https://owl.english.purdue.edu/owl/resource/717/11/.

Exercise 5: As an individual, create a classroom presentation of not more than 5 minutes that explains the historical-cultural highlights you discovered from your Genesis passage. In addition to content, other aspects graded will be creativity, accuracy, and organization in your presentation. Handouts are optional.

"RESEARCH AS INQUIRY" RUBRIC HANDOUT FOR A GENESIS CLASS

Name: _____ Group: _____ Date: _____

Student Learning Outcome: Information literacy learners are able to locate, access, evaluate, and synthesize new information from diverse sources, from multiple perspectives, and multiple media, both formal and informal; effectively compare and contrast their accuracy and relevancy.

Assignment: Find at least two books, two peer-reviewed articles, and two non-academic Internet sources on a given topic and reorganize the content into a literature review following the Turabian citation style.

Standards of Evaluation	Accomplished	Proficient	Developing	Novice
GROUP: APPLYING AND CREATING Finding 2+ peer-reviewed articles and citing in correct style	Found two or more appropriate articles and created two or more accurate and complete citations	Found one appropriate article and created one accurate and complete citation	a) Article is appropriate but citation not accurate/complete, or b) article not appropriate but citation accurate/complete	Created none
Score:	15–20	10–14	5–9	0–4
GROUP: APPLYING and CREATING Finding 2+ books and citing in correct style	Found two or more appropriate books and created two or more accurate and complete citations	Found one appropriate book and created one accurate and complete citation	a) Book is appropriate but citation not accurate/complete, or b) book not appropriate but citation accurate/complete	Created none
Score:	15–20	10–14	5–9	0–4
GROUP: APPLYING and CREATING Finding two or more non-academic Internet sources, each with five or more credibility strengths and citing in correct style	Found two or more non-academic Internet sources with five or more credibility strengths and created two or more accurate and complete citations	Found one non-academic Internet source with five or more credibility strengths and created one accurate and complete citation	a) Resource has 5+ credibility strengths but citation is not accurate/complete, or b) resource does not have 5+ credibility strengths but citation is accurate/complete	Created none

Standards of Evaluation	Accomplished	Proficient	Developing	Novice
Score:	15–20	10–14	5–9	0–4
INDIVIDUAL: EVALUATING **Three- to four-page quality literature review**	Lit review included a) three to four pages, b) Turabian style, c) two or more articles, two or more books, two or more social media, d) no spelling/grammar errors	Lit review strong in three of the four areas	Lit review strong in two of the four areas	Lit review strong in one of the four areas
Score:	15–20	10–14	5–9	0–4
INDIVIDUAL: CREATING **Quality of 5-minute presentation**	Presentation a) w/in 5 minutes, b) covered content well, c) creative, accurate, well organized	Presentation strong in two of three areas	Presentation strong in one of three areas	Presentation strong in none of three areas
Score:	15–20	10–14	5–9	0–4
Total Score: /100				
Comments:				

⊚ Teaching the Frame "Scholarship as Conversation"

Distinctions Found in the Frame "Scholarship as Conversation"

Among the six frames, classroom faculty may notice that the frame "Scholarship as Conversation" (ACRL, 2015) is most like the *habits of mind* problem-solving skill of thinking interdependently, which includes processes of engaging over long periods of time with colleagues who are like-minded and those who are not, resulting in a spectrum of discoveries and not necessarily findings that everyone agrees with (Costa and Kallick, 2000). Librarians and some classroom faculty may see similarities between this frame and the third competency in the 2000 *Standards*, "Evaluate Information and Its Sources Critically and Incorporate Selected Information into His or Her Knowledge Base" (ACRL, 2000). For a detailed depiction of this and other similarities between the 2000 *Standards* and the 2015 *Framework*, see tables 2.2 and 2.3 in chapter 2, as well as appendix C, "Thematic Coding of the 2000 *Standards* as Found in the 2015 *Framework*."

Unique concepts expressed in the frame "Scholarship as Conversation" include (see also figure 9.1):

- attribution
- discovery
- multiple perspectives
- privileged voices
- sustained discourse.

Experts who practice the concepts found in "Scholarship as Conversation" know that some issues may appear to have settled answers, but others, when immersed in an extended process involving "Scholarship as Conversation," may not have a single answer—or any definitive answer. Because of this, experts seek out perspectives that are like their own as well as different from their own. While both experts and novice learners can participate in the conversation, certain authorities can control the conversation such that it may marginalize certain views and privilege others. Novice learners, in order to more effectively enter and participate in the conversation, will learn how to successfully maneuver in the discourse.

Faculty/Librarian Brainstorming Scenario for Teaching "Scholarship as Conversation" for an Adult Learner Online Master's in Nursing Education Program

A newly graduated library student has been hired as a library faculty at a growing mid-sized university. Her first responsibility is to create an information literacy learning experience for adult students in an online master's degree in nursing education program. No small task. The following is the conversation between the librarian, the lead nursing faculty member, and all three of the full-time online faculty who teach the program; two of the faculty have joined via videoconferencing and introduced themselves to the librarian, and the other two are physically present in the room.

Lead Nursing Faculty: OK, let's see if we can get started. As you are all aware, one of the provost's initiatives for this year is information literacy education. How that works out is up to each program, with the program's librarian as collaborator. As you just heard, we are very fortunate to have our new librarian with us today, and fresh from library school! We are delighted you could join us to help us fulfill this new initiative. As you and I spoke earlier on the phone, let's not forget that all our online students are adult learners who are nurses in their own right, some having practiced for decades, and now want to turn a corner and get a master's in nursing education to teach nursing in an academic, vocational, or health care organization.

Librarian: Yes, I'm very excited to work out some ideas with you. I'm hoping we can not only move forward on your information literacy goals for the provost's initiative, but deliver it in an experience that is adult-friendly.

Nursing Faculty 2 (videoconferencing): If you can help us pull that off, I'll take you out to lunch next time I'm on campus!

Librarian: Thanks, I'll hold you to that! So, in a nutshell here's the idea. Information literacy needs to be experienced by our wonderful adult student learners as well as undergraduates. I'd like to suggest that every one of your students take an online library tutorial at some point in the Research for Evidence-Based Practice course. Students will work through an assignment that walks them through starting a Twitter journal club that could continue after graduation. They will be evaluating a clinical trial study or evidence-based practice article. There are six variables students will use to assess the articles to determine if a given article is credible and if it is relevant to clinical practice. From our collaboration today, we can brainstorm ideas for an assignment that incorporates information literacy along with its corresponding rubric.

Nursing Faculty 3: Yes, we're familiar with journal clubs, but we haven't been successful in getting students to keep participating in them. Most of our techniques have involved using threaded discussions as the medium. Personally, I hadn't thought of using social media. Tell us more.

Librarian: In addition to watching a short video tutorial on how to find relevant manuscripts or articles, students will read two articles that explain what a journal club is and how to get started in one on Twitter. Three students in class would be assigned as "chairs" of the journal club. It's the chairs' job, along with faculty input and approval, to find an appropriate clinical trial study or evidence-based practice article and to send the other students a link to the full text. The chairs will also act as facilitators during the Twitter chats. There would be three journal club experiences over the course of the class. Students will have enough time to apply six variables to the piece as they prepare for their Twitter discussions.

Nursing Faculty 2 (videoconferencing): I love the idea. But where do students go if they have technical issues, as I know they will?

Librarian: I've spoken with the IT department, and they are ready to assist your online students with questions about Twitter or getting connected to library databases.

Nursing Faculty 1: What databases are you suggesting?

Librarian: How about PubMed and Cochrane. Both are known for their evidence-based practice approaches, and both are covered in the video tutorial.

Nursing Faculty 3: Yes, I agree—I think those are appropriate. What six variables should be assessed?

Lead Nursing Faculty: I was thinking of: purpose of the study, population selection, controls of the study, randomization, results, and author's conclusions.

Nursing Faculty 3: Those are pretty standard for accessing studies, but I'd also want to include methodology. Students need to know if the specific data collection used is appropriate to the study and if the statistics used are measuring what authors say they are attempting to measure.

Librarian: Good idea. I'll add methodology to the list.

Creating an SLO for Teaching "Scholarship as Conversation"

The group continues to think through the details of the assignment (a social media journal club) and then, looking at each of the six frames in the *Framework*, chooses as the best fit the frame "Scholarship as Conversation." From that frame's *Knowledge Practices*, the librarian suggests that the fourth statement would most closely align with the intended students' experience: "Critically evaluate contributions made by others in participatory information environments." The group continues to collaborate to create the student learning outcome: "In a participatory information environment of a specific medium, whether formal or informal, academic or non-academic, evaluate the value and accuracy of information by its a) purpose, b) methodology and statistics, c) population selection, d) controls, e) randomization, f) results, and g) conclusions" (table 9.3).

Librarian: This has been very productive. I think we are at a good stopping point. If you like, I can take all we've agreed on and put together drafts of the assignment and the rubric to discuss and finalize at our next meeting.

Lead Nursing Faculty: That would be wonderful. Let's plan to get back together again and look at the drafts for these ideas and finalize our ideas. How about a month from now?

Faculty/Librarian Collaboration Scenario for Teaching "Scholarship as Conversation" for an Adult Learner Online Master's in Nursing Education Program

A month later, the collaborative team of four online faculty in the master's in nursing education program and their program's librarian meet to look over the drafts of the assignment and rubric as they move forward on implementing an information literacy experience for all their adult nursing student learners. The same two nursing faculty from earlier are attending via videoconferencing, along with two faculty in person. The following is from that conversation.

Lead Nursing Faculty: Well, nice to finally get back together again. I hope everyone had a pleasant term so far. Lots happening! We had a great time collaborating last time to create an information literacy assignment and rubric for our students, and our librarian has kindly put together drafts from our work together, which we will discuss and finalize today. We're currently thinking of including the assignment as part of the Research for Evidence-Based Practice course so that students will have an incentive to finish up the 100-point exercises. [Turning to the librarian] Thank you so much for your assistance.

Librarian: Glad to be here. I've brought along print copies of the two documents, or you can look at the digital copies I sent last week. What do you think? [Note: see "'Scholarship as Conversation' Assignment Handout for an Adult Learner Online Master's in Nursing Education Program," and "'Scholarship as Conversation' Rubric Handout for an Adult Learner Online Master's in Nursing Education Program."]

Nursing Faculty 2 (videoconferencing): We really appreciate the work you've put into this and your expertise. You really listened to our input and captured what is important to our discipline and applied it specifically to our information literacy needs. I must say I was a little skeptical at our last meeting; I wasn't exactly sure what you were talking about. But using Twitter appears to be quite doable.

Nursing Faculty 3: Yes, it seems quite sound. I do have a problem with the amount of work and time it takes to educate our adult student learners and make them successful in this potentially anxiety-producing experience. I have doubts about placing this in the already packed content of Research for Evidence-Based Practice course, although arguably that's the most obvious place to put it.

Nursing Faculty 4 (videoconferencing): I can't agree with you more. This is a heck of a lot of work. As you all know, I teach two sections of the evidence-based course, and this will overwhelm my students, guaranteed.

Lead Nursing Faculty: Well, maybe we need to reconsider if this is a good idea in the first place. For all its liabilities, its promise really strikes at the core of information literacy practice for our students. It's obviously very tied to the frame "Scholarship as Conversation." I dare say there are few other approaches like an online journal club using social media that meet the concepts found in that frame, the way I read it.

Nursing Faculty 3: I think I have a solution. We are still looking to fulfill two units in our program, now that we've reconfigured our required units. This assignment could actually meet those two units with not much more work. Maybe just rename it Twitter Journal Club and list it with the other courses. We'll start as a part of orientation in the summer. Then for four terms, students must participate to receive a half-point per term. We'll just increase the number of chairs to eight and have it occur twice each term. It may even be a recruiting tool for us when prospective students see it. And it helps us meet our tuition threshold.

Lead Nursing Faculty: Brilliant idea! I love the idea.

Nursing Faculty 2 (videoconferencing): Absolutely! That will work!

Nursing Faculty 3: I agree!

Librarian: Wow, for a moment there I thought I was out of a job! Adding chairs is a no-brainer. But what do you think of the content of the assignment draft? And the rubric?

Nursing Faculty 4 (video): I've looked at it a great deal, and except for the extra credit part, which is problematic, I see no other concerns or changes. It's a solid piece of work I think. It not only accomplishes our information literacy agenda but, as I see the direction we are going, it embeds the journal club idea into the curriculum. If it's as good as we hope it to be, maybe it will be sustainable in some form after our students graduate.

Lead Nursing Faculty: I see no problem in giving students who are the "chairs" the extra credit points. They still have to do all the other work, as I understand it. And having such a role throughout the two years may come in handy for deserving students. We'll have to see. So, if everyone is ready, I make a motion that we implement the Twitter Journal Club with those few changes mentioned and make this a new part of the program. Any further discussion? Hearing none, all those in favor, say aye!

All Four Faculty: Aye, Aye, Aye, Aye.

Lead Nursing Faculty: OK, it's unanimous. I will submit this to faculty governance tonight for its next meeting. [Turning to the librarian] Your hard work has paid off!

Librarian: OK great! Thanks!

Lead Nursing Faculty: No, thank you! Meeting adjourned.

View the results of these discussions in the "'Scholarship as Conversation' Assignment Handout for an Adult Learner Online Master's in Nursing Education Program," and "'Scholarship as Conversation' Rubric Handout for an Adult Learner Online Mas-

Table 9.3. The Frame "Scholarship as Conversation" Sample SLOs Adapted from Its *Knowledge Practices* and *Dispositions*

SCHOLARSHIP AS CONVERSATION			
KNOWLEDGE PRACTICES SLOS INFORMATION LITERACY LEARNERS ARE ABLE TO . . .	*KNOWLEDGE PRACTICES* INFORMATION LITERACY LEARNERS ARE ABLE TO . . .	*DISPOSITIONS SLOS* INFORMATION LITERACY LEARNERS ARE ABLE TO . . .	*DISPOSITIONS* INFORMATION LITERACY LEARNERS ARE ABLE TO . . .
1. Understand and execute one or more citation styles accurately and fully and demonstrate knowledge of one or more authoritative sources for accessing the style	Cite the contributing work of others in their own information production	1. Design an intuitive timeline that clearly follows the evolution of a topic's change or ebb and flow of thought with appropriate attributions	Recognize they are often entering into an ongoing scholarly conversation and not a finished conversation
2. Demonstrate appropriate scholarly discourse by word choices, tone, and level of diction for chosen medium of communication	Contribute to scholarly conversation at an appropriate level, such as local online community, guided discussion, undergraduate research journal, conference presentation/poster session	2. Describe in depth the relevant characteristics of a topic's stakeholders that may impact or influence where they are located along different spectrums such as education, socioeconomic status, race, religiosity, affiliations, significant life events, disabilities, gender, etc.	Seek out conversations taking place in their research area
3. Demonstrate flexibility and adaptability in scholarly discourse in order to adjust to changes in a scholarly discourse; demonstrate knowledge of the "rules of culture" in a scholarly community in order to gain and maintain acceptance into that community	Identify barriers to entering scholarly conversation via various venues	3. Demonstrate evidence of information contributions that express their own opinions, evaluations, or analyses of chosen areas of interest, expertise, or scholarship	See themselves as contributors to scholarship rather than only consumers of it
4. In a participatory information environment of a specific medium, whether formal or informal, academic or non-academic, evaluate the value and accuracy of information by its: a) purpose, b) methodology and statistics, c) population selection, d) controls, e) randomization, f) results, and g) conclusions	Critically evaluate contributions made by others in participatory information environments	4. Evaluate a venue for scholarly conversation with appropriate criteria and demonstrate an understanding of its culture or milieu by choosing the appropriate venue of a given information output and participating appropriately	Recognize that scholarly conversations take place in various venues

5. Identify and articulate a specific contribution on a disciplinary topic in terms of (a) defining what it adds to the knowledge base, (b) describing how that additional knowledge affects or changes the conversation, (c) presenting any questions it answers within the knowledge base, and (d) posing any new questions it asks	Identify the contribution that particular articles, books, and other scholarly pieces make to disciplinary knowledge	5. Demonstrate evidence of actively seeking out multiple and alternative perspectives as well as evidence of acknowledging diversity in perspectives without prejudice before expressing conclusions; express those conclusions with appropriate and relevant qualifiers, and acknowledging own limitations of understanding	Suspend judgment on the value of a particular piece of scholarship until the larger context for the scholarly conversation is better understood
6. Create a robust, intuitive timeline that shows the changes in scholarly perspectives of a topic by identifying and describing a) its beginning with authoritative seminal works, b) succeeding works that quote or refer to the seminal works, and c) the distribution of works that contribute to the topic	Summarize the changes in scholarly perspective over time on a particular topic within a specific discipline	6. Create accurate and complete records when engaging in information sharing and give proper credit to others' intellectual property	Understand the responsibility that comes with entering the conversation through participatory channels
7. Demonstrate a clear understanding of a topic from a given scholarly work and then locate and articulate other scholarly works whose perspectives agree, disagree, or give additional, relevant, and mitigating information on the topic not covered in the original work; demonstrate a well-reasoned understanding of the merit and level of acceptance of a given perspective	Recognize that a given scholarly work may not represent the only or even the majority perspective on the issue	7. Critically evaluate user-generated content (such as customer reviews, forums, blog responses, and star-rated critiques) to discern trustworthiness and value	Value user-generated content and evaluate contributions made by others
		8. Demonstrate sensitivity when analyzing research by considering when an information system may privilege some authorities according to various factors, including language fluency and technological fluency and, when relevant, articulating the influence and impact of these factors	Recognize that systems privilege authorities, and that not having fluency in the language and process of a discipline disempowers their ability to participate and engage

These *Knowledge Practices* and *Dispositions* originate from the frame "Scholarship as Conversation" in the *Framework for Information Literacy for Higher Education* (ACRL, 2015). Used with permission from the American Library Association.

ter's in Nursing Education Program." These teaching aids are designed to be used as is, or adapted as needed for either online or on-the-ground instruction. Copies of both the assignment and rubric documents, in a PDF and a Word version, are available on the book's website (https://implementingtheinformationliteracyframework.wordpress.com/) or https://tinyurl.com/ya6h4vyq) under chapter 9.

"SCHOLARSHIP AS CONVERSATION" ASSIGNMENT HANDOUT FOR AN ADULT LEARNER ONLINE MASTER'S IN NURSING EDUCATION PROGRAM

Name: _____ Date: _____

Student Learning Outcome: Information literacy learners are able to, in a participatory information environment, of a specific medium, whether formal or informal, academic or non-academic, evaluate the value and accuracy of information.

Assignment: Evaluate information by its: a) purpose, b) methodology and statistics, c) population selection, d) controls, e) randomization, f) results, and g) conclusions.

Exercise 1: The purpose of this assignment is to introduce you to critically evaluating a clinical trial study or evidence-based practice article for its own validation, using a Twitter journal club approach. First read these two articles: a) C. Ferguson, M. DiGiacomo, L. Gholizadeh, L. E. Ferguson, and L. D. Hickman, (2017), "The Integration and Evaluation of a Social-Media Facilitated Journal Club to Enhance the Student Learning Experience of Evidence-Based Practice: A Case Study," *Nurse Education Today* 48, 123–28; b) P. D. Bowles, K. Marenah, D. M. Ricketts, and B. A. Rogers (2013), "How to Prepare for and Present at a Journal Club," *British Journal of Hospital Medicine* 74, no. 10, C150–C152. In this week's threaded discussion, reflect on some of the main points from these two articles, showing you understood them.

Exercise 2: Read how to search the database PubMed (https://www.nlm.nih.gov/bsd/disted/pubmedtutorial/cover.html) and watch the three-part tutorial on how to search the Cochrane Library (go to http://www.cochranelibrary.com/ and click Help, then click "How to use the Cochrane Library," and then scroll down to "Online self-paced tutorials"). In this week's threaded discussion, also reflect on what you learned from these instructions. Even if you are not involved in exercise 4a, it is still expected that you learn how to use these two databases.

Exercise 3: If you do not already have a Twitter account, go to twitter.com and sign up. On the same page read "First steps after you've created your account." In this week's threaded discussions, also reflect on any part of your Twitter experience (before the beginning of the Twitter journal club).

Exercise 4a: Determine from your professor if you are one of the three "chairs" for: a) using PubMed or the Cochrane Library, locate one clinical trial study or evidence-based practice article to discuss in the Twitter journal club; b) send a link of the full text or an attachment of the full text to your student peers; and c) be prepared to facilitate the discussion in the Twitter posts at the assigned time. You can receive extra credit for these roles. You will also do exercise 4b for all three studies/articles.

Exercise 4b: Wait until you receive the first of three studies or articles from a "chair." Read the article and apply what you learned in exercise 1 by writing a summary of your **critiques** for each of the three studies/articles covering the following seven areas, labeling each: a) purpose, b) methodology and statistics, c) population selection, d) controls, e) randomization, f) results, and g) conclusions. If any area appears to be missing, then note that in your document. Before the assigned deadlines, turn in your summary document for grading. Grading will follow the "Scholarship as Conversation" rubric.

"SCHOLARSHIP AS CONVERSATION" RUBRIC HANDOUT FOR AN
ADULT LEARNER ONLINE MASTER'S IN NURSING EDUCATION PROGRAM

Name: _____   Date: _____

Student Learning Outcome: Information literacy learners are able, in a participatory information environment, of a specific medium, whether formal or informal, academic or non-academic, to evaluate information by its: a) purpose, b) methodology and statistics, c) population selection, d) controls, e) randomization, f) results, and g) conclusions.

Standards of Evaluation	Accomplished	Proficient	Developing	Novice
INDIVIDUAL: UNDERSTANDING Read the two articles in exercise 1 and posted reflections in threaded discussions	Read both articles and posted meaningful, insightful reflections in threaded discussions	Read both articles and for one posted meaningful, insightful reflections in threaded discussions	Read both articles but did not post meaningful, insightful reflections in threaded discussions	Read none or one article but did not post meaningful, insightful reflections in threaded discussions
Score:	15–20	10–14	5–9	0–4
INDIVIDUAL: UNDERSTANDING Read/watched both tutorials on how to search PubMed and Cochrane Library	Read/watched both tutorials and posted meaningful, insightful reflections in threaded discussions	Read/watched both tutorials and for one posted meaningful, insightful reflections in threaded discussions	Read/watched both tutorials but did not post meaningful, insightful reflections in threaded discussions	Read/watched none or one tutorial but did not post meaningful, insightful reflections in threaded discussions
Score:	15–20	10–14	5–9	0–4
INDIVIDUAL: CREATING Created a Twitter account, or had one	Created a Twitter account and a) posted something and b) followed someone	Created a Twitter account but only did a) or b), not both	Created a Twitter account but did not do either a) or b)	Did not create a Twitter and did not do either a) or b)
Score:	15–20	10–14	5–9	0–4
INDIVIDUAL: APPLYING Found an appropriate study or article for the Twitter journal club as a "chair"	a) Found an appropriate study or article for the Twitter journal club, b) sent it to peers, and c) facilitated the postings	Did two of a), b), or c)	Did one of a), b), or c)	Did not do a), b), and c)
Score:	15–20 extra points	10–14 extra points	5–9 extra points	0–4 extra points

Standards of Evaluation	Accomplished	Proficient	Developing	Novice
INDIVIDUAL: EVALUATE **Participated in all three Twitter journal club experiences**	Participated meaningfully in all three Twitter journal club experiences	Participated meaningfully in two of three Twitter journal club experiences	Participated meaningfully in one of three Twitter journal club experiences	Participated in none of the three Twitter journal club experiences OR participation was substandard
Score:	15–20	10–14	5–9	0–4
INDIVIDUAL: EVALUATE AND APPLY **Wrote a summary critique of all three studies/articles covering all seven areas**	Wrote a complete summary critique of all three studies/articles covering all seven areas	Wrote a complete summary critique of two of three studies/articles OR did all three but lacked one or two of the seven areas	Wrote a complete summary critique of one of three studies/articles OR did all three but lacked three or four of the seven areas	Wrote a complete summary critique of one or none of three studies/articles AND if one, lacked five or six of the seven areas
Score:	15–20	10–14	5–9	0–4
Total Score: /100				
Comments:				

⑥ Teaching the Frame "Searching as Strategic Exploration"

Distinctions Found in the Frame "Searching as Strategic Exploration"

Among the six frames, classroom faculty may notice that the frame "Searching as Strategic Exploration" (ACRL, 2015) is most like a kind of social learning called *situated learning*, in which the learner starts as a novice working from the outside toward becoming a legitimate member of a *Community of Practice (CoP)*. In this way, they achieve deeper involvement with experts in the *CoP*, which takes place in a knowledge society (Brown, Collins, and Duguid, 1989; Lave and Wenger, 1991). Librarians and some classroom faculty may also note the similarities between this frame's distinctions and both the second competency from the now rescinded 2000 *Standards*, "Access the needed information effectively and efficiently," and the first half of the third competency, "Evaluate Information and Its Sources Critically" (ACRL, 2000). For a detailed depiction of this and other similarities between the *Standards* and the *Framework*, see tables 2.2 and 2.3 in chapter 2, as well as appendix C, "Thematic Coding of the 2000 *Standards* as Found in the 2015 *Framework*."

Unique concepts expressed in this frame, "Searching as Strategic Exploration," include (see also figure 9.1):

- *Community of Practice (CoP)*
- flexibility
- mindfulness
- research
- serendipity.

Experts known for understanding the concepts found in the frame "Searching as Strategic Exploration" acknowledge that searching occurs in a context, that it is complex, and that it involves the searchers' own cognition, their own feelings, and their own *Community of Practice* journey. On the more concrete side of this frame, experts search deeper and wider, with a carefully chosen set of different tools and approaches, whereas novice learners search with more impulsive, shallower, restrictive behaviors, with less intentionality and focus, and fewer search strategies and tools.

Faculty/Librarian Brainstorming Scenario for Teaching "Searching as Strategic Exploration" for a Dissertation Literature Review

A librarian has been recently studying how to use a *Community of Practice* as a conceptual approach to help advanced students create literature reviews. He chooses to introduce the idea at the next faculty meeting for one of his liaison areas, the doctoral psychology faculty. The following is that conversation.

Psychology Department Director: OK, I believe that's the last piece from our curriculum review committee. Next on the agenda I'd like to introduce the librarian who liaisons with our department. He not only coordinates purchasing all our e-book requests, but teaches many of our library tutorial sessions. Today he wants to float an idea that might provide an information literacy exercise to our master's and doctoral students as they work on their literature reviews. Let's give him a warm department welcome!

Librarian: Thanks everyone. I appreciate the few minutes I have on the agenda. I'd like to explain an idea to strengthen your students' literature review skills for their dissertations while also providing an information literacy experience. With the renewal of our national accreditation in a few years, there's a need to show data on how we are doing on the core competency of information literacy. OK, so the student who wants to produce a quality literature review, in many ways, is on a *Community of Practice (CoP)* journey. As most of you know, a *CoP* model has two pieces: novices, who are the students, and experts, who are the source material behind lit reviews. Novices begin as peripheral participants, searching their topics, topics that are unknown (to the students) but in practice have a well-defined, shall we say, knowledge society. Oh, sorry, you have a question?

Faculty 1: Well, more of a comment. Sounds like you've been doing some reading from two of our basic textbooks, Lave and Wenger as well as Brown, Collins, and Duguid's work [Brown, Collins, and Duguid, 1989; Lave and Wenger, 1991].

Librarian: Yes, that's true. I can't say I understand everything, but recently I've seen a connection between what they write about in regard to *CoPs* and one of the concepts—or frames—in the *Framework for Information Literacy for Higher Education*. There are six of these new frames, and one is called "Searching as Strategic Exploration." Students are already doing searching for their lit reviews. With a little more instruction, I believe, they can also fulfill an information literacy student learning outcome. So, I'd like to help one of you create a basic assignment that could be used as a lit review project with an information literacy assessment component for accreditation data. Anyone interested?

Faculty 2: Sure, I might be willing! It does sound interesting. I have a sabbatical coming up next term and I haven't fleshed out all my to-dos. I'm interested in doing more with information literacy, if for no other reason than to help me with my future accreditation responsibilities when I return.

Librarian: That sounds excellent. I'll get together with you after the meeting.

Creating an SLO for Teaching "Searching as Strategic Inquiry"

The librarian and the psychology faculty member connect after the faculty meeting and set an initial time to meet two weeks later to talk about plans for the lit review assignment. At that meeting, the librarian shares more about the new *Framework*, explaining its six frames, and their *Knowledge Practices* and *Dispositions*. As they scan through each of the *Knowledge Practices* and *Dispositions* for the frame "Searching as Strategic Exploration," both land on the fourth bulleted *Knowledge Practice*, "Match information needs and search strategies to appropriate search tools." Together they work up a draft student learning outcome and place it in a Google Doc, which later is refined to the following statement (see table 9.4):

> For a specific information need, identify and utilize relevant search strategies and search strings, and effectively search proprietary databases, free databases, or other formally or informally archived information sources to retrieve information relevant to the information need and context.

Table 9.4. The Frame "Searching as Strategic Exploration" Sample SLOs Adapted from Its *Knowledge Practices* and *Dispositions*

SEARCHING AS STRATEGIC EXPLORATION			
KNOWLEDGE PRACTICES SLOS INFORMATION LITERACY LEARNERS ARE ABLE TO . . .	*KNOWLEDGE PRACTICES* INFORMATION LITERACY LEARNERS ARE ABLE TO . . .	*DISPOSITIONS SLOS* INFORMATION LITERACY LEARNERS ARE ABLE TO . . .	*DISPOSITIONS* INFORMATION LITERACY LEARNERS ARE ABLE TO . . .
1. At the beginning of a search process, determine approximate boundaries for a given information need, such as date range, time limits for project, depth of research, number and types of sources needed, purpose of and audience for a deliverable, complexity of a deliverable, and timeliness of accessibility for any information source	Determine the initial scope of the task required to meet their information needs	1. Demonstrate evidence of changes made during the search process, such as logs of search words, databases used, notes from consultations with information experts, narratives exploring the search process and any experiments attempted, summative or evaluative notes on research, and any other metacognitive techniques used	Exhibit mental flexibility and creativity
2. Search a topic in any information archive and identify keywords or keyword phrases, organizations, stakeholders, recognized experts, and other relevant verifiable information connected to the topic; then locate and retrieve the information needed derived from these elements	Identify interested parties, such as scholars, organizations, governments, and industries, who might produce information about a topic and then determine how to access that information	2. Manage time and priorities in order to allow for the developmental nature of research and anticipate and plan for multiple search times; plan for an execute time for regular evaluative summaries after a search session in order to search more effectively the next time	Understand that first attempts at searching do not always produce adequate results
3. When searching, design and utilize both divergent (creative, non-traditional) approaches as well as convergent (traditional, common sense) approaches	Utilize divergent (e.g., brainstorming) and convergent (e.g., selecting the best source) thinking when searching	3. Explain what might be the "best" results for a given information need, then when looking at different available information sources determine each's strengths and weaknesses (in light of usefulness for the need) for providing the "best" results	Realize that information sources vary greatly in content and format and have varying relevance and value, depending on the needs and nature of the search

Disposition	Description
Seek guidance from experts, such as librarians, researchers, and professionals	4. Recognize the need for expert guidance, then arrange, attend, and participate in a collaborative session with the appropriate expert; prepare for the session with evaluative notes on the search process taken so far and on the ability to explain in sufficient terms the information need as well as the deliverable
Recognize the value of browsing and other serendipitous methods of information gathering	5. Demonstrate intellectual curiosity and media literacy by routinely browsing for needed information with whatever information device or source (e.g., talking/listening to people) may be available
Persist in the face of search challenges and know when they have enough information to complete the information task	6. Determine and articulate criteria for ending the search process, including whether the information was available and why this determined the end

Knowledge Practice	Description
Match information needs and search strategies to appropriate search tools	4. For a specific information need, identify and utilize relevant search strategies and search strings, and effectively search proprietary databases, free databases, or other formally or informally archived information source to retrieve information relevant to the information need and context
Design and refine needs and search strategies as necessary, based on search results	5. Based on an initial search result, effectively narrow or refine these results to locate sources that are more relevant; when results are unsatisfactory, demonstrate creativity and flexibility to redesign the search to locate and access new information sources
Understand how information systems (i.e., collections of recorded information) are organized in order to effectively access the information	6. After a search is conducted with results, analyze how the records are arranged and utilize this analysis to effectively access the most helpful information
Use different types of searching language (e.g., controlled vocabulary, keywords, natural language) appropriately	7. For a given topic in a given database, keep a record of search results as determined by such factors as controlled vocabulary like subject headings, keywords, keywords plus subject headings, and natural language; analyze the results of each technique and utilize the results to more effectively search
Manage searching processes and results effectively	8. Track each searching attempt according to date, searching source, search strings used, number and quality of results, regular evaluative summaries of process, and ideas for next searches

These *Knowledge Practices and Dispositions* originate from the frame "Searching as Strategic Exploration" in the *Framework for Information Literacy for Higher Education* (ACRL, 2015). Used with permission from the American Library Association.

Faculty/Librarian Collaboration Scenario for Teaching "Searching as Strategic Exploration" for a Dissertation Literature Review

The librarian and faculty member agree to meet once a week for the next few months to iron out an appropriate assignment that can provide data for any future accreditation reports. See the results in the "'Searching as Strategic Exploration' Assignment Handout for a Dissertation Literature Review" and "'Searching as Strategic Exploration' Rubric Handout for a Dissertation Literature Review." These teaching aids are designed to be used as is or adapted as needed for either online or on-the-ground instruction. Copies of both the assignment and rubric documents, in a PDF and a Word version, are available on the book's website (https://implementingtheinformationliteracyframework.wordpress .com/ or https://tinyurl.com/ya6h4vyq) under chapter 9.

"SEARCHING AS STRATEGIC EXPLORATION" ASSIGNMENT
HANDOUT FOR A DISSERTATION LITERATURE REVIEW

Name: _____ Date: _____

Student Learning Outcome: Information literacy learners are able to identify and utilize relevant search strategies and search strings and effectively search proprietary databases, free databases, or other formally or informally archived information sources to retrieve information relevant to the information need and context.

Assignment: Meet with a librarian to assist you in three search strategies, three search strings, and three tools to search.

Exercise 1: Write your working topic or research question here: _____

_____

Meet with a librarian until all four exercises are complete. Below write a minimum of three search strategies for your topic (Google "search strategies" if needed for ideas):

-
-
-

Exercise 2: Below write a minimum of three search strings for your topic:

-
-
-

Exercise 3: Below write a minimum of three tools to search for your topic:

-
-
-

Exercise 4: Attach to this assignment a worksheet that you and the librarian used in finding quality resources (books, articles, other dissertations/theses, blogs, social media, and other sources). In your first meeting with the librarian, please show this assignment worksheet to him or her so you both know what is required. Continue to apply these techniques to find quality resources for your topic/research question and consult the librarian as needed.

"SEARCHING AS STRATEGIC EXPLORATION" RUBRIC
HANDOUT FOR A DISSERTATION LITERATURE REVIEW

Name: _____ Date: _____

Student Learning Outcome: Information literacy learners are able to identify and utilize relevant search strategies and search strings and effectively search proprietary databases, free databases, or other formally or informally archived information sources to retrieve information relevant to the information need and context.

Assignment: Meet with a librarian to assist you in three search strategies, three search strings, and three tools to search.

Standards of Evaluation	Accomplished	Proficient	Developing	Novice
MEETING **Meeting with the librarian for an information need**	Met with the librarian until all four exercises were complete	Met with the librarian until three of four exercises were complete	Met with the librarian until two of four exercises were complete	Met with the librarian until one of four exercises were complete
Score:	15–20	10–14	5–9	0–4
CREATING **Creating three or more search strategies for an . . .**	Created three or more search strategies	Created two of three search strategies	Created one of three search strategies	Created no search strategies
Score:	15–20	10–14	5–9	0–4
CREATING **Creating three or more search strings for an . . .**	Created three or more search strings	Created two of three search strings	Created one of three search strings	Created no search strings
Score:	15–20	10–14	5–9	0–4
CHOOSE **Choosing three or more tools to search for an . . .**	Chose three or more tools to search	Chose two of three tools to search	Chose one of three tools to search	Chose no tools to search
Score:	15–20	10–14	5–9	0–4
FINDING **Finding relevant resources**	Found ___ or more resources	Found ___ of ____ resources	Found ___ of ____ resources	Found ___ of ____ resources
Score:	15–20	10–14	5–9	0–4
Total Score: /100				
Comments:				

⊚ Key Points

Chapter 9 has been about practical teaching applications for the last three information literacy frames of the *Framework* model, including suggested learning outcomes, sample assignments, and corresponding sample rubrics for the information literacy frames "Research as Inquiry," "Scholarship as Conversation," and "Searching as Strategic Exploration."

- Four teaching aids guide the discussion for each frame: a) a diagram illustrating its distinctions, b) a table of student learning outcomes derived from its *Knowledge Practices* and *Dispositions*, c) a sample assignment handout, and d) an accompanying sample rubric handout.
- Along with each frame's four teaching aids, presented are two discipline-specific or curriculum-level librarian and classroom faculty scenarios that becomes the background for each frame's sample assignment and sample rubric.
- The first scenario demonstrates a faculty/librarian brainstorming session with the goal of finding common ground between a syllabus assignment and a frame's descriptions, followed later by a faculty/librarian collaborative scenario with the goal of modifying an assignment and building a corresponding rubric.
- The fourth frame, "Research as Inquiry," is introduced conceptually as an intellectual process of listening and thoughtful questioning and is followed by a proposed student learning outcome that assesses students' abilities to "locate, access, evaluate, and synthesize new information from diverse sources, from multiple perspectives, and from multiple media, both formal and informal [and] effectively compare and contrast their accuracy and relevancy." It ends with a sample assignment and its rubric and is intended for a first- or second-year student taking a Genesis Bible course in which students watch a library tutorial that helps them find books, articles, and non-academic media related to the historical cultural background of their Genesis passage.
- The fifth frame, "Scholarship as Conversation," is most like the *habits of mind* problem-solving skill of thinking independently and interdependently with others of similar or dissimilar perspectives. Its suggested student learning outcome assesses students' abilities "in a participatory information environment, of a specific medium, whether formal or informal, academic or non-academic, to evaluate the value and accuracy of information by its: a) purpose, b) methodology and statistics, c) population selection, d) controls, e) randomization, f) results, and g) conclusions." The sample assignment and its rubric are designed for an adult learner population of online master's in nursing education students.
- The sixth frame, "Searching as Strategic Exploration," is distinguished conceptually as the ability of master's and doctoral students to see themselves as members of *Communities of Practice* as they create their literature reviews. The suggested student learning outcome is aimed at developing their abilities "to identify and utilize relevant search strategies and search strings, and effectively search proprietary databases, free databases, or other formally or informally archived information sources to retrieve information relevant to the information need and context," demonstrated by a sample assignment and its rubric intended for master's or doctoral students who meet with a librarian to begin their literature reviews.

Chapter 10 takes a look back and a look forward at the current intellectual culture of information literacy, with recommendations for all stakeholders in the educational process of developing information-literate graduates and citizens.

⊚ References

ACRL (Association of College & Research Libraries). 2000. *Information Literacy Competency Standards for Higher Education*. American Library Association. http://www.ala.org/acrl/standards/informationliteracycompetency.

ACRL (Association of College & Research Libraries). 2015. *Framework for Information Literacy for Higher Education*. American Library Association. http://www.ala.org/acrl/standards/ilframework.

Bowles, P. D., K. Marenah, D. M. Ricketts, and B. A. Rogers. 2013. "How to Prepare for and Present at a Journal Club." *British Journal of Hospital Medicine* 74, no. 10 (October): C150–C152.

Brown, John Seely, Allan Collins, and Paul Duguid. 1989. "Situated Cognition and the Culture of Learning." *Educational Researcher* 18, no. 1 (January–February): 32–42. http://www.jstor.org/stable/1176008.

Costa, Arthur L., and Bena Kallick. 2000. "Habits of Mind." Adapted from *Habits of Mind: A Developmental Series*. Alexandria, VA: Association for Supervision and Curriculum Development. http://www.chsvt.org/wdp/Habits_of_Mind.pdf.

Ferguson, Caleb, Michelle DiGiacomo, Leila Gholizadeh, Leila E. Ferguson, and Louise D. Hickman. 2017. "The Integration and Evaluation of a Social-Media Facilitated Journal Club to Enhance the Student Learning Experience of Evidence-Based Practice: A Case Study." *Nurse Education Today* 48 (January): 123–28. http://www.nurseeducationtoday.com/article/S0260-6917(16)30231-3/fulltext?rss=yes.

Lave, Jean, and Etienne Wenger. 1991. *Situated Learning: Legitimate Peripheral Participation*. New York: Cambridge University Press.

⊚ Further Reading

Tam, Ka-Wai, Lung-Wen Tsai, Chien-Chih Wu, Po-Li Wei, Chou-Fu Wei, and Soul-Chin Chen. 2011. "Using Vote Cards to Encourage Active Participation and to Improve Critical Appraisal Skills in Evidence-Based Medicine Journal Clubs." *Journal of Evaluation in Clinical Practice* 17, no. 4: 827–31.

Moving Forward in Creating *Framework*-Based Information Literacy Instruction

---

IN THIS CHAPTER

▷ What kind of information literacy instruction is needed today?

▷ Moving forward at the library level

▷ Moving forward at the institutional level

What Kind of Information Literacy Instruction Is Needed Today?

WHAT KIND OF information literacy instruction does your institution provide? Does it prepare your students to understand their world, to make sound decisions based on valid information that they have the intellectual capital to competently discover, discern, and interpret? When they come to you for research assistance, are they asking the deeper questions about the nature of the information they are looking at and about the significance of the information? Do they ask, is it true, is it complete, is it fair and balanced, is it accurate, *is it relevant*? Do they ask questions about who is producing the information and what is valued versus what is discounted or left out? Do they ask, who refutes this information, and why? Or are you and your students satisfied with simply bringing up the right database, typing in appropriate-sounding keywords, and compiling a stack of electronic texts that "fit the bill." The assignment states they need four peer-reviewed journal articles and—1, 2, 3, 4—they're done!

Maybe you don't want to teach the theoretical, rhetorical concepts at the core of ACRL's *Framework*. Maybe you are far more comfortable showing students how to use subject headings and Boolean operators, showing them the best database for their needs. Or far more comfortable lecturing on the content of the course you are teaching. Maybe students are asking for information, you find it for them, and simply give it to them. Maybe that's as far as you have time to go.

Then who will teach information literacy as a liberal art, as a life skill, as a set of intellectual competencies or *habits of mind*? Somebody has to.

One dominant characteristic of the 2016 U.S. presidential election was the proliferation of "fake news," which has engendered rampant discussion over its impact on the election itself and raised serious questions by many about the American public's ability to distinguish exaggeration and distortion from objective presentation and analysis. Was it just passions out of control, or does it indicate a more pervasive and discouraging low level of information literacy and critical thinking by the American population?

Writing for *Forbes* magazine in December 2016 under the headline, "Americans Believe They Can Detect Fake News: Studies Show They Can't," Brett Edkins referenced three studies—one by the Pew Research Center, another from Stanford University, and a third by the marketing research firm Ipsos—that cast serious doubt on Americans' ability to detect and *disregard* false information. As Edkins describes the Ipsos poll, "Respondents were shown six headlines—three false and three true. If they recalled seeing the story before, they were asked if the headline was accurate. Respondents believed the fake headlines were 'somewhat' or 'very' accurate 75 percent of the time" (Edkins, 2016).

In fact, the "fake news" phenomenon during the 2016 presidential election prompted Facebook and Google to make changes to try to stymie fake news. As Edkins explained, Facebook will

> partner with third party fact-checkers to flag fake articles and alert users before they share fake news . . . Facebook will also "rank 'disputed' stories lower in news feed[s] and will not allow 'disputed' stories to be turned into ads and promoted." . . . Meanwhile Google has said it would prevent websites selling fake news from using its advertising network. (2016)

Writing for the *Wall Street Journal* about Stanford University's Graduate School of Education study of 7,804 preteens and teens released at the end of 2016 (Wineberg and McGrew, 2016), Sue Shellenbarger reported:

> Some 82% of middle schoolers couldn't distinguish between an ad labeled "sponsored content" and a real news story on a website. . . . More than two out of three middle-schoolers couldn't see any valid reason to mistrust a post written by a bank executive, arguing that young adults need more financial-planning help. And nearly four in 10 high school students believed, based on the headline, that a photo of deformed daisies on a photo-sharing site provided strong evidence of toxic conditions near Fukushima Daiichi nuclear plant in Japan, even though no source or location was given for the photo. (2016)

Shellenbarger (2016) also noted that at that moment in time, Stanford University's "free social studies curriculum that teaches students to judge the trustworthiness of historical sources has been downloaded 3.5 million times." Put together by the Stanford History Education Group (SHEG) and named *Reading Like a Historian*, the curriculum is available online at https://sheg.stanford.edu/rlh. The curriculum guides teachers in instruction on "Home Page Analysis," "Evaluating Evidence," and "Claims on Social Media." The staff includes many notable historians, scholars, and educators, but no librarians.

Another interpreter and instructor in information literacy, with expressed concepts closely aligned with those in the ACRL *Framework*, is the field of composition. Generally, instruction in information literacy as found in writing courses is nested within those student learning outcomes intended to produce graduates competent in "twenty-first-century skills" or "habits of mind" in order to be successful through college and for the rest of their lives. In 2011, three key national organizations—the Council of Writing Program Administrators (WPA), the National Council of Teachers of English (NCTE), and the National Writing Project (NWP)—created their own framework, the *Framework for Success in Postsecondary Writing*. Under the section "Developing Critical Thinking through Writing, Reading, and Research," this framework identifies eight learning outcomes, which include these three that are close fits to concepts in ACRL's *Framework*:

- "evaluate sources for credibility, bias, quality of evidence, and quality of reasoning"
- "conduct primary and secondary research using a variety of print and non-print sources"
- "generate questions to guide research" (WPA, NCTE, and NWP, 2011: 7).

This framework document was adapted from and aligned with the Writing Program Administrators' *WPA Outcomes Statement for First-Year Composition* (updated and adopted in July 2014). Under its section, "Critical Thinking, Reading, and Composing," it identifies four learning outcomes, one of which is "locate and evaluate (for credibility, sufficiency, accuracy, timeliness, bias, and so on) primary and secondary research materials, including journal articles, essays, books, scholarly and professionally established and maintained databases or archives, and informal electronic networks and internet sources" (WPA, 2014: 2).

Historians, composition instructors, and other disciplines, in various stages of development, are working with information literacy through the lens of their discipline. Educators, generally, are working with information literacy with the lens of education. Librarians, too, have their lens. And with varying terminology, pedagogical approaches, and degrees of clarity, they are all aimed at the same goal: helping their students achieve competency in information literacy as part of the education process.

⑥ Moving Forward at the Library Level

The Shadow of the *Standards*

More for academic librarians than their classroom educator counterparts in other disciplines, the *Information Literacy Competency Standards for Higher Education* of 2000 cast a long shadow. The *Standards* are what were taught by librarians—in some form—for decades. Today, regarding a *Framework* for information literacy instruction, the older expectations held by both librarians and classroom educators need to be broken down, especially if so much of what library and information science has to offer is to be harvested for information literacy instruction with the *Framework*. In some institutions—possibly those with strong liberal arts traditions—librarians will need to be far more proactive in repositioning themselves as credible educators who are capable of helping faculty to integrate the more complex ideas of the *Framework* into a wide range of disciplines.

Therefore, it is practical and far more productive to be patient with the transition from *Standards* to *Framework*, particularly if an institution has an especially robust information literacy program based on the *Standards*. Keep in mind that though the *Standards* have been rescinded by ACRL, the *Framework* still represents an evolution from the *Standards*, and thus analogies and comparisons are helpful, just as they are in other situations of transition. And, as shown with a simple coding technique (see appendix C), the *Standards* are clearly represented in the *Framework*'s six frames. Teaching by analogy—a technique of going from the familiar to the unfamiliar—is a proven and common technique in teaching.

In addition, becoming information literate is a developmental process, and it is perfectly appropriate to begin with more basic representations and scaffold to the more complex. Initiating discussions in information literacy with a more basic, *Standards*-like perspective can make for a good beginning, a fitting springboard for deeper discourse.

Finally, nothing proceeds from a vacuum or void. Particularly with adult learners, crossing a threshold implies moving from something old to something new and that there is some essence that transcends the finite limits of language and finds new expression that captures new understanding and knowledge. Librarians, information specialists, and interested educators have been on a journey from the *Standards* to the *Framework*, and it is reasonable to acknowledge that those now making the same journey will evolve in a similar fashion.

Partnering with Accrediting Agencies on Information Literacy

At the postsecondary level, the U.S. Department of Education recognizes a number of accrediting agencies, including these regional six: a) the Higher Learning Commission (HCL), b) the Middle States Commission on Higher Education (MSCHE), c) the New England Association of Schools and Colleges (NEASC), d) the Northwest Commission on Colleges and Universities (NWCCU), e) the Southern Association of Colleges and Schools (SACS), and f) the Western Association of Schools and Colleges (WASC). Information literacy is addressed in varying degrees, so the work of the educational institution in responding to information literacy instruction will vary as well. All six agencies recognize the concept of information literacy in some form, with NWCCU and HCL only going as far as to say the institution should teach the effective use of information resources. MSCHE is the most robust, using the term "information literacy" 12 times in its accreditation manual and posting on its website a 118-page document entitled "Developing Research & Communication Skills: Guidelines for Information Literacy in the Curriculum." Of course, at the time this book is being written, none has made a formal response or adjustments for the new *Framework*.

It is clear from looking at the presence of information literacy in current accreditation handbooks, which are as yet *Standards*-based and rather nascent in development, that the landscape for the *Framework* is wide open. Accreditation processes vary as well, if the length or brevity of a given accreditation handbook is any indication; the HCL document is 238 pages, while the NWCCU work is 15. Thus, it is relevant for administrators and stakeholders (which include librarians) involved in an institution's accreditation process to know and understand the criteria that must be met. Certainly, accreditation expectations can be exceeded, but often the people doing the accreditation work focus on what has to be done, rather than looking for ways to do more than what is required. But generally, institutions look to their libraries to guide, if not lead, in meeting accreditation expectations in regard to information resources and information literacy. Therefore campus librarians and library administrators should be fully invested and exceedingly proactive in this opportunity. Don't wait to be asked, and when asked, go as far and wide as you possibly can in helping with the deliverables. Be curious, ask questions, volunteer. Likewise, accreditation administrators and others involved in the accreditation process should get their libraries on board as soon as possible and make it clear that they value the library's robust participation. By simply being as inclusive as possible as well as open to co-equal collaboration with their libraries, campus leadership will help enrich and energize the development of cross-disciplinary information literacy instruction.

Making (More) Room for the *Framework* in Library Schools

Writing in 2005, Heidi Julien studied the websites of 93 library schools globally to examine what, if any, training has been offered to library school students in information literacy instruction. She concluded at that time that there was "inadequate formal preparation for professional librarians doing instructional work" (2005: 210).

Since her study, there has been modest, yet steady progress. Certainly, if information literacy is to be fully realized within the general education curriculum of postsecondary schools—as today's ACRL *Framework for Information Literacy for Higher Education* would necessitate—then library school programs need to improve their efforts in preparing librarians for their more significant roles in the broader education process in terms of ongoing curriculum development, classroom instruction, and faculty collaboration. If the number of ALA-accredited library schools offering courses in information literacy instruction is an indication, this process is well under way. Of the more than 50 accredited library schools, nearly half have specific courses in information literacy instruction and many more in instructional design and teaching in general. In addition, the Instruction Section website (part of the ACRL website) offers a rich menu of teaching tools, instruction models, and other resources that are easily accessible to educational administrators, classroom instructions, and librarians.

More work needs to be done, however. Though the research is slim, courses in information literacy for library science students, especially those that are distinct from bibliographic instruction, do not appear to be strongly emphasized (Yi and Turner, 2014; Hall, 2009). All library schools need to make information literacy education—as exemplified in the *Framework*—a core objective for graduates. Additionally, as demonstrated by some of the pushback to the new *Framework*, some current librarians may feel that the "rules" have changed as to what constitutes a librarian's job. A significant minority feel that the *Framework* is too much of a departure from the more skills-based *Standards* as well the longer tradition of bibliographic instruction, and they see themselves as being asked to prepare a kind of instruction they had not been equipped to deliver. Thus, it is important to not just bolster and adapt library school curriculum to help prepare new graduates to work in today's *Framework* and emerging information ecosystem but also to have accessible professional development opportunities to help current librarians be successful in working with the *Framework*. Ideally, these opportunities would be online to accommodate working professionals.

There also should be occasions for non-librarians to find relevant post-graduate coursework in information literacy, such as the University of Rhode Island's Information Literacy Instruction Certification Program, open to non-MLIS students. Information literacy education for educators can be done within an institution with the help of librarians or through partnerships with local library schools or specific library school faculty.

Library schools themselves, already embedded within a university culture, can create opportunities for education in information literacy instruction for their own university faculty colleagues. This can be achieved generally through such existing agencies as faculty development offices, like the six-week professional development course for faculty created by the Center for Teaching and Learning at Moraine Valley Community College (Swanson, 2017). Or the library school could create stand-alone courses or workshops available to interested faculty or administrators. And finally, library school faculty could create short programs within specific departments—ideally ones that can be delivered by the departments themselves.

⑥ Moving Forward at the Institutional Level

Enhancing Co-Equal Collaboration between Libraries and Other Academic Agencies

Collaboration allows the accomplishment of goals that would not be done otherwise. Teaching the kind of information literacy envisioned in today's ACRL *Framework* will require collaboration among librarians, classroom faculty across the disciplines, and institutional agencies to be fully realized. At the same time, collaboration among faculty has long been acknowledged as critical for educational institutions to achieve the kind of learning outcomes that create lifelong learners (Nelson, 2015). But, as previously mentioned, too often trying to get faculty to collaborate is much like herding cats:

> Teacher collaboration does not occur naturally; it runs against prevailing norms of teacher isolation and individualistic approaches to teaching. Without specific training, teachers often lack the necessary collaboration skills as well as skills in collecting data, making sense of the information, and figuring out its implications for action. (David, 2008/2009: 87)

While it may be overly optimistic to ask librarians or individual faculty to be proactive in helping to create a more collaborative academic environment at their institutions, a few enthusiastic participants and active seekers can be all it takes to get things moving in the right direction. If you can't lead the charge yourself, solicit those agencies within your institution whose leading may be more appropriate (such as faculty development or centers for teaching, learning, and assessment) to implement opportunities and activities to build a more collaborative culture.

On a smaller, less formal scale, a coffee date to discuss an interesting article on collaboration or possibly inviting a colleague to share in an online webinar on collaboration also may help to ignite enthusiasm. Regardless, reading the articles or viewing the webinars alone are useful activities in personal professional development. Collaboration done well can create powerful and effective solutions, while attempting to collaborate without insight into the process can derail matters quickly and possibly poison future collaborations for months to come.

But there are additional reasons to collaborate. While the main purpose of collaboration is to achieve a common goal, Roger Baldwin and Deborah Chang have identified three additional motivating purposes: "increasing prestige or influence, sharing resources and reducing costs, and facilitating learning. Each of these motivators is a pillar supporting the overall incentive for collaboration: the desire for greater achievement through working with others" (2007: 27).

Baldwin and Chang examined how the Andrew Mellon Foundation supported collaborations in higher education in seven ways through its Faculty Career Enhancement Program. Applying for a Mellon grant—or for similar grant programs—to facilitate the development of collaboration at your institution is a good idea, but at least three of the grant ideas can be developed within an institution using internal resources:

1. Scholarly consultation grants: "modest funds to enable professors to travel to consult with colleagues elsewhere . . . or to bring that colleague to the grant recipient's home campus"
2. Field/interest-based conferences or workshops: "faculty [come] together to design conferences and workshops focusing on shared subject specializations or common interdisciplinary or pedagogical interests"
3. Support for intellectual community: "a portion of their grant is used to create space and time on their campuses for intellectual community . . . [faculty] formed reading or discussion groups around broad-based themes" (Baldwin and Chang, 2007: 28–29).

Supported by funds from internal groups such as faculty development or a grants office, all of these ideas can be adapted to form collaborative opportunities in cross-disciplinary information literacy instruction.

Preparing for Change from Non-Library Stakeholders

Collaboration, arbitration, negotiation—what do these terms have in common? They are all processes of change in which the ownership of the process of change is shared. Sharing means compromise and consensus, two practices that require patience and trust. It is a trust that the decisions made are the best possible for all. Whether a librarian or an administrator or a classroom instructor, educators can have strong opinions about the way things must be talked about and done, but understanding is usually limited by personal perspectives and, where understanding is incomplete, so are the solutions.

Co-equal collaboration means that end products may not seem to be everything an individual stakeholder wants, and other things may not be perceived as necessary. It will be something else, something unanticipated, because at the beginning of the process you didn't know all that the other stakeholders needed. As the Rolling Stones song goes, "You can't always get what you want. But if you try sometime, you find you get what you need." It can be nerve-wracking because you are not in control, and you cannot predict the end results. But isn't that the way it needs to happen when you are working for a goal that has to meet the needs that the *situation* requires and not what is perceived to be required by any one individual or any one group?

Librarians, with their long tradition in bibliographic instruction and a decade and a half of experience with the *Standards*, are challenged possibly more than other stakeholders to think outside their box, and that's uncomfortable. But it's necessary if information literacy instruction is to be truly cross-disciplinary and embedded within curricula and syllabi. It's necessary to be open-minded and inquisitive—in fact, to practice many of the *Dispositions* articulated by the *Framework*.

Ultimately, a program of information literacy instruction at any given institution will be unlike any other program at another institution, and those working for it need to understand, anticipate, and welcome the changes to be made to create that program.

Assessment: It's How We Know It's Working

Especially within the realm of library and information science, there is an abundance of material addressing information literacy. To a lesser degree, yet at an increasing pace, the other disciplines are warming up to the discourse. A visit to the Instruction Section of the ACRL website or to any of the major websites dealing with information literacy will provide more information, possibly, than a person can intelligently digest.

What is not nearly so rich are tools for assessment, particularly in regard to the *Framework*. In the same study, Julien remarked:

> These results show that (as far as it was possible to determine) fewer than half the courses offered include basic information literacy concepts, outcomes evaluation, needs assessment, or web-based instructional strategies. The omission of needs assessment begs the question of how it is that librarian instructors will develop instructional objectives that will indeed meet the needs of their clients. . . . Failing to teach librarian instructors how to conduct outcomes evaluation is equally problematic. . . . Previous research shows that outcomes evaluation in library instructional activities is rare. (2005: 214–15)

This, of course, is changing, but for now, one of the most significant concerns is how to assess information literacy with the same rigor and specificity that other disciplines, such as nursing or accounting, require. Assessing information literacy skills in terms of learning outcomes is a different measurement than the more common data offered to quantify information literacy instruction, including the number of bibliographic instruction sessions, the number of reference questions, total reference hours, the number of LibGuides or other resources created, or a count of how many times these materials are accessed. This is all helpful information, but what is needed is assessment of the information literacy competency levels of the students themselves. Educational agencies must quantify the student learning outcomes, not the materials or activities meant to instruct:

> Beyond the responsibility for simply instructing students in certain skills however, many accrediting organizations call for assessment of student learning outcomes, defined as a change in knowledge or attitude as a result of interaction with the library, a call which is again echoed throughout higher education literature. (Saunders, 2007: 319)

Given the theoretical character of the *Framework*, much of today's discourse has revolved around how to create assessment tools to provide quantitative data. But more critical to the mission is to implement assessment methods that can quantify the information literacy skills that are inherent in the *habits of minds* that higher education holds as mission-critical to creating lifelong learners for the twenty-first century. Just as the *Framework* broadens the concept of information literacy to exemplify a liberal art, rather than only a set of library-based skills, so also assessment must include the measurement of these broader, beyond-the-library elements of information literacy that prepares the student for the workplace, for self-government, and for personal fulfillment.

Co-equal collaboration is necessary to deliver information literacy instruction that is embedded in classrooms outside the library, managed by disciplines other than library and information science. This means that assessment, too, will come from these classrooms. Thus, collecting assessment data may come largely at the institutional level or the academic department level rather than from the library. This is a challenge that librarians and classroom faculty will need to meet together.

🌀 Key Points

This chapter has discussed some of the main concerns in going forward with implementing *Framework*-based information literacy instruction:

- As exemplified by today's ACRL *Framework*, the type of information literacy is far broader than bibliographic instruction under ACRL's 2000 *Standards* and requires a cross-disciplinary, liberal arts approach in instruction; this is a challenge that all educators must work together to implement.
- The principles found in the *Standards* are still useful instructionally to help learners develop their intellectual skills as they evolve from a more novice starting point to deeper understandings of information literacy. Going from the known (skills-based *Standards*) to the unknown (theory-based and metaliteracy-based *Framework*) is sound pedagogical practice.
- Information literacy is on the radar of all major higher educational regional accrediting agencies, but the details are generally sketchy and, as of yet, based on ACRL's 2000 *Standards*. Librarians and educators alike have a significant opportunity to proactively shape information literacy education to satisfy accreditation demands.
- Library schools in general must work diligently to formally prepare their library school students, as well as practicing librarians and partnering stakeholders, in *Framework* information literacy instruction skills, including assessment practices.
- All information literacy stakeholders need to foster, support, and develop skills for co-equal collaboration.
- Co-equal collaboration means sharing ownership of the process and anticipating the changes needed by partnering stakeholders; it requires training in the collaboration process and practice in many of the *Knowledge Practices* and *Dispositions* articulated in the *Framework*.
- Ubiquitous, practical, rigorous, quantitative assessment based on conventional and normed student learning outcomes is greatly needed. The sooner this can be accomplished, the easier it becomes to work with the *Framework*—for librarians transitioning from the *Standards* and for classroom educators coming up to speed on information literacy concepts but comfortable with discipline-specific educational practices.

🌀 References

Baldwin, Roger G., and Deborah A. Chang. 2007. "Collaborating to Learn, Learning to Collaborate." *Peer Review* 9, no. 4 (Fall): 26–30.

Council of Writing Program Administrators (WPA). 2014. *WPA Outcomes Statement for First-Year Composition* (V3.0). Council of Writing Program Administrators. July 17. http://wpacouncil.org/positions/outcomes.html.

Council of Writing Program Administrators (WPA), National Council of Teachers of English (NCTE), and National Writing Project (NWP). 2011. *Framework for Success in Postsecondary Writing.* Council of Writing Program Administrators. January. http://wpacouncil.org/framework.

David, Jane L. 2008/2009. "What Research Says About / Collaborative Inquiry." *Educational Leadership* 66, no. 4 (December–January): 87–88.

Edkins, Brett. 2016. "Americans Believe They Can Detect Fake News: Studies Show They Can't." *Forbes,* December 20. http://www.forbes.com/sites/brettedkins/2016/12/20/americans-be lieve-they-can-detect-fake-news-studies-show-they-cant/#57ad0d1f54a4.

Hall, Russell A. 2009. "Exploring the Core: An Examination of Required Courses in ALA-Accredited." *Education for Information* 27, no. 1: 57–67.

Julien, Heidi. 2005. "Education for Information Literacy Instruction: A Global Perspective." *Journal of Education for Library and Information Science* 46, no. 3 (Summer): 210–16.

Nelson, Jennie. 2015. "'It Takes a Whole Campus': Information Literacy in Composition and across the Curriculum." *Journal of Teaching Writing* 28, no. 1: 85–116.

Saunders, Laura. 2007. "Regional Accreditation Organizations' Treatment of Information Literacy: Definitions, Collaboration, and Assessment." *Journal of Academic Librarianship* 33, no. 3: 317–26.

Shellenbarger, Sue. 2016. "Most Students Don't Know When News Is Fake, Stanford Study Shows. *Wall Street Journal,* November 21. https://www.wsj.com/articles/most-students-dont -know-when-news-is-fake-stanford-study-finds-1479752576.

Swanson, Tony. 2017. "Sharing the ACRL Framework with Faculty: Opening Campus Conversations." *College & Research Libraries News* 78, no. 1 (January): 12–14, 48.

Wineberg, Sam, and Sarah McGrew. 2016. "Evaluating Information: The Cornerstone of Civic Online Reasoning (Executive Summary)." https://sheg.stanford.edu/upload/V3LessonPlans/ Executive%20Summary%2011.21.16.pdf.

Yi, Kwan, and Ralph Turner. 2014. "The Current Landscape of the School Librarianship Curricula in USA." *Journal of Education for Library and Information Science* 55, no. 4 (October): 303–21.

⦿ Further Reading

American Academy for Liberal Education. 2013. *Program Standards of Excellence in Liberal Education.* Alexandria, VA: American Academy for Liberal Education. http://www.aale.org/docs/ Program%20Stds.Oct%202013.pdf.

Bailey, Edgar C. 2010. "Educating Future Academic Librarians: An Analysis of Courses in Academic Librarianship." *Journal of Education for Library and Information Science* 51, no. 1 (Winter): 30–42.

Hill, Lott, Soo L. Kim, and Robert Lagueux. 2007. "Faculty Collaboration as Faculty Development." *Peer Review* 9, no. 4 (Fall): 17–19.

Koltay, Tibor. 2011. "The Media and the Literacies: Media Literacy, Information Literacy, Digital Literacy." *Media, Culture & Society* 33, no. 2 (March): 211–21.

Pashaie, William. 2005. *Academic Libraries, Information Literacy, and Higher Education Accreditation.* Master's thesis, University of California, Los Angeles. https://openlibrary.org/authors/ OL7174828A/William_Pashaie.

Thompson, Gary B. 2002. "Information Literacy Accreditation Mandates: What They Mean for Faculty and Librarians." *Library Trends* 51, no. 2 (Fall): 218–41.

Wiebe, Todd J. 2016. "The Information Literacy Imperative in Higher Education. *Liberal Education* 101/102, no. 4/1 (Fall 2015/Winter 2016): 52–57. http://digitalcommons.hope.edu/cgi/ viewcontent.cgi?article=2521&context=faculty_publications.

Appendix A

What Is Information Literacy?
A Short Guide for Faculty
and Librarians

WHILE INFORMATION LITERACY HAS a history dating back to the 1970s in library and information science, it is less developed in terms of being an established and core aspect of an individual's education. Across the curriculum, faculty are very much in favor of the concept of information literacy but generally are not very clear on how that translates into typical classroom instruction within a given discipline. How do you go about embedding information literacy instruction within your course in, say, history, biology, technology, or music? If you are that faculty member, this guide is for you.

Published in early 2017 by Dave Harmeyer, an academic librarian, and Janice J. Baskin, a classroom faculty, "What Is Information Literacy? A Short Guide for Faculty and Librarians" was originally issued as a six-part series in Azusa Pacific University's bimonthly *Provost Newsletter*. The following resource is provided as one example of how to introduce one or more of the six frames of the 2015 Association of College & Research Libraries (ACRL) *Framework for Information Literacy for Higher Education* to classroom faculty in any discipline. Each essay has two parts. The first half is a faculty-friendly introduction to one of the six frames, explaining more fully what it means, contextualizing it and demonstrating how it is relevant to lifelong learning and to an overall education program. The second half is a scenario between an academic librarian and a classroom faculty member collaborating to plan and implement an information literacy class assignment. Assignments are within one of six discipline-specific courses and delivered in the context of one of three different student classifications (freshmen, advanced undergraduate, or graduate levels). Table A.1 gives an overview of which student type and which course is covered in each of the six essay scenarios. Finally, each essay ends with a rubric handout to be used for assessing the information literacy assignment that resulted from the conversation.

Table A.1. Student Classification and Course Title for Each Scenario in "What Is Information Literacy?"

FRAME	STUDENT CLASSIFICATION	COURSE TITLE
Part 1: Authority Is Constructed and Contextual	Undergraduates—mid to higher level	English Literature
Part 2: Information Creation as a Process	Freshmen	Biology
Part 3: Information Has Value	Master's program students	Seminar in Music History
Part 4: Research as Inquiry	Lower division accounting students	Accounting—section on ethics
Part 5: Scholarship as Conversation	Freshmen and sophomores	Exploring Genesis (Bible)
Part 6: Searching as Strategic Exploration	Adult learners, online	Public Communication

The following six essays are intended to be used as conversation starters between librarians and classroom faculty. One or more of the articles, in the context of faculty-librarian collaboration, can help both come up with creative ideas to be adapted into a classroom setting, on-the-ground or online. In this way, every student will have an information literacy experience that benefits him or her in the development of information skills as well as the capacity to think more conceptually as an information-literate person, criteria highly sought by employers hiring college graduates.

In addition to being used as a six-part, bimonthly email to faculty, other uses of the essays include adding them to a LibGuide on information literacy, uploading the entire document to a campus Google Drive, or create a print or online faculty guidebook. Any use of one or more of the essays will also need to include the following attribution: Reproduced from *Implementing the Information Literacy Framework: A Practical Guide for Librarians* by Dave Harmeyer and Janice J. Baskin. © 2018 Rowman & Littlefield Publishers.

Both PDF and Word versions of "What Is Information Literacy? A Short Guide for Faculty and Librarians" are available on the book's website: https://implementingtheinfor mationliteracyframework.wordpress.com/ or https://tinyurl.com/ya6h4vyq.

What Is Information Literacy? A Short Guide for Faculty and Librarians

Part 1: Authority Is Constructed and Contextual

What is information literacy? Many times, faculty think of it as library instruction. But, in fact, it is a much broader idea today both in education and in library and information science. Information literacy is now defined as a set of intellectual skills that students need to successfully navigate their lives as citizens, consumers, and individuals in pursuit of happiness. All decisions—medical, financial, civic, career, and more—are predicated on a person's ability to define, choose, and gather relevant information; evaluate and analyze that information; and then synthesize and create new information—in a world overflowing with information from countless sources utilizing myriad technologies. Accrediting bodies like the Western Association of Schools and Colleges (WASC) and global agencies like the United Nations Educational, Scientific and Cultural Organization (UNESCO) recognize that education should prepare the individual to be lifelong learners, in part through being information literate.

Faculty may be familiar with the five *Information Literacy Competency Standards for Higher Education* as approved by the ACRL in 2000. These *Standards* are skills-based and help assure that an information-literate person is able to:

- Determine the nature and extent of information needed
- Access needed information effectively and efficiently
- Evaluate information and its sources critically and incorporate selected information into his or her knowledge base and value system
- Use information effectively to accomplish a specific purpose
- Understand the economic, legal, and social issues surrounding the use of information, and access and use information ethically and legally.

But in 2015 that changed—radically. ACRL replaced the five *Standards* with the six frames of the *Framework for Information Literacy for Higher Education*, based on the idea of threshold concepts, "those ideas in any discipline that are passageways or portals to enlarged understanding or ways of thinking and practicing within that discipline." That is, there are now six concepts that are said to encompass information literacy, and these concepts change the very nature of information literacy instruction. These frames, listed here, are theory-based rather than focused on skills as the *Standards* were often perceived:

- Authority Is Constructed and Contextual
- Information Creation as a Process
- Information Has Value
- Research as Inquiry
- Scholarship as Conversation
- Searching as Strategic Exploration.

Thus, each frame is adaptable and relevant to any discipline. Let's take a closer look at the first one listed: "Authority Is Constructed and Contextual." ACRL states:

Information resources reflect their creators' expertise and credibility, and are evaluated based on the information need and the context in which the information will be used. Authority is constructed in that various communities may recognize different types of authority. It is contextual in that the information need may help to determine the level of authority required. (ACRL, 2015)

What does this mean to your discipline and what does it look like in your classroom? Librarians today will need to help faculty and administrators explore and determine how these *habits of mind* will be developed and assessed through their courses, their programs, and their schools. The concepts are meant to be embedded in learning outcomes, threaded through course assignments, and explicitly addressed in curriculum.

So, to help begin this conversation, let's look at a practical classroom example in the field of English literature that investigates the frame "Authority Is Constructed and Contextual."

* * *

A librarian and a classroom faculty member are discussing a classroom exercise that the faculty member recently used to teach the ACRL information literacy frame "Authority Is Constructed and Contextual." Let's listen in on part of their conversation.

Jack Lewis, classroom faculty: Of the six information literacy frames, the first one, "Authority Is Constructed and Contextual," seemed to be a good fit for my English Literature course.

Rhett Sarch, librarian: So, what did you do to start off?

Jack: I divided the class into groups of four or five and had one student in each group take notes on a Word document from an email I sent everyone before class. The document had a place for student names, plus two columns. One column was labeled "Author Guidelines" and the other, "Rationale." The guidelines were broken into sections titled "Mission," "Scope," "Style," and so on.

Then I explained that each group represents an editorial board for a scholarly journal called the *Journal of Christianity & English Literature*. I also sent them, ahead of time, a link to the journal's actual author guidelines as a model to follow in order to create their own set of guidelines. After 25 minutes, note takers shared with the entire class one section of their group's "Author Guidelines" and its corresponding "Rationale."

Rhett: How were you able to teach about the context of an author's authority?

Jack: That was easy. Based on what students learned in the exercise, I then led them in a discussion of what items a curriculum vitae of a potential author of the journal article might include. I listed each criterion as a bulleted item on the whiteboard.

Rhett: That's impressive, Jack. But how did you measure student learning?

Jack: Like you said, information literacy is only as good as what you can assess. During the last few minutes of class, I gave them a prompt for a reflective exercise for which they wrote one new thing learned from the theme, "Authority Is Constructed and Contextual," which they turned in. Also, this exercise was followed up with further reflection in that week's threaded discussions in Sakai.

Rhett: OK, so you ended up with three artifacts for measuring learning: first, the group-designed Author Guidelines; second, the list of author criteria; and third, the students' written reflections. How did you work out an assessment of all that?

Jack: I created a simple rubric. [See "Rubric Handout for Author Guideline Exercise."] Then, for each student I checked the relevant box and wrote a few thoughts in the comment box. So this assignment ended up being an element of the entire course grade, yet it is also individual data that could be used for other assessment needs, including accreditation.

Reference

Association of College & Research Libraries (ACRL). 2015. *Framework for Information Literacy for Higher Education*. American Library Association. http://www.ala.org/acrl/standards/ilframework.

RUBRIC HANDOUT FOR AUTHOR GUIDELINE EXERCISE

Name: _____ Date: _____

Standards of Evaluation	Accomplished	Proficient	Developing	Novice
GROUP: ANALYZE At what level did the student's group cover: mission, scope, style, and authority in the new author guidelines	a) Brief but clear mission, b) clearly defined scope of English Lit (dates), c) style of writing MLA/APA correct, and d) a sense of author authority	Strong in three of the four areas	Strong in two of the four areas	Strong in none or one of the four areas
Score:	20–25	15–19	10–14	5–9
GROUP: EVALUATE Level of convincing argument in the RATIONALE column	a) Thoughtful, b) persuasive, c) often multiple parts, and d) all parts of the model guidelines mentioned	Strong in three of the four areas	Strong in two of the four areas	Strong in none or one of the four areas
Score:	20–25	15–19	10–14	5–9
INDIVIDUAL: COMPREHENSION Based on reflective exercise, level of comprehending an important part of the whole lesson	Clearly stated one of the important parts of the lesson	Stated one important part of the lesson but not clearly	Stated something that was of minor importance	Missed stating any important parts of the lesson
Score:	45–50	40–44	35–39	30–34

Total Score: /100

Comments:

ⓖ What Is Information Literacy? A Short Guide for Faculty and Librarians

Part 2: Information Creation as a Process

Many college courses require writing, and all require reading. But the skills of reading and writing critically at the college level are much different than those of reading, say, a popular magazine, or writing out directions to a friend's house, or sending a series of texts to decide which restaurant to eat at or movie to see. To be information literate, according to the ACRL, a person needs to understand what's involved in creating the information received as well as the information he or she intends to deliver. Inside its new *Framework for Information Literacy for Higher Education*, ACRL identifies one of six information literacy frames it calls "Information Creation as a Process" and defines it:

> Information in any format is produced to convey a message and is shared via a selected delivery method. The iterative processes of researching, creating, revising, and disseminating information vary, and the resulting product reflects these differences. (ACRL, 2015)

The first thing that may come to mind when considering applications for this frame is a freshman writing class or a course with a research paper assignment. A second thing may be the feeling that this frame is really more about being able to write a college paper than it is about information literacy. But writing—or communicating—is only part of this frame.

Just as important—or perhaps more so—is understanding how any information you receive got to you. It also means understanding the implications of the format of a piece of information. What are the differences between a blog and an academic journal article or a report on a website funded by a pharmaceutical company and a mainstream newspaper article? What sort of review process or gatekeeping is involved? How do you find background on how any piece of information was created (and what does it mean if you can't)? What happens when the format of a message changes—how do perceptions change when the same information is delivered in the *Los Angeles Times* versus a radio talk show? And even in similar formats, how is the same information framed differently in each? What are the criteria for credibility, reliability, and authenticity for any given format? How transparent is the process—who can impact it or influence it negatively or positively? When is the immediacy of the format important, and when does it impair or corrupt discourse?

The information-literate person will know what formats or modes are relevant to any information need and adapt accordingly, both in terms of accepting information as valid or sound and in terms of choosing the right vehicle for communicating his or her created information to others. He or she also has the intellectual skill to evaluate emerging forms and modes of information delivery and to utilize them appropriately and ethically. The information-literate individual also has the awareness to detect relevant new modes.

So, like the other five ACRL information literacy frames, this one goes far beyond knowing how to locate an acceptable source and how to properly cite that source in a paper. Whether studying to be a psychologist, a computer programmer, or a business executive, understanding the culture of communication in a particular field is one of the keys to future career success. For a practical illustration of this frame, let's look at a classroom exercise on "Information Creation as a Process" in the discipline of biology.

＊　＊　＊

A librarian and a classroom faculty member are discussing a classroom exercise that the faculty member recently used in class to teach some of the concepts included in the ACRL information literacy frame "Information Creation as a Process."

Chuck Warind, classroom faculty: After our discussion on the new information literacy frames, I decided that "Information Creation as a Process" was a good fit for an assignment I give to my freshmen biology class.

Rhett Sarch, librarian: So, how did you introduce the idea within this class assignment?

Chuck: First, I introduced the class to the overall concept of "Information Creation as a Process" and discussed how it pertains to the field of biology. I broke the class into small groups to create guidelines for using this lens, as you call it, for managing information in field of biology. We then pooled our ideas together as a class and created a one-page guide for the main assignment.

Rhett: You've got my interest. What was your big assignment?

Chuck: The term assignment required a self-publishing exercise with two other classmates. Each student needed to create a *Wikipedia* entry for a newly discovered species of mammals he or she picked from a list.

Rhett: I didn't know there were new species being discovered. Where do you find them?

Chuck: New species are reported by Sci-News.com. I check to see if these have been added to *Wikipedia* before making a list. Each group of three students regularly met online using Padlet, a digital bulletin board, using the "Information Creation as a Process" guide for biology that we created as a class to direct their progress and thoughts.

Rhett: How did you grade each student and assess their information literacy progress?

Chuck: I used a simple rubric to score students in three areas: the number and quality of resources they found about their species, the level of relevant postings in Padlet, and their final entry in *Wikipedia*. [See "Rubric Handout for *Wikipedia* Species Entry Assignment."] The three categories are scored as numbers and entered into my grade book and added to aggregate university data for reports. The rubric was included in the assignment.

Reference

Association of College & Research Libraries (ACRL). 2015. *Framework for Information Literacy for Higher Education*. American Library Association. http://www.ala.org/acrl/standards/ilframework.

RUBRIC HANDOUT FOR *WIKIPEDIA* SPECIES ENTRY ASSIGNMENT

Name: _____ Date: _____

Standards of Evaluation	Accomplished	Proficient	Developing	Novice
RESOURCES **Number and quality**	Found up to three evidences from highly reputable sources; APA/MLA style correct	Found up to two evidences from good sources; APA/MLA style mostly correct	All evidences from mediocre sources and/or APA/MLA style incorrect	All evidences from questionable sources and/or APA/MLA style mostly incorrect
Score:	20–25	15–19	10–14	5–9
FRAMEWORK POSTINGS IN PADLET **Number and quality mentioning "Information Creation as a Process"**	More than three clear, thoughtful references to "Information Creation as a Process"	Three clear, thoughtful references to "Information Creation as a Process"	Less than three references to "Information Creation as a Process"	No references to "Information Creation as a Process"
Score:	20–25	15–19	10–14	5–9
***WIKIPEDIA* ENTRY** **Inclusion of "Information Creation as a Process"**	Clearly included one or more concepts in "Information Creation as a Process"	In between Accomplished and Developing	In between Proficient and Novice	No clear evidence that "Information Creation as a Process" was included
Score:	45–50	40–44	35–39	30–34
Total Score: /100				
Comments:				

⑥ What Is Information Literacy? A Short Guide for Faculty and Librarians

Part 3: Information Has Value

As citizens in a democratic society, we need to understand the importance of information—the false or misleading, as well as the true. We are not merely consumers of information, isolated and transitory, like taking a morning cup of coffee, unaware that the information received and the information created by us has a positive or negative effect. Writing classes teach about the purposes of information to entertain, to inform, to influence, to self-express. Political science and journalism classes discuss the barriers to freedom of information, whether human or technological, and the ramifications of withheld, inaccessible, or managed information. As the ACRL expresses it in its *Framework*, those expert in information literacy "understand that [information's] value may be wielded by powerful interests in ways that marginalize certain voices" and that information's value "may also be leveraged by individuals and organizations to effect change, and for civic, economic, social, or personal gains" (ACRL, 2015). Imagine what kind of choices are made if a person does not have the intellectual tools to gauge the value of so much information that is thrust upon him or her daily in today's oversaturated information environment. Consider the reading of your Miranda rights—what good does that do if you don't comprehend its value?

ACRL defines the information literacy frame "Information Has Value" as follows:

> Information possesses several dimensions of value as a commodity, as a means of education, as a means to influence, and as a means of negotiating and understanding the world. Legal and socioeconomic interests influence information production and dissemination. (ACRL, 2015)

In regard to this frame, novice learners see information sources with little sophistication. Information typically is seen as equal and offered transparently without any guile. If criteria for evaluation are used, they tend to be self-serving, egocentric, and ethnocentric. Critical reasoning skills are nascent, and thus judging a source as trustworthy is largely an emotional decision. There is little, if any, "reading against the grain," and research is viewed as a hunt for ammunition to buttress a currently held opinion rather than an inquiry or participation in a discourse for the development of new knowledge or discovery of truth. Claims without support, or with invalid or hidden premises, go unnoticed. The ethical imperative to consider a diversity of sources is also unrecognized and unrealized.

Particularly important in today's information environment or ecosystem is understanding how personal information is commodified and how, good or bad, the newer forms of media feed information to those who are linked in. Whether you are looking for new tires or interested in a cause, you can find yourself the target of a relentless stream of unsolicited information of varying degrees of worth. Being information literate today also means knowing how to protect your identity against misuse and theft, knowing what can happen to your comments, posts, tweets, texts, and emails, and knowing how to act ethically. As the ACRL asserts regarding this frame, "Experts [on information literacy] also understand that the individual is responsible for making deliberate and informed choices about when to comply with and when to contest current legal and socioeconomic practices concerning the value of information" (2015).

Because information *has* value, the information producer and user both have an ethical responsibility to control his or her information behavior, to protect one's own privacy as well as respect that of others, and to respect the ideas of others—their intellectual property. Especially today, when so much information is electronic, stealing another's information—and worse, misusing it through distortion or misrepresentation—can seem an invisible crime. Abiding by intellectual property laws can be difficult without a well-developed sense of intellectual and academic integrity. Teaching our students academic integrity is one of our most important tasks as educators. All disciplines can be damaged by the lack of academic integrity.

The concept of "Information Has Value" goes far beyond simply choosing a relevant and trustworthy source for an academic assignment. From voting for a candidate to trusting the new drug your doctor prescribed to buying a phone or car that doesn't explode, being able to accurately appraise the value of information and then appropriately using it is key. To help illustrate this frame, here is a classroom exercise on "Information Has Value" in the discipline of music.

*   *   *

A librarian and a classroom faculty are discussing a classroom exercise that the faculty recently used in class to teach the ACRL information literacy frame "Information Has Value."

Wolfgang K. Browne, classroom faculty: Of the six information literacy frames, the third one, "Information Has Value," seemed to be a good fit for an assignment in my master's level Seminar in Music History course.

Rhett Sarch, librarian: So, how did you introduce the frame within a class session?

Wolfgang: I asked the class to break into groups of two or three. By then each student had chosen a topic related to music history. I passed out to everyone a 3 × 5 card and a handout which had a copy of the 10-source annotated bibliography assignment from the syllabus, which included the two-paragraph description from the frame "Information Has Value."

I asked the groups to take 15 minutes to read through and discuss the frame's description together in light of the assignment, which instructed students to write 2–4 sentence annotations summarizing each of the 10 sources, in light of the frame's two-paragraph description. By the end of the 15 minutes, every student was to write down on a 3 × 5 card one statement that related to what they just learned or a question they had and then pass their cards to me.

Rhett: Great idea. It engages each student to think about a frame and express an opinion without risking embarrassment in a public discussion. How did you further integrate the frame into your class time?

Wolfgang: After briefly looking over the cards, I used students' statements and questions as springboards into a class discussion on "Information Has Value." For example, one card asked: "How does a marginalized music history idea get noticed if only certain other ideas get published?"

I explained to the class that using this frame, we can see that any music history idea, as information, has value and that there are non-traditional ways that are used as means of influence. I then asked students what non-traditional ways might be used to increase the influence of such an idea. They suggested social media like Facebook or Twitter, as well as creating a free blog.

White, Harry. "The Oratorios of Johann Joseph Fux and the Imperial Court in Vienna."
Studies in Music from the University Of Western Ontario 15, (1995): 1-17. Accessed
February 10, 2017. http://0-
search.ebscohost.com.patris.apu.edu/login.aspx?direct=true&db=
rih&AN=A172660&site=eds-live&scope=site.

White's views describe the significant influences of both the Catholic Church as well
as the Imperial Court in Vienna had on the 17th century composer Johann Joseph Fux. In
White's opinion, the environmental forces not only "confirm[s] the authenticity of Vienna as
a distinctive voice" in the "bewildering musical plurality of the Baroque ear" but also
demonstrates the influences of these two world views being produced and disseminated
throughout the history of Baroque style and especially upon its many composers.

Figure A.1. Annotated citation of White's "The Oratorios of Johann Joseph Fux."

Rhett: Can you give me an idea of what an annotation looks like written with this frame in mind?

Wolfgang: Sure, I have a copy on my phone of the three I shared in class. Here's the first one [see figure A.1]. As you see it, begins with the citation in Chicago style, followed by my annotation with underlines showing where it refers to the frame "Information Has Value."

Rhett: So, as students write their annotations they are using the frame as a lens through which to do so. How did you then assess their learning?

Wolfgang: On the handout with the frame's definitions I included a rubric used to score the assignment. And, as I said, I required students to highlight in color that part of each annotation that referenced the frame. And here's a copy of that rubric. [See "Rubric Handout for an Annotated Bibliography Assignment."]

Reference

Association of College & Research Libraries (ACRL). 2015. *Framework for Information Literacy for Higher Education*. American Library Association. http://www.ala.org/acrl/standards/ilframework.

RUBRIC HANDOUT FOR AN ANNOTATED BIBLIOGRAPHY ASSIGNMENT

Name: _____ Date: _____

Standards of Evaluation	Accomplished	Proficient	Developing	Novice
RESOURCES **Number and quality**	All 10 were from highly reputable sources	Eight or nine were from good sources	Six or seven were from good sources	Five or fewer were from good sources
Score:	20–25	15–19	10–14	5–9
FRAME IN ANNOTATIONS **Number and quality mentioning "Information Has Value"**	All 10 annotations had clear, thoughtful references to "Information Has Value"	Eight or nine annotations had clear, thoughtful references to "Information Has Value"	Six or seven annotations had references to "Information Has Value"	Five or fewer annotations had references to "Information Has Value"
Score:	45–50	15–19	10–14	5–9
STYLE **Level of accuracy and completeness of citations**	All 10 citations were accurate and complete	Eight or nine citations were accurate and complete	Six or seven citations were accurate and complete	Five or fewer citations were accurate and complete
Score:	20–25	15–19	10–14	5–9
Total Score: /100				
Comments:				

What Is Information Literacy? A Short Guide for Faculty and Librarians

Part 4: Research as Inquiry

There is an old joke that goes something like this: Just after dark, a little boy is crawling on all fours all around a street corner, intensely searching for something. A police officer stops and asks the boy, "What are you doing?" The boy responds, "I lost a dollar at Fifth and Main and I am looking for it." "But this is Fourth and Main," the officer replies, "why are you looking here?" Says the boy: "Because the light's better."

Good research begins when you know what you are looking for and where to look for it. But knowing these two things requires practicing several other intellectual skills, including knowing how to define a problem, knowing how to ask relevant questions, and being able to organize, analyze, and interpret information in order to ask deeper, more complex questions. It means being able to assess the validity and worth of sources and any given line of thinking along the way in order to avoid being misled or falling into fallacious or irrelevant thinking. Good research means knowing the difference between declaring "there wasn't any information" and more humbly stating "I can't find the information" and then seeking assistance.

Above all, research requires intellectual curiosity—maintaining a healthy skepticism in order to not only ask why, but why not? It is open-ended, open-minded, tolerant of ambiguity, persistent, and innovative. In light of this, the ACRL defines the frame "Research as Inquiry" as follows:

> Research is iterative and depends upon asking increasingly complex or new questions whose answers in turn develop additional questions or lines of inquiry in any field. (ACRL, 2015)

Novice researchers tend to take a write-and-stuff approach to research papers and assignments. That is, they put the majority of the paper together first, then go on a hunt for the requisite number of sources to interject into the text. With this write-and-stuff approach, they are much less open to finding and considering information that may challenge or alter their thesis and are often unaware of the need to examine and discuss any refutation to their work. As the song goes, "A man hears what he wants to hear, and disregards the rest." To become effective researchers, we need to take the harder, more disruptive path and seek answers to the questions we sometimes would rather not ask.

Effective research is iterative. It is iterative because it is developmental. But breaking through the crash-course mentality of students, who often procrastinate until the eleventh hour to complete an assignment—a strategy unlikely to allow the intellectual development of a research idea—can be tough. By way of an analogy, let's say your assignment is for students to paint a picture of a fish. The first time they paint it, it is basically recognizable. You see the tail, the fins, some representation of the scales, the fish mouth. No, you say to students, you have missed so much. You point out several things, and then say, "Go back and look again, and then paint again." This happens several times. By the sixth or seventh time students' eyes begin to open: They notice the iridescence in the scales, the way they curve around the body, the musculature of the tail, the graceful feathering of the fins. And your students begin to develop new drawing strategies to capture these qualities and thus begin to apprehend and know what a fish is.

So it is with the ideas found in the frame "Research as Inquiry." Students' first questions are basic, straightforward, and often oversimplified. As they proceed in their inquiries, they begin to recognize that some of these first questions were inaccurate or incomplete, and they ask better questions, more nuanced, drawing on the new language of their topic, building on the fundamental knowledge gained by their first iterations, crossing new thresholds of understanding to create more meaningful questions, and synthesizing valid ideas from pertinent information. These are the intellectual skills individuals will need to meet the challenges in their lives; they will need to develop the intellectual patience to investigate problems fully, to suspend judgment as they work through the inquiry process, and to come to a more comprehensive understanding so that they can craft the most effective solutions. What follows is a scenario to illustrate the information literacy frame "Research as Inquiry."

* * *

As the liaison librarian for the School of Business, Rhett Sarch has determined that the frame "Research as Inquiry" is the inroad that will offer accounting students an information literacy experience and one that can be measured. Rhett spent time looking over the frame's definitions, *Knowledge Practices*, and *Dispositions*, jotting down notes and highlighting certain words and phrases. He then looked over a couple of the accounting course syllabi and reflected on the program description and course descriptions. One topic that appeared to be common to all documents was that of ethics; for example, ethical accounting and the statement found in Research as Inquiry: "Learners who are developing their information literate abilities . . . follow ethical and legal guidelines in gathering and using information" (ACRL, 2015).

The next day, having done his homework, Rhett made an appointment with one of the accounting professors. The following is their conversation.

Rhett Sarch, librarian: Thanks, Luca, for making time in your schedule to brainstorm some ideas together to add an information literacy component to your lower division accounting classes.

Luca Pacioli, classroom accounting faculty: Sure, you're welcome. But like I said, I'm pretty skeptical we can come up with something. There's precious little time to get through all my normal class content.

Rhett: I certainly understand. What I propose is a kind of flipped classroom experience for students, something that is completely outside of class but graded, like a regular assignment. And something that incorporates content you already intend to cover.

Luca: OK, can you show me what you mean?

Rhett: I've studied up on a couple of your syllabi, the program's description, and class descriptions. One thing that's common to all, and to the information literacy frame "Research as Inquiry," is ethics. I think this frame might be a catalyst to provide your students with an information literacy learning experience.

Luca: Yes, the ethics of accounting is a topic that never seems to go away! I don't cover it extensively in my course content. What ideas do you have?

Rhett: It's a simple idea. Students in a class are randomly divided into two teams. One team will take the perspective that ethics in accounting is a good thing, the other team takes the perspective that ethics in accounting is not as good as it seems. Both teams will be given a link to the frame "Research as Inquiry." They will be graded by the quality and depth of using the frame in the process of researching their assigned perspective and the final deliverables, which will be: a bibliography of at least five resources in APA style, a three-minute video illustrating their point of view on ethics in accounting, and a simple descriptive timeline (a page or less) showing some sense of an iterative process in their team's experience. Students could do something as fun as a mannequin challenge or as conventional as a recorded presentation. The three items are turned in by a deadline and graded by a rubric. All members of a team receive the same grade based on the rubric.

Luca: So let me get this straight, this is entirely outside of class? Who grades it?

Rhett: That's up to you. Maybe have one team grade the other team, or let your grad assistant do it, or you.

Luca: What about the rubric?

Rhett: I'm working on a draft and will send it to you for your consideration in the next few days. [See "Rubric Handout for Ethics of Accounting: Pro/Con Assignment."]

Luca: I suppose if it goes well I may show the videos in class, do a re-cap of the topic, and add any material not covered. I love it!

Rhett: Thanks, Luca. Let's set a meeting for next week for any loose ends.

Reference

Association of College & Research Libraries (ACRL). 2015. *Framework for Information Literacy for Higher Education*. American Library Association. http://www.ala.org/acrl/standards/ilframework.

RUBRIC HANDOUT FOR ETHICS OF ACCOUNTING: PRO/CON ASSIGNMENT

Team: _____ Date: _____

Standards of Evaluation	Accomplished	Proficient	Developing	Novice
BIBLIOGRAPHY Number and quality of resources (articles/books); resources do not need to support either position	Five or more articles/books from highly reputable sources and APA style correct	Articles/books from good sources and/or APA style mostly correct	Most articles/ books from mediocre sources and/or APA style somewhat incorrect	Most articles/books from questionable sources and/or APA style mostly incorrect
Score:	20–25	15–19	10–14	5–9
VIDEO Number and quality of mentioning concepts found in "Research as Inquiry"	More than three clear, thoughtful connections to "Research as Inquiry"	Three clear, thoughtful connections to "Research as Inquiry"	Less than three connections to "Research as Inquiry"	No connections to "Research as Inquiry"
Score:	20–25	15–19	10–14	5–9
TIMELINESS	Both bibliography and video turned in on time	Only bibliography turned in on time	Only video turned in on time	Neither bibliography nor video turned in on time
Score:	20–25	15–19	10–14	5–9
TIMELINE Quality of explaining some sense of an iterative process in students' bibliography/ video experience	Timeline shows five or more developments that show a progressive iterative process	Timeline shows less than five developments that show an iterative process	Timeline appears more confusing than clearly showing an iterative process	Timeline shows no clear iterative process
Score:	20–25	15–19	10–14	5–9
Total Score: /100				
Comments:				

Part 5: Scholarship as Conversation

The only constant is change, declared Heraclitus, a Greek philosopher (500 BCE), and that, perhaps, is a fitting characterization for the fifth "frame" of information literacy, "Scholarship as Conversation." As anyone who has reentered a conversation (much changed from its start) knows, talking changes things. Discourse is dynamic—while the reasons we share information may be murky, we are compelled to share. Being information literate in scholarly or professional discourse means that you understand the process required to participate successfully as well as benefit from the conversation and that the nature of the discourse is to change or evolve.

What changes discourse is a number of things, all inherent in the information-literate mind: to understand that the conversation is not finished, but ongoing; to not just value different perspectives, but seek them out; to both contribute to and evaluate contributions to the conversation; to tolerate ambiguity, suspend judgment, and exercise responsibility during the process; and finally, to recognize that the purpose of the process is to "negotiate meaning" among your community.

Whether a gang of video gamers or a task force of neurosurgeons, groups of people with common interests and common goals talk to others within the group in specialized ways with specialized rules of evidence and authority and specialized language. In rhetoric, these are known as "discourse communities," and the ACRL definition for "Scholarship as Conversation" demonstrates strong similarities to these:

> Communities of scholars, researchers, or professionals engage in sustained discourse with new insights and discoveries occurring over time as a result of varied perspectives and interpretations. (ACRL, 2015)

Information-literate individuals have learned the skills and developed the appropriate mind-sets to enter into a scholarly or professional conversation, comprehend its milieu, participate successfully, and make relevant and valuable contributions to the knowledge base. More than that, they understand that not being able to do so disempowers the individual. Information-literate people comprehend that if they don't know the language of their discourse communities or its unique modes of communication, they are hampered, if not barred, from communication.

Since all students aspire to enter some profession, the ability to hear and be heard within that professional community is vital to career success. Also essential is students' ability to follow the development of important issues in the field they are pursuing, to recognize the key contributors to those issues, as well as to recognize new voices in whatever venue and from any valid, though possibly differing, perspectives. Innovation often comes from unexpected places, so the ability to take in information from unexpected places is key.

In addition to their relevance in workplace and professional conversations, the information literacy skills practiced from the frame "Scholarship as Conversation" are also important for civic life and for any situation where a discourse community has formed. In fact, for any leadership role, whether church elder, community organizer, or humanitarian advocate, the ability to effectively manage the professional conversation can mean the difference between truly changing a situation and merely being busy.

Now let's take a look at a scenario that helps illustrate how a librarian and faculty member might collaborate to teach the information literacy frame "Scholarship as Conversation."

* * *

Rhett has been teaching one-shot library instruction sessions for the Department of Biblical and Religious Studies (DBRS) for 10 years. In compliance with the university's new information literacy initiative, Rhett and his fellow librarians are working more collaboratively with faculty in order to implement a new information literacy model. The director of DBRS has shared with Rhett all current Old Testament undergraduate syllabi. Working together, Rhett and the director are identifying one course that has a large number of course sections taught to mostly undergraduate DBRS majors. The two are looking for something that might work well as a broad-based information literacy student experience. They settle on the course Exploring Genesis, which all DBRS students take before their junior year. A large number of sections are taught, with one-third taught by adjuncts.

Rhett then meets with the lead faculty for the Exploring Genesis course, who not only manages changes in the course content but also teaches three sections a year herself, coordinates all the adjuncts, and knows Rhett as a librarian colleague. As they spend several hours working on the details, she and Rhett also collaborate to set up a large meeting with all of the instructors of the course, not only to bring them on board regarding the new information literacy model but to walk the faculty through what an information literacy student learning experience might look like for the course. Let's follow what happened at the meeting, called by the lead faculty herself, and situated at a local, popular family restaurant's banquet room on a Saturday at 4:00 p.m.

Sarah Hueglad, Old Testament classroom faculty: OK, everyone, I think we can get started. But, please, continue to enjoy the refreshments. In a moment our department librarian, Rhett, will share a few things about connecting information literacy to the Exploring Genesis course that we all teach. Rhett and I met a couple of times and have designed an information literacy experience assignment for the course, along with a model for a rubric. We began the process by choosing the information literacy concept called "Scholarship as Conversation." It seemed like a good fit for the class and for the assignment we eventually created. The idea of "Scholarship as Conversation" is one of six frames that make up an information literacy model coming recently from the Association of College & Research Libraries called the *Framework for Information Literacy for Higher Education*.

As you know, this course has four core student learning outcomes that we are required to teach to. We also have the option to add up to two more of our own learning outcomes. A new book on this new information literacy model has a large number of sample SLOs for each of the six frames. Adapting one of them to the new assignment seemed like the best way to go. So, for this assignment, we added the SLO: "Information literacy learners are able to create a chronological narrative of significant historic milestones on a topic in a particular discipline."

To teach to this SLO, we suggest replacing the Genesis Person of the Year Award assignment with a new Chronological Narrative assignment. Students will be assigned one of the themes in Genesis (creation, sibling rivalry, infertility, covenants, lies/deceits, and so forth). After watching a video on how to search for scholarly resources, they will locate and analyze at least four scholarly journal articles and then write a three-page, Turabian citation style reflective paper exploring the "conversation" on their theme in terms of the history of its development and the scholarly perspectives that helped shape it. After their paper is completed, students will be placed into groups of two or three according to their common theme. Each group will be required to create one deliverable that explains their collective insights regarding the scholarly conversations they discovered from their theme. Deliverables can be a PowerPoint presentation, a short video, a play, an interpretive dance (just kidding), or other approved end products. Rhett, maybe you can explain a little more.

Rhett: Thanks, Sarah. It's nice to see so many familiar faces on this Saturday afternoon and I'm especially grateful so many of our adjuncts could come. I'm glad the time we chose made it possible for all of you to attend.

OK, so on your handouts are two things: the assignment Sarah just summarized and the rubric we worked on for both the three-page student paper and the students' final deliverable. [See "'Scholarship as Conversation' Assignment Handout for the Genesis Thematic Chronological Narrative" and "Rubric Handout for the Genesis Thematic Chronological Narrative Assignment."] The rubric helps in two ways: first, it simplifies your grading, and second, it easily collects information literacy data for accreditation and other campus uses. Notice the rubric has four sets of scores. Each will be used both as an initial baseline for each student and an aggregated baseline for the course sections as a whole. The student data remains confidential even as we work with the Office of Institutional Research and Assessment to gather longitudinal data over the educational experience of each student. I see we have a question.

Faculty 1: Doesn't this add to our workload? How will we be compensated?

Sarah: Since one assignment is replaced with another, there is no change in workload. In fact, the older assignment had a time-consuming, threaded discussion component that the new one does not.

Faculty 2: Why did THIS particular course get singled out in OUR department? Is it because so many students take the class?

Rhett: Yes, one reason this course was chosen was because it affected a large student population. In fact, the other departments across campus also are collaborating with their librarians to do similar information literacy assignment modifications to one or more courses. The university hopes to integrate information literacy assignments into as many courses as possible, including those online.

Faculty 3: Well, I for one appreciate this plan. It's a lot clearer to me now—how I can do this thing called information literacy. I'm looking to trying it out.

Sarah: Any more questions? Great, meeting adjourned!

Reference

Association of College & Research Libraries (ACRL). 2015. *Framework for Information Literacy for Higher Education*. American Library Association. http://www.ala.org/acrl/standards/ilframework.

"SCHOLARSHIP AS CONVERSATION" ASSIGNMENT HANDOUT
FOR THE GENESIS THEMATIC CHRONOLOGICAL NARRATIVE

Name: _____ Group: _____ Date: _____

Student Learning Outcome: Information literacy learners are able to create a chronological narrative of significant historic milestones on a topic in a particular discipline.

This assignment has three components:

1. After being assigned one of a dozen themes found in the book of Genesis and watching this video on how to search for scholarly resources, you will find and study at least four peer-reviewed, scholarly journal articles that discuss the history or development of your theme, articles that together should include more than one perspective on your theme.
2. You will individually write a three-page reflective paper discussing these perspectives as a scholarly conversation, using Turabian citation style.
3. You will be assigned to a group, and your teammates' papers and research collectively will inform your group final deliverable project. You will be working with your group to come up with a creative way to communicate to the rest of the class what you discovered from the literature regarding your thematic chronology in Genesis. Examples of what can be used include PowerPoint, a short video, a play, or other approved end product. Presentations should be 10 minutes or less. Grading will be assessed by a rubric.

Reproduced from *Implementing the Information Literacy Framework: A Practical Guide for Librarians* by Dave Harmeyer and Janice J. Baskin. © 2018 Rowman & Littlefield Publishers.

RUBRIC HANDOUT FOR THE GENESIS THEMATIC CHRONOLOGICAL NARRATIVE ASSIGNMENT

Student Learning Outcome: Information literacy learners are able to create a chronological narrative of significant historic milestones on a topic in a particular discipline.

Student: _____ Group: _____ Date: _____

Standards of Evaluation	Accomplished	Proficient	Developing	Novice	Scores/ Comments
BIBLIOGRAPHY Number and quality of resources	Four or more resources: a) topically relevant, b) current, c) scholarly, and d) correct Turabian style	Lacking in one of the four categories: a), b), c), or d)	Lacking in two of the four categories: a), b), c), or d)	Lacking in all four categories: a), b), c), and d)	
Score 1:	15–20	10–14	5–9	0–4	1:
PAPER Quality of three-page Genesis thematic chronological narrative paper	a) Identified three or more insights on the theme, b) identification and comparison of scholar perspectives is clear and well-supported from the journal texts, c) chronology of theme development is highly accurate, well detailed, and highly relevant	a) Identified at least two insights on the theme, b) identification and comparison of scholar perspectives is present with adequate text support, c) chronology of development is basically accurate, sufficient detail and relevancy	a) Identified at least one insight on the theme, b) identification and comparison of scholar perspectives is barely perceptible with minimal text support, c) chronology of development has some inaccuracy, minimal detail, relevancy uneven	a) Attempt at insight is present but undeveloped, b) attempt at identification and comparison of scholar perspectives is present but undeveloped, inappropriate, or no text support, c) chronology of development is inaccurate, detail is inappropriate or irrelevant or missing	
Score 2:	30–40	20–29	10–19	0–9	2:

Standards of Evaluation	Accomplished	Proficient	Developing	Novice	Scores/Comments
GROUP PROJECT **Quality of demonstrating connections between what was discovered in the literature and final deliverable to the class**	a) Clearly demonstrated learning from the literature, b) high creativity, c) all members involved	a) Demonstrated learning from literature, b) some creativity, c) not all members involved	a) Unclearly demonstrated learning from literature, b) low creativity, c) not all members involved	a) No clear demonstration of learning from literature, b) no creativity, c) all members not involved	
Score 3:	30–40	20–29	10–19	0–9	3:
Total Score: /100					
Additional Comments:					

Note to faculty: When submitting final grades in the form, there are three additional columns for individual student's chronological assignment scores (Score 1, Score 2, and Score 3).

Part 6: Searching as Strategic Exploration

How do you teach someone how to look? How do you find a new lead when you are in the library databases and your search results are negligible? How do you think strategically about the information you already have and the need to discover new places to look and new sources to pursue? This kind of critical thinking is key to problem solving and essential for innovation. The information literacy frame "Searching as Strategic Exploration" is all about the intellectual skills needed to "think outside the box."

Ask any seasoned journalist, investigator, or scientific researcher. How do you figure out whom to ask and what to ask when all you have is a problem and no idea of a solution? How do you gain access to the sources that may likely contain answers when you haven't found the right language to unlock the information door?

Sometimes it means looking again, even when you don't think there's anything else to see. Sometimes it means digging into unlikely places, talking it through, breaking it down with those who share your perspective and those who don't to, perhaps, grasp new insights. Sometimes you need a little "serendipity," says the ACRL in its 2015 *Framework for Information Literacy for Higher Education*, which briefly defines the frame "Searching as Strategic Exploration" thusly:

> Searching for information is often nonlinear and iterative, requiring the evaluation of a range of information sources and the mental flexibility to pursue alternate avenues as new understanding develops. (ACRL, 2015)

So, how do you teach someone how to look? Once again, as with the five other frames, this frame touches on concepts inherent in several other disciplines. Being able to dig up the right information is a vital skill in journalism, where students are trained to ask who, what, where, why, when, and how as the first step in good reporting. The techniques for brainstorming in composition are essential to help students discover and identify material to write about and how to write about it. *Inventio*, one of the five canons of classical rhetoric organized by Cicero (86–82 BCE), involves searching and discovering the information needed to create an effective argument. Discovery in law is essential in being able to gather the relevant evidence required to win a case. Effective diagnosis in medicine means being able to utilize divergent and convergent thinking, order the right tests to collect the needed data, and interpret that data with precision and accuracy. Doing all of these things well means understanding "Searching as Strategic Exploration."

To teach this frame, faculty need to create assignments that give students the opportunities to explore information systems and practice searching strategies—assignments whose primary purpose is to provide students robust feedback on their developing search skills. Interactive activities and discussion groups, online and in-class, can create the learning spaces students need to discover from each other new ideas for searching. Progressive assignments can also be a good fit for students to experience the developmental nature of research. All it takes is keeping this aspect of information literacy in mind when creating adaptable assignments. For an example, let's look at an online communications studies class.

* * *

Rhett has been the online librarian for the older campus's newer online university since it began eight years ago. It has grown, and over half of the students are adult learners (students typically over the age of 25 and returning to school). He's had the opportunity to interact with a number of these adult learners via email, chat, and Google Hangouts. He realizes these students are different from the traditional undergraduates, as well as credential, master's, and doctoral students. These online students need more scaffolding as they enter into the weird world of proprietary online databases. Knowing this, Rhett is excited about meeting the information literacy needs of such a diverse population as he collaborates by email with the faculty of record for the communications studies course that most students at the online university take in their first term. The following email is the result of that collaboration:

From: Michele Watanabe [online university faculty member]
Date: Wed, Apr 19, 2017 at 7:03 PM
To: Rhett Sarch [librarian]
Subject: Re: Information Literacy experience for your students

Hey Rhett, nice to hear from you. I read over your proposal to add an information literacy learning experience into my COMM 111 Public Communication course. I love your suggestion that I choose one of my assignments that fits well with one of those six frame descriptions you sent me. I so appreciate your guidance in creating an SLO and a rubric [see "Rubric Handout for Communication Theorist Assignment"] for scoring. I've chosen the last frame, "Searching as Strategic Exploration," as being closest to one of my assignments, and after our collaboration, I agree, I think the third bulleted item in the *Knowledge Practices* list will work best as an SLO:

Information literacy learners are able to collaborate using both differing techniques and common ground techniques when searching a topic.

So, taking your advice, I'm changing up my theorists' assignment to integrate this information literacy SLO as an experience students can learn from. There are three parts to the assignment. First, students are randomly assigned into groups of three. Then, from a group of 73 communication theorists found on the *Wikipedia's* site, https://en.wikipedia.org/wiki/Category:Communication_theorists, each group is given a range of theorists to work with based on the alphabet (theorists whose last names end in A–B, C–F, and so forth). The student groups brainstorm to choose up to three theorists whom they believe would be best to interpret an assigned current event. Then in part 2, students individually choose one of their top theorists and discover resources that examine that theorist's theory and approach to a current national event or issue. For part 3, students write a reflection of three pages in the frame of that theorist for that assigned current event.

Your expertise has been invaluable in helping me build a solid information literacy experience into my course. Who knew! And thanks for your help with the rubric. Here's my current form. Let me know if you have any further comments or recommendations.

Reference

Association of College & Research Libraries (ACRL). 2015. *Framework for Information Literacy for Higher Education*. American Library Association. http://www.ala.org/acrl/standards/ilframework.

RUBRIC HANDOUT FOR THE COMMUNICATION THEORIST ASSIGNMENT

Name: _____   Date: _____

Standards of Evaluation	Accomplished	Proficient	Developing	Novice
GROUP: ANALYZE At what level did the student's group cover the elements of Part 1 of the assignment?	a) Well-developed list of pertinent resources, b) clearly articulated rationale for choosing their theorists, c) well-developed analysis of the fit of the theorists to the current event, d) excellent use of proper citing	Strong in three of the four areas	Strong in two of the four areas	Strong in none or one of the four areas
Score:	20–25	15–19	10–14	5–9
INDIVIDUAL: EVALUATE chosen theorist in terms of discovered resources and validity of theorist's theory and approach to chosen current event	a) Thoughtful and articulate, b) persuasive and relevant, c) multiple levels or parts, d) all parts of the model guidelines addressed	Strong in three of the four areas	Strong in two of the four areas	Strong in none or one of the four areas
Score:	20–25	15–19	10–14	5–9
INDIVIDUAL: COMPREHENSION Based on reflective exercise, level of comprehending an important part of the whole lesson	Clearly identified and comprehensively discussed at least one of the important parts of the lesson, with details and examples	Identified and discussed one important part of the lesson with sufficient detail and examples	Identified and discussed a part of the lesson, though not a major element; detail and examples present but insufficient	Missed stating any important parts of the lesson
Score:	40–50	30–39	20–29	10–19
Total Score: /100				
Comments:				

Appendix B
Flashcards for the Six Frames

FLASHCARDS? YES, the flashcard has a long and successful history. So why not employ the technique with the six frames? Let's be honest—the six frames and their short definitions are not easy to remember. Also, once in a convenient pocket form, the cards can be easily accessed a) in conversations about the six frames, b) when making decisions about which frame to apply to which syllabus assignment, and c) as an icebreaker when speaking to the next *Framework* advocate.

Find on the next page the six frames in boxes that can be copied, cut out, and taped on the back of business cards. The small images in the upper-right corner of each flashcard are suggested as further mnemonic guides. Carry these flashcards wherever you go for those serendipitous moments to talk the *Framework* walk.

Authority Is Constructed and Contextual

Information resources reflect their creators' expertise and credibility, and are evaluated based on the information need and the context in which the information will be used. Authority is constructed in that various communities may recognize different types of authority. It is contextual in that the information need may help to determine the level of authority required.

Information Creation as a Process

Information in any format is produced to convey a message and is shared via a selected delivery method. The iterative processes of researching, creating, revising, and disseminating information vary, and the resulting product reflects these differences.

Information Has Value

Information possesses several dimensions of value, including as a commodity, as a means of education, as a means to influence, and as a means of negotiating and understanding the world. Legal and socioeconomic interests influence information production and dissemination.

Research as Inquiry

Research is iterative and depends upon asking increasingly complex or new questions whose answers in turn develop additional questions or lines of inquiry in any field.

Scholarship as Conversation

Communities of scholars, researchers, or professionals engage in sustained discourse with new insights and discoveries occurring over time as a result of varied perspectives and interpretations.

Searching as Strategic Exploration

Searching for information is often nonlinear and iterative, requiring the evaluation of a range of information sources and the mental flexibility to pursue alternate avenues as new understanding develops.

Images are from public domain http://www.clipshrine.com/.
Reproduced from *Implementing the Information Literacy Framework: A Practical Guide*, by Dave Harmeyer and Janice J. Baskin. © 2018 Rowman & Littlefield Publishers.

Appendix C

Thematic Coding of the 2000 *Standards* as Found in the 2015 *Framework*

IN ADDITION TO the mapping between the 2000 *Standards* and the 2015 *Framework* documented in chapter 2 of this book, *Implementing the Information Literacy Framework: A Practical Guide for Librarians*, the following subjective thematic coding demonstrates that the five *Standards* are indeed found throughout the *Framework*. Also, the results of this exercise helped determine which *Standards* matched to which frames in the distinctions sections of chapters 8 and 9 of the book. This document is also on the book's website (https://implementingtheinformationliteracyframework.wordpress.com/ or https://tinyurl.com/ya6h4vyq), where you can see the color rendering throughout the *Framework*'s six frames and definitions.

The key and subsequent coding are rendered in a) highlighted colors as well as b) bracketed numbers so that a black-and-white display (print book) or a color display (e-book) of the data can be read and understood by both modalities. Also, the concepts of *experts* and *novice learners* are italicized to more clearly distinguish these two important categories found in each frame's definition. The six frames are listed alphabetically, the same order they are found in the Association of College & Research Libraries' *Framework for Information Literacy for Higher Education*. To help understand the coding, an example would be: Standard 3.1: "Evaluate information and its sources critically" (highlighted in green) is thematically coded to "Authority Is Constructed and Contextual [3.1]," because similar concepts are found in both.

The following is the key to the five *Standards*, which are then thematically coded within the *Framework*'s six frames and their two-part definitions/descriptions. As noted above, this subjective exercise demonstrates that the enduring concepts of the 2000 *Standards* are clearly continued in the 2015 *Framework*.

1) Determine the extent of information needed
2) Access the needed information effectively and efficiently
3.1) Evaluate information and its sources critically
3.2) Incorporate selected information into one's knowledge base
4) Use information effectively to accomplish a specific purpose
5) Understand the economic, legal, and social issues surrounding the use of information, and access and use information ethically and legally

Authority Is Constructed and Contextual [3.1]

Information resources reflect their creators' expertise and credibility [3.1] and are evaluated [3.1] based on the information need and the context in which the information will be used [1]. Authority is constructed in that various communities may recognize different types of authority [3.1]. It is contextual in that the information need may help to determine the level of authority required [1].

Experts understand that authority is a type of influence recognized or exerted within a community [3.1]. *Experts* view authority with an attitude of informed skepticism and an openness to new perspectives [3.1], additional voices, and changes in schools of thought [3.1]. *Experts* understand the need to determine the validity of the information created by different authorities [3.1] and to acknowledge biases [3.1] that privilege some sources of authority over others, especially in terms of others' worldviews, gender, sexual orientation, and cultural orientations. An understanding of this concept enables *novice learners* to critically examine all evidence [3.1]—be it a short blog post or a peer-reviewed conference proceeding—and to ask relevant questions about origins, context [3.1], and suitability for the current information need [1]. Thus, *novice learners* come to respect the expertise that authority represents [3.1] while remaining skeptical of the systems that have elevated that authority and the information created by it [3.1]. *Experts* know how to seek [2] authoritative voices [3.1] but also recognize that unlikely voices can be authoritative [3.1], depending on need [1]. *Novice learners* may need to rely on basic indicators of authority [3.1], such as type of publication or author credentials [3.1], where *experts* recognize schools of thought or discipline-specific paradigms [3.1].

Information Creation as a Process [4]

Information in any format is produced to convey a message [4] and is shared via a selected delivery method [2]. The iterative processes of researching, creating, revising [4], and disseminating information [2] vary, and the resulting product [4] reflects these differences.

The information creation process [4] could result in a range of information formats [4] and modes of delivery [2], so *experts* look beyond format [2] when selecting resources to use [1 & 2]. The unique capabilities and constraints [5] of each creation process [4] as well as the specific information need [1] determine how the product is used [4]. *Experts* recognize that information creations [4] are valued differently in different contexts [3.1], such as academia or the workplace [3.1]. Elements that affect or reflect on the creation [4], such as a pre- or post-publication editing or reviewing process, may be indicators of quality [3.1]. The dynamic nature of information creation [4] and dissemination [2] requires ongoing attention [3.1] to understand evolving creation processes [4]. Recognizing the nature [3.1 & 5] of information creation [4], *experts* look to the underlying processes [3.1] of creation as well as the final product [4] to critically evaluate [3.1] the usefulness of the information [1, 3.1, & 4]. *Novice learners* begin to recognize the significance [3.1] of the creation process [4], leading them to increasingly sophisticated choices [1, 2, 3.1, & 5] when matching [1, 2, & 3.1] information products [4] with their information needs [1].

Information Has Value [3.1, 4, & 5]

Information possesses several dimensions of value, including as a commodity [3.2 & 4], as a means of education [4], as a means to influence [4], and as a means of negotiating and understanding the world [4]. Legal and socioeconomic interests [5] influence information production [4] and dissemination [2].

The value of information is manifested in various contexts, including publishing practices [4], access to information [2], the commodification of personal information [4], and intellectual property laws [5]. The novice learner may struggle to understand the diverse values of information in an environment where "free" information and related services are plentiful [2] and the concept of intellectual property is first encountered through rules of citation or warnings about plagiarism and copyright law [5]. As creators and users of information [4], *experts* understand their rights and responsibilities [5] when participating in a community of scholarship [3.2 & 4]. *Experts* understand that value may be wielded by powerful interests in ways that marginalize certain voices. However, value may also be leveraged by individuals and organizations to effect change and for civic, economic, social, or personal gains [3.2, 4, & 5]. *Experts* also understand that the individual is responsible for making deliberate and informed choices [3.2, 4, & 5] about when to comply with and when to contest current legal and socioeconomic practices [5] concerning the value of information.

Research as Inquiry [1 & 3.1]

Research is iterative and depends upon asking increasingly complex or new questions [1 & 3.1] whose answers in turn develop additional questions or lines of inquiry [3.1] in any field.

Experts see inquiry as a process that focuses on problems or questions in a discipline or between disciplines that are open or unresolved [1 & 3.1]. *Experts* recognize the collaborative effort within a discipline to extend the knowledge in that field [4]. Many times, this process includes points of disagreement where debate and dialogue work to deepen the conversations around knowledge [3.1 & 3.2]. This process of inquiry extends beyond the academic world to the community at large [4], and the process of inquiry may focus upon personal, professional, or societal needs [1]. The spectrum of inquiry ranges from asking simple questions that depend upon basic recapitulation of knowledge to increasingly sophisticated abilities [1 & 3.1] to refine research questions [4], use more advanced research methods [2 & 4], and explore more diverse disciplinary perspectives [2 & 4]. *Novice learners* acquire strategic perspectives on inquiry [1 & 3.1] and a greater repertoire of investigative methods [1 & 3.1].

Scholarship as Conversation [3.2]

Communities of scholars, researchers, or professionals engage in sustained discourse with new insights and discoveries occurring over time [3.2 & 4] as a result of varied perspectives and interpretations.

Research in scholarly and professional fields is a discursive practice in which ideas are formulated, debated, and weighed against one another over extended periods of time [3.1]. Instead of seeking discrete answers to complex problems, *experts* understand that a given issue may be characterized by several competing perspectives [3.1] as part of an ongoing conversation in which information users and creators come together and negotiate meaning [3.1 & 4]. *Experts* understand that, while some topics have established answers [1 & 4] through this process, a query may not have a single uncontested answer [3.1]. *Experts* are therefore inclined to seek out many perspectives, not merely the ones with which they are familiar [1, 2, 3.1, & 3.2]. These perspectives might be in their own discipline or profession [3.2] or may be in other fields. While *novice learners* and *experts* at all levels can take part in the conversation, established power and authority structures may influence their ability [3.1] to participate [2] and can privilege certain voices and information. Developing familiarity with the sources of evidence, methods, and modes of discourse in the field [4] assists *novice learners* to enter the conversation. New forms of scholarly and research conversations provide more avenues in which a wide variety of individuals may have a voice in the conversation [2]. Providing attribution to relevant previous research is also an obligation of participation in the conversation [5]. It enables the conversation to move forward and strengthens one's voice in the conversation [3.2].

Searching as Strategic Exploration [2 & 3.1]

Searching for information is often nonlinear and iterative [2], requiring the evaluation of a range of information sources [3.1] and the mental flexibility to pursue alternate avenues [2 & 3.1] as new understanding develops [2 & 3.1].

The act of searching often begins with a question that directs the act of finding needed information [1]. Encompassing inquiry, discovery, and serendipity, searching identifies both possible relevant sources as well as the means to access those sources [2 & 3.1]. *Experts* realize that information searching is a contextualized, complex experience [2] that affects, and is affected by, the cognitive, affective, and social dimensions of the searcher [3.2]. *Novice learners* may search a limited set of resources [1 & 2], while *experts* may search more broadly and deeply to determine the most appropriate information within the project scope [1 & 2]. Likewise, *novice learners* tend to use few search strategies, while *experts* select from various search strategies, depending on the sources, scope, and context of the information need.

Appendix D
Bookmarks

THIS TWO-SIDED SAMPLE bookmark was designed using a common word cloud generator with words found from the titles of the six *Framework for Information Literacy for Higher Education* frames. To help market your campus information literacy initiative, bookmarks will connect students and faculty to information literacy and libraries in a personal and ongoing way.

This bookmark example serves as a simple reminder to the concepts that make up the information literacy *Framework*. Another example of a bookmark might contain a URL link to a LibGuide on information literacy. Other types could include the library's website logo, phone number, web address, or links to librarian liaisons. A PDF of the bookmarks can be found on the book's website (https://implementingtheinformationliteracyframe-work.wordpress.com/ or https://tinyurl.com/ya6h4vyq) for easier as-is copying.

Strategies for using bookmarks include:

- Keeping some at the circulation/reference/information desks
- Using one during a reference interview
- Posting on bulletin boards throughout campus
- Adding to student and faculty orientation packets
- Passing them out at faculty meetings, faculty development seminars, during faculty departmental meetings (see suggested talking points below)
- Making them available at the campus writing center, learning enrichment center, or other appropriate places and events.

Having a ready-made statement when you hand a faculty member a bookmark can help you engage them in a conversation about information literacy or your campus information literacy initiative. Possible talking points include:

- This term the library is beginning to implement a new campus-wide information literacy initiative. Your librarian liaison can tell you more about it and how it fits with your course.

- This bookmark is a simple reminder of the six concepts that make up the *Framework for Information Literacy for Higher Education*. Your librarian liaison can tell you more about these concepts and which are most relevant to your course.
- There is also this web link to the library's information literacy LibGuide. The LibGuide includes six short, introductory essays, one on each of the six concepts [see appendix A].
- A simple way to incorporate a measurable information literacy experience into your course is to slightly modify one of your current assignment. Your librarian liaison can help you do this. Shall I let her know to contact you?

Suggested instructions for creating bookmarks from the template:

1. Copy each page onto an 8 ½- by 11-inch sheet of paper. In order for each bookmark to line up with its matching front and back as a double-sided copy, all side margins must align as closely as possible.
2. Center the two images from top to bottom.
3. Using a color printer, copy these two pages onto 8 ½- by 11-inch cardstock. The front of the bookmarks will be on one side of the cardstock and the back of the bookmarks on the other side.
4. The front and back of each bookmark should match for precise cutting.

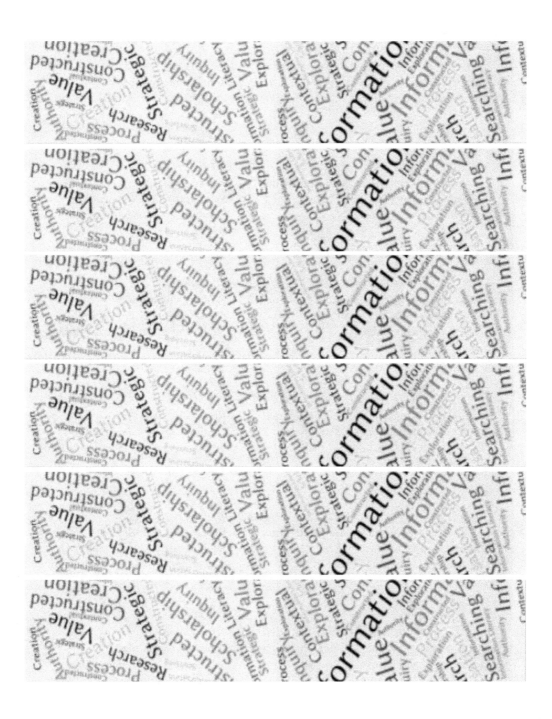

The Six Frames for Information Literacy
Authority Is Constructed and Contextual   **Research as Inquiry**
Information Creation as a Process   **Scholarship as Conversation**
Information Has Value   **Searching as Strategic Exploration**

The Six Frames for Information Literacy
Authority Is Constructed and Contextual   **Research as Inquiry**
Information Creation as a Process   **Scholarship as Conversation**
Information Has Value   **Searching as Strategic Exploration**

The Six Frames for Information Literacy
Authority Is Constructed and Contextual   **Research as Inquiry**
Information Creation as a Process   **Scholarship as Conversation**
Information Has Value   **Searching as Strategic Exploration**

The Six Frames for Information Literacy
Authority Is Constructed and Contextual   **Research as Inquiry**
Information Creation as a Process   **Scholarship as Conversation**
Information Has Value   **Searching as Strategic Exploration**

The Six Frames for Information Literacy
Authority Is Constructed and Contextual   **Research as Inquiry**
Information Creation as a Process   **Scholarship as Conversation**
Information Has Value   **Searching as Strategic Exploration**

The Six Frames for Information Literacy
Authority Is Constructed and Contextual   **Research as Inquiry**
Information Creation as a Process   **Scholarship as Conversation**
Information Has Value   **Searching as Strategic Exploration**

Index

Page references for figures are italicized.

About the Authors

Dave Harmeyer is professor and associate dean of university libraries at California's Azusa Pacific University (APU) and chairs the campus information literacy committee. Dave has a master of library science degree from University of California, Los Angeles, and a doctorate in educational technology from Pepperdine University. His dissertation on chat reference won the Beta Phi Mu Doctoral Dissertation Scholarship Award for 2006. He has taught the Library Media Technologies course in APU's online Master of Arts in Education: School Librarianship/Teacher Librarian Services Credential program since it began in 2001. He has written more than a dozen articles for his reference interview column in *The Reference Librarian* and has a 2014 book with Rowman & Littlefield, *The Reference Interview Today: Negotiating and Answering Questions Face to Face, on the Phone, and Virtually*. Dave also has co-authored articles with classroom faculty touching on such topics as constructivist-based teaching in Second Life (in *i-manager*'s *Journal of Educational Technology*) and enhancing student learning in online courses using Twitter #hashtags (in the *International Journal of Distance Education Technologies*).

Janice J. Baskin is a retired professor of English and communications and taught English composition for 14 years, which included instruction in research and information literacy. She also taught courses in basic writing skills, advanced rhetoric, literature, public relations, radio, television, and film, oral communication, skills for lifelong learning, skills for professional development, research and information utilization, teamwork and conflict resolution, popular culture, and critical thinking. She holds a master of science degree in journalism from the University of Illinois at Urbana-Champaign, and a master of arts degree in rhetoric from California State Polytechnic University, Pomona. As a faculty in the Azusa Pacific University Libraries, she was a member of the information literacy committee and served as chair of the Undergraduate Studies Council, where she worked to help implement information literacy instruction across the curriculum. Prior to her career in academia, Janice worked as a writer, editor, and producer in the news media and in public relations, where the abilities to retrieve relevant information, evaluate it, and utilize it appropriately to create new information are key journalistic and communication skills. She has co-authored articles in teaching and education. Currently, she works as an academic editor.

CPSIA information can be obtained
at www.ICGtesting.com
Printed in the USA
LVHW100231200819
628260LV00007B/142/P

9 781538 107577